INTRODUCTION TO
MACHINE LEARNING

Dr. Bechoo Lal

TAP

Toronto Academic Press

INTRODUCTION TO MACHINE LEARNING

Dr. Bechoo Lal

Toronto Academic Press
4164 Lakeshore Road
Burlington ON L7L 1A4
Canada
www.tap-books.com

Email: orders@arclereducation.com

ISBN: 978-1-77956-300-2

Toronto Academic Press publishes wide variety of books and eBooks. For more information about Toronto Academic Press and its products, visit our website at www.tap-books.com.

ABOUT THE AUTHOR

Bechoo Lal, PhD. became a Member (M) of IAENG: International Association of Engineers, USA with membership (108820) in 2010, a Senior Member (SM) in 2019. I am doctorate PhD in Computer Science, PhD- Information System from University of Mumbai, Master from Banaras Hindu University (BHU), PGP- Data Science from Purdue University, USA. Currently working as a Associate Professor in Department of Computer Science & Engineering, KLEF- KL University Vijayawada Campus Andhra Pradesh, India. His research areas are data science, big data analytics and Machine Learning.

Table of Contents

List of Figures

List of Tables

PREFACE

Even since computers were invented many decades ago, many researchers have been trying to understand how human beings learn and many interesting paradigms and approaches towards emulating human learning abilities have been proposed. The ability of learning is one of the central features of human intelligence, which makes it an important ingredient in both traditional artificial intelligence (AI) and emerging cognitive science.

Machine learning (ML) draws upon ideas from a diverse set of disciplines, including AI, probability and statistics, computational complexity, information theory, psychology and neurobiology, control theory and philosophy. ML involves broad topics including fuzzy logic, neural networks, evolutionary algorithms, probability and statistics, decision trees, etc. Real-world applications of ML are widespread such as pattern recognition, data mining, gaming, bio-science, telecommunications, control and robotics applications. Designing an intelligent machine involves a number of design choices, including the type of training experience, the target performance function to be learned, a representation of this target function and an algorithm for learning the target function from training. Depending on the resources of training, ML is always categorized as supervised learning, unsupervised learning and reinforcement learning. It is interesting to note that human beings adopt more or less these three learning paradigms in our learning process.

This book comprises of eight-chapters. Chapter 1 lays the foundation by introducing essential concepts, including different types of machine learning models, validation and testing techniques, and the critical process of data cleaning. In Chapter 2, the topics such as feature scaling, K-means clustering, and the curse of dimensionality, along with alternative clustering approaches, are thoroughly explored.

Chapter 3 provides an in-depth look at learning from labeled data. It covers linear regression, addressing issues like the dummy variable trap and regularization techniques. Advanced topics such as ridge regression, lasso regression, and elastic net regression are also discussed. Chapter 4 highlights the univariate and multivariate decision trees, including classification and regression trees. It addresses pruning techniques, rule extraction, and learning rules from data, offering practical insights into one of the most interpretable machine learning models.

Chapter 5 examines the role and design principles of neural networks. Chapter 6 introduces the concept and its key elements, such as policy, reward function, value function, and model. Examples and an extended case study on Tic-Tac-Toe illustrate these concepts in practice, providing a hands-on understanding of reinforcement learning. In Chapter 7 we discuss the practical applications of machine learning across different industrial sectors. Chapter 8 addresses the broader societal implications of machine learning. Topics include data privacy, biases, ethical considerations, transparency, adversarial machine learning, legal issues, and the human vs. machine debate. This chapter encourages critical thinking about the responsible use and potential challenges of machine learning.

This book provides a thorough and accessible introduction to machine learning, offering valuable insights for students and experienced researchers.

-Author

CHAPTER

1 Introduction to Machine Learning

LEARNING OBJECTIVES

After studying this chapter, you will be able to:

- Understand the concept of machine learning;
- Identify and comprehend different types of machine learning models;
- Comprehend the importance of validation and testing in the machine learning model development process;
- Understand the concept of data cleaning in machine learning; and
- Comprehend various real-world applications of machine learning across different sectors.

KEY TERMS FROM THIS CHAPTER

Cross- validation

Machine learning

Overfitting

Supervised learning

Data cleaning

Outliers

Reinforcement learning

Unsupervised learning

UNIT INTRODUCTION

Machine learning is gaining significant popularity in the business world, with its impact expected to reach almost all employees in the coming years. Machine learning focuses on utilizing extensive data sets to understand the connections between variables, make accurate predictions, and make informed decisions in a dynamic setting. The amount of data for machine learning is increasing at a remarkable pace. It is expected that within a span of two years, the amount of data generated will be nine times greater than the data available at the start of those two years (Badillo et al., 2020).

Companies already possess a greater amount of data than ever before regarding their clients and their buying patterns. Hedge funds and pension plans have the capacity to collect substantial quantities of data and expert opinions regarding the companies in which they make investments. Recent improvements in computer processing speeds and decreases in data storage expenses enable us to analyze this data and draw conclusions in ways that were previously impossible (Smola & Vishwanathan, 2008).

Comprehending the fundamental principles of machine learning is essential for students and researchers in this quickly developing domain. This chapter seeks to offer a thorough introduction to the fundamental principles and techniques that form the foundation of machine learning. In this analysis, many categories of machine learning models, such as supervised, unsupervised, and reinforcement learning, each designed for certain objectives and uses will be examined (Lemm et al., 2011).

An essential element in the development of efficient machine learning models is guaranteeing their performance and ability to generalize. The discussion will focus on validation and testing strategies that minimize overfitting and ensure a fair assessment of model accuracy. Furthermore, the significance of data quality cannot be exaggerated. Data cleaning is a crucial step in the development of reliable and capable machine learning systems. It encompasses the preprocessing and preparation of raw data (Simeone, 2018).

The wide range of applications for machine learning demonstrates its versatility, spanning across industries such as healthcare, finance, retail, and transportation. Through an analysis of these applications, one can acquire valuable insights into the impact of machine learning on driving innovation and enhancing efficiency in diverse sectors (Mitchell, 1997).

Did you know?

The term "machine learning" was coined by Arthur Samuel in 1959. Samuel was a pioneer in the field of artificial intelligence, known for his work in developing one of the first self-learning programs, a checkers-playing program.

1.1. CONCEPT OF MACHINE LEARNING

Machine learning is a subdivision of artificial intelligence (AI). Artificial intelligence (AI) focuses on the development of methods for machines to replicate human intelligence, potentially surpassing it. Machine learning is developing artificial intelligence by acquiring knowledge from extensive datasets. Perhaps this invention is the most thrilling advancement in artificial intelligence, having the potential to completely revolutionize every element of a business (Carbonell et al., 1983). What are the societal benefits of replacing human decision-making with machines? One benefit is the ability to perform tasks quickly. Machines possess the ability to rapidly analyze data and reach conclusions at a far faster rate compared to humans. The outcomes generated by a machine exhibit a high degree of consistency and can be readily reproduced on alternative machines. In contrast, people exhibit occasional irregular behavior, and educating a human for a task can be both time-consuming and costly (Yang et al., 2019). When it comes to distinguishing machine learning from other AI approaches, let's take the example of programming a computer to play tic tac toe (also known as noughts and crosses). One possible method involves creating a reference table that outlines the different positions that may occur and the corresponding moves that a skilled human player would make in each of those positions (Kuznetsov, 2004). One approach is to develop a multitude of games for the computer, such as having it play against itself numerous times, allowing it to learn and determine the optimal move. The second approach involves the utilization of machine learning techniques. Both methods can effectively be used with simple games like tic tac toe. Complex games like chess and Go have demonstrated the effectiveness of machine learning techniques, as they exceed traditional approaches (Kulesza et al., 2014). Language translation serves as an excellent example of machine learning's capabilities. How is it possible to train a computer to translate, say, from English to French? Giving the computer an English to French dictionary and teaching it to translate words for words is one idea. sadly, the outcome is terrible. Creating a look-up table to translate phrases rather than words is an obvious extension of this idea (Das & Behera, 2017). The results obtained are better than before, although there is still room for improvement. Google has made significant advancements in utilizing machine learning techniques. The announcement was made in November 2016 and it is referred to as "Google Neural Machine Translation" (GNMT). A computer is provided with a substantial amount of English material along with its French translation. The system learns from the provided material and develops its own set of complex translation rules. The outcomes of this have shown significant progress compared to earlier methods (El Naqa & Murphy, 2015).

Data science encompasses a wide range of tasks, including setting objectives, implementing systems, and communicating with stakeholders. Machine learning is a component of data science, but the field itself is often seen as more comprehensive. In this book, the terms "machine learning" and "data science" are used interchangeably. It is crucial for machine learning specialists to actively contribute to their employers' objectives in order to be effective in the business world (Dietterich, 1990).

Did you know?

Artificial neural networks, a key machine learning technique, were inspired by the structure and functioning of the human brain? These networks consist of layers of nodes (neurons) that process information in a manner similar to biological brains.

Machine learning or data science can be seen as a modern interpretation of statistics. In statistics, there has been a long-standing focus on various subjects including distributions of probabilities, confidence intervals, significance tests, and linear regression. Understanding these subjects is crucial, as one now can extract insights from vast datasets in ways that were previously unimaginable. For example (Wang et al., 2009):

i. One can create models that are not linear in nature to enhance forecasting and make better decisions.

ii. Searching for patterns in data can enhance a company's comprehension of its customers and the surrounding business landscape.

iii. It is possible to create decision rules that can adapt to a dynamic environment (El Misilmani & Naous, 2019).

As previously stated, the advancements in computer processing speeds, decreasing data storage costs, and the growing availability of data have made these applications of machine learning feasible. When someone with a background in statistics or econometrics explores machine learning, they may find the terminology unfamiliar at first. As an example, statisticians and econometricians discuss independent variables and dependent variables, whereas decision scientists refer to features and targets (Kuznetsov, 2001).

1.2. TYPES OF MACHINE LEARNING MODELS

Machine learning models can be classified into four main categories (Figure 1.1):

i. Supervised learning
ii. Unsupervised learning
iii. Semi-supervised learning
iv. Reinforcement learning

The goal of supervised learning is to use data to forecast outcomes. The application of a basic regression model for salary prediction is demonstrated in the next section. An illustration of supervised learning is this. Models for classification can be distinguished from supervised learning models that are used to forecast a variable that can take a continuum of values, such a person's income or the cost of a house. In machine learning, classification models are rather prevalent (Ayodele, 2010).

The goal of unsupervised learning is to identify patterns in data. Predicting a specific variable is not the primary goal. Instead, it is to gain a deeper understanding of the environment that the data represents. Think of a business that sells a variety of goods to customers. Purchase data could be utilized to identify the traits of customers who purchase various goods.

Consequently, this could impact the manner in which the products are promoted. Clustering serves as the primary mechanism used for unsupervised learning. The dataset for supervised learning consists of features and labels. The labels represent the goal values that need to be forecasted. The characteristics represent the variables that will be used to make predictions (Song et al., 2017).

As an example, with predicting house prices, the factors to consider may include the living space area, the number of bedrooms and bathrooms, the garage size, and whether the basement is finished, among others. The house price would serve as the label. In unsupervised learning, the data comprises of features without any accompanying labels. This is because the focus of the model is to recognize patterns rather than making predictions. One could utilize an unsupervised learning model to gain insights into the houses present in a specific neighborhood, without the intention of making price predictions. It is possible to observe a group of houses that have a living space ranging from 1,500 to 2,000 square feet, three bedrooms, and a one-car garage. Additionally, there is another group of houses with a living area of 5,000 to 6,000 square feet, six bedrooms, and a two-car garage (Jamal et al., 2018).

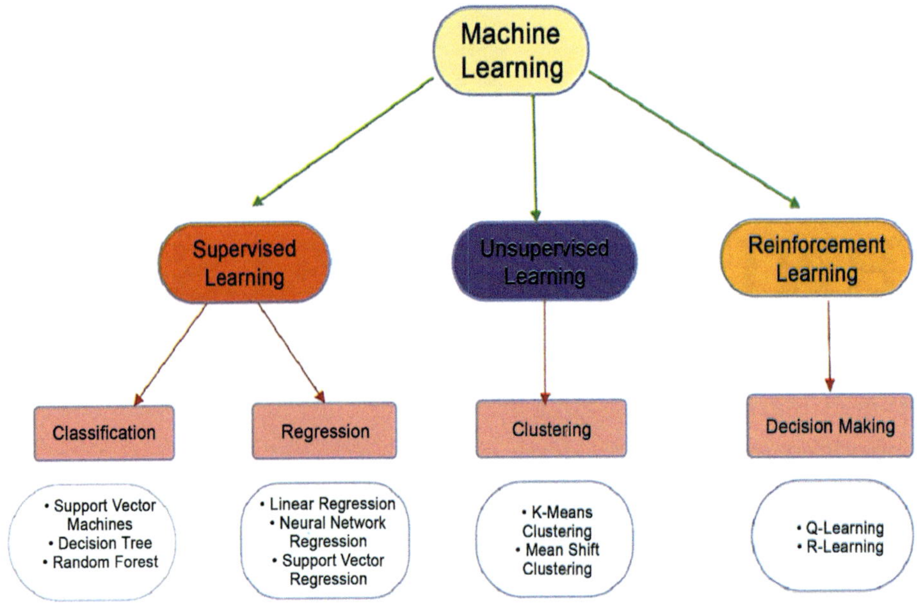

Figure 1.1. *Illustration of different types of machine learning models.*

Source: Shruti Singh, Creative Commons License.

Semi-supervised learning lies at the intersection of supervised and unsupervised learning. It occurs when attempting to make predictions with a combination of labeled data (data with target values) and a larger amount of unlabeled data. One might argue that the unlabeled data lacks value, but that is not always true. Utilizing both labeled and unlabeled data can enhance prediction by generating clusters (Jordan & Mitchell, 2015).

Suppose we want to forecast whether a consumer will buy a specific product based on factors like age, income level, and other relevant characteristics. Additionally, let's assume that we possess a limited quantity of labeled data, which includes information about customer characteristics and their purchase behavior, and a significantly larger quantity of unlabeled data, which only includes information about potential customer characteristics without indicating their purchase behavior. Unsupervised learning can be applied in a given circumstance (Chatzimparmpas et al., 2020):

i. The complete data set contains two distinct clusters, labeled A and B.
ii. The buyers from the labeled data are all associated with points in Cluster A, while the non-buyers from the labeled data are all associated with points in the opposite Cluster B.

It is reasonable to categorize all individuals in Cluster A as purchasers and all persons in Cluster B as non-buyers. Humans use semi-supervised learning. Consider a scenario where you are not familiar with the terms "cat" and "dog," but possess keen powers of observation. You observe two clearly defined groupings of domesticated animals in your local area. Finally, someone identifies two specific creatures, explicitly stating that one is a feline (cat) and the other is a canine (dog) (Suthaharan, 2016). Applying labels to all the other animals you have seen becomes effortless when utilizing semi-supervised learning. It should come as no surprise that machines can also utilize semi-supervised learning, just like humans. Several machine learning algorithms are derived from studying the mechanisms of human brain data processing (Wexler et al., 2019).

Reinforcement learning is the last category of machine learning that focuses on circumstances where a sequence of decisions needs to be made. The environment undergoes dynamic and unpredictable changes as decisions are made. Autonomous vehicles utilize reinforcement learning techniques. The algorithms provide the basis of the programs mentioned above designed for playing games like Go and chess. Additionally, they are used for some trading and hedging determinations (Janiesch et al., 2021).

Remember

Machine learning models can introduce biases and ethical issues. It's important to consider these aspects when developing and deploying models to ensure fairness and transparency.

1.3. VALIDATION AND TESTING

When a data set is utilized for predicting or establishing a decision strategy, there is a risk that the machine learning model will perform effectively for the data set, but will not exhibit strong generalization capabilities for other data. A crucial aspect to consider is the necessity for the data utilized in a machine learning model to accurately reflect the scenarios in which the model will be implemented.

Using data from a location with wealthy clients to forecast national product sales is likely to yield biased outcomes. Statisticians have long recognized the importance of conducting out-of-sample testing for models. By this, we are referring to the need for the model to be evaluated using data that is distinct from the sample data used to establish the model's parameters (Xie et al., 2011).

Data scientists are generally inclined to explore multiple models rather than focusing on evaluating just one. Typically, they use multiple models, evaluate and compare them, and subsequently assess the accuracy of the selected model. In order to accomplish this, they require three sets of data:

i. A training set
ii. A validation set
iii. A test set

The training set is utilized to figure out the parameters of the models being considered. The validation set is used to assess the generalization performance of each model on a distinct dataset. The test set is reserved to assess the accuracy of the selected model (Chorev et al., 2022). Lets demonstrate this using an easy example. Assume our objective is to forecast the incomes of individuals employed in a specific occupation within a particular region of the United States based on their age. We gather data from a randomly selected group of 30 individuals. This is a little dataset developed to provide a simple example. The data sets utilized in machine learning often exceed this size. The initial 10 observations, also known as instances in the field of machine learning, will be utilized to create the training set. The subsequent 10 observations will be utilized to compose the validation set, while the final 10 observations will be utilized to compose the test set (Vabalas et al., 2019). The training set is displayed in Table 1.1 and displayed in Figure 1.2. Many individuals are often attracted to pick a model that exhibits a high level of accuracy when trained on a specific dataset. Based on some experimentation, it appears that a polynomial of degree five achieves this. Here is the model:

$$Y = a + b_1X + b_2X^2 + b_3X^3 + b_4X^4 + b_5X^5$$

When considering the relationship between salary and age, it is important to note that Y represents salary while X represents age. Figure 1.3 displays the outcome of fitting the polynomial to the data (Burzykowski et al., 2023). The model demonstrates a strong alignment with the data. The root-mean-squared error (RMSE) for the 10 individuals in the training data set is $12,902. It represents the standard deviation of the difference between the model's predicted salary and the actual salary. However, it is possible that one has over-fitted the data, which goes against common sense. (This is because the curve in Figure 1.3 appears to be unreal. The pattern fluctuates, rises, fluctuates, and then rises again with increasing age. One should evaluate the model's performance on unseen data. In order to effectively utilize the language of data science, it is crucial to assess the model's ability to generalize to a validation data set that differs from the training set mentioned in Table 1.1 (Jacobs, 2018).

Table 1.1. *Representation of Training Data Set: Salaries for a Random Sample of 10 people*

Age (years)	Salary ($)
25	135,000
55	260,000
27	105,000
35	220,000
60	240,000
65	265,000
45	270,000
40	300,000
50	265,000
30	105,000

Source: Peter Hull, Creative Commons License.

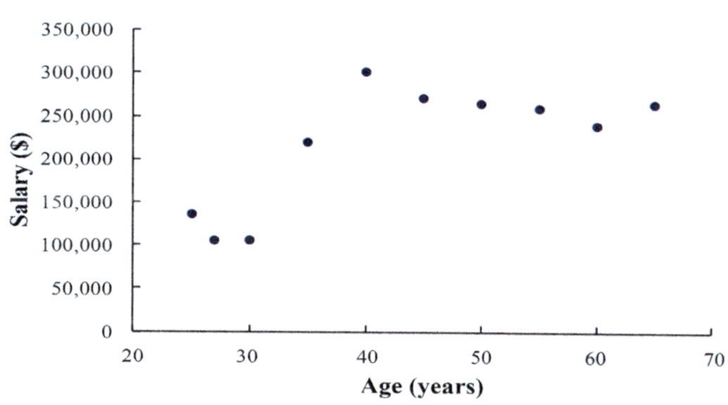

Figure 1.2. Scatter plot of the training data set given in Table 1.1.

Source: John Hull, Creative Commons License.

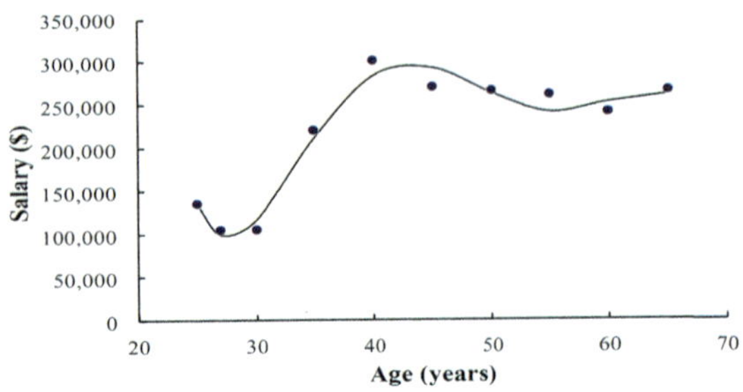

Figure 1.3. *Result of fitting a polynomial of degree 5.*

Source: Jay Cao, Creative Commons License.

Table 1.2 displays the validation set. Figure 1.4 displays the scatter plot for this data. When utilizing the model shown in Figure 1.3 with this dataset, it becomes apparent that the root mean square error (rmse) is approximately \$38,794, which is significantly greater than the \$12,902 achieved with the training data set outlined in Table 1.1. It is obvious that the model shown in Figure 1.3 is suffering from over-fitting, as it fails to effectively generalize to unseen data (Polyzotis et al., 2019).

Table 1.2. *Representation of the Validation Data Set*

Age (years)	Salary ($)
30	166,000
26	78,000
58	310,000
29	100,000
40	260,000
27	150,000
33	140,000
61	220,000
27	86,000
48	276,000

Source: Eddie Mizzi, Creative Commons License.

It is logical to explore an easier model as the next course of action. Based on the scatter plot shown in Figure 1.2, it appears that a quadratic model could be a suitable choice. This model is:

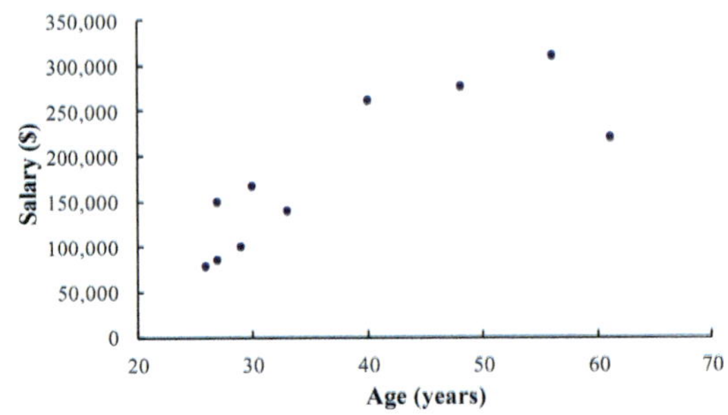

Figure 1.4. *Scatter plot the data set given in Table 1.2.*

Source: Jeff Li, Creative Commons License.

$$Y = a + b_1 X + b_2 X^2$$

i.e., a polynomial of degree two. The quadratic model that best fits the training data set from Figure 1.2 is shown in Figure 1.5. The fit to the training set is naturally not as strong as the model in Figure 1.3. The error's standard deviation is \$32,932. Nevertheless, the model demonstrates a satisfactory ability to generalize to unfamiliar data. The quadratic model's standard deviation of errors for the validation data set in Table 1.2 and Figure 1.4 is \$33,554, which is slightly higher than the \$32,932 for the training data (Ferdinandy et al., 2020).

Based on the given information, it can be concluded that the quadratic model has a better generalization compared to the more complex model shown in Figure 1.3. The model shown in Figure 1.5 is more simple compared to the model shown in Figure 1.3, and it demonstrates strong generalization capabilities when applied to the validation set. Nevertheless, it should be noted that simpler models do not always outperform more complex models. For the data at hand, a linear model could be used. These predictions can be observed in Figure 1.6.

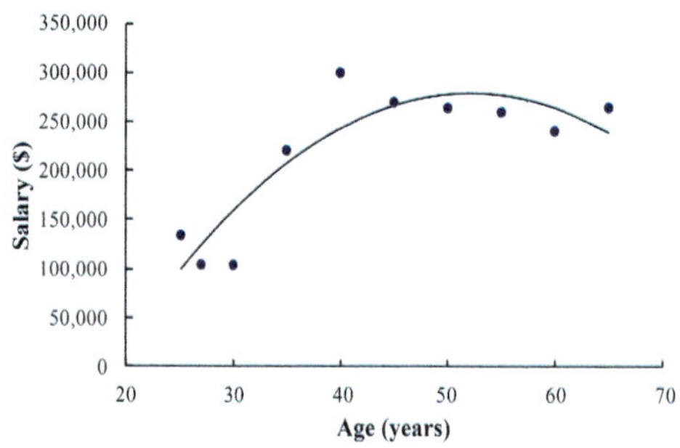

Figure 1.5. *Result of fitting a quadratic model to the data.*

Source: Niti Mishra, Creative Commons License.

It is evident from the visual representation that this model fails to accurately depict the decrease in salaries as individuals progress beyond the age of 50. This observation is supported by the standard deviation of the error for the training data set, which is $49,731, significantly higher than that for the quadratic model (Maleki et al., 2020).

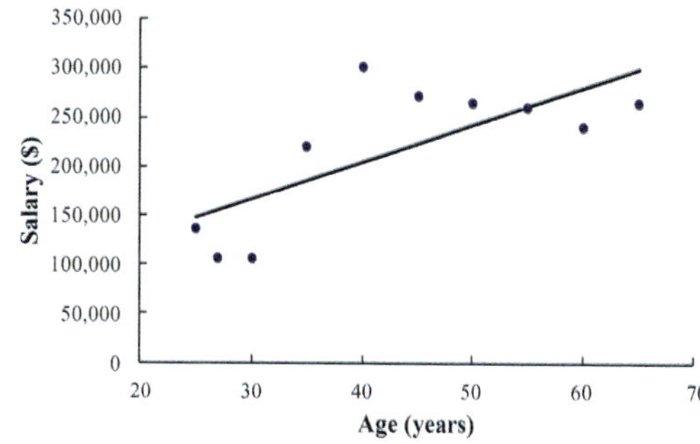

Figure 1.6. *Result of fitting a linear model to training data.*

Source: John Hull, Creative Commons License.

Table 1.3 provides a summary of the root mean square errors obtained from the three models that were examined. It is worth noting that both the linear model and the quadratic model demonstrate strong generalization capabilities on the validation data set. However, the quadratic model is favored due to its superior accuracy. In contrast, the five-degree polynomial model does not have good generalization. The model tends to overfit the training data, while the linear model tends to underfit the training data.

Table 1.3. *Representation of Root Mean Square Errors.*

	Polynomial of degree 5	**Quadratic Model**	**Linear model**
Training Set	12,902	32,932	49,731
Validation Set	38,794	33,554	49,990

Source: Jun Yuan, Creative Commons License.

What is the level of accuracy of the quadratic model? We can trust the findings from the validation set. However, the utilization of the validation set in the model selection process might lead to an overestimation of the model's accuracy. Consequently, the test data set is utilized to generate an accuracy measure. Up until now, this data set has not been utilized in any analyses. Suppose the test data set results are shown in Table 1.4 (Vishnukumar et al., 2017). The test set's root mean squared error is $34,273. It is important to base the presentation of the chosen model's performance on results from the test data set, rather than relying on the validation set or training set. What is the optimal way to strike a balance between over-fitting and under-fitting? This is a crucial matter in machine learning. Machine learning algorithms, like neural networks, often require a significant number of parameters to be effective. Over-fitting can be a common issue, even when dealing with a large training data set (El Naqa et al., 2018).

Table 1.4. *Representation of Errors When a Quadratic Model is Applied to the Test Set*

Age (years)	Salary ($)	Predicted Salary ($)	Error ($)
26	110,000	113,172	−3,172
52	278,000	279,589	−1,589
38	314,000	230,852	+83,148
60	302,000	264,620	+37,380
64	261,000	245,457	+15,543
41	227,000	249325	−22,325
34	200,000	199,411	+589
46	233,000	270,380	−37,380
57	311,000	273,883	−37,117
55	298,000	277,625	+20,375

Source: Niti Mishra, Creative Commons License.

Figure 1.7 provides a visual representation of this rule. The figure suggests that there is a range of models that become increasingly complex. For every model, a measure of the model's error is computed, such as root-mean-square error, for both the training set and the validation set. When the model's complexity is below a certain threshold, it exhibits strong generalization capabilities. The error on the validation set is only slightly higher than that on the training set. When the model complexity surpasses a certain threshold, the errors for the validation set begin to rise (Cabitza et al., 2021).

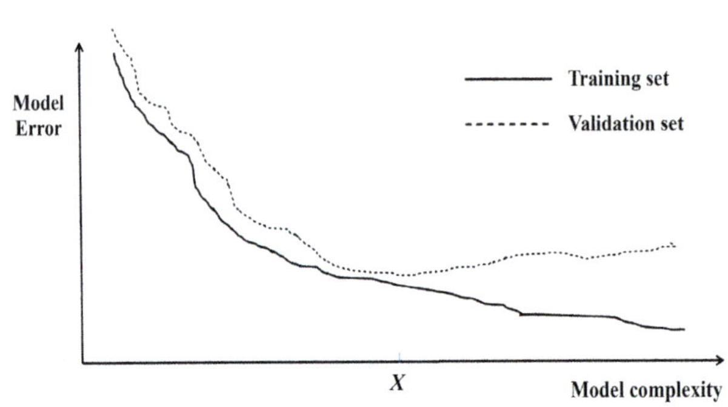

Figure 1.7. *Errors of a model for the training set and the validation set.*

Source: Emilio Barone, Creative Commons License.

The optimal model is the one that exhibits a certain level of model complexity. This is because the model demonstrates the lowest error rate for the validation set. As the complexity increases, the errors decrease for the training set but rise for the validation set. This suggests that over-fitting may be occurring (Straub, 2021).

Striking the perfect balance between under-fitting and over-fitting is commonly known as the bias-variance trade-off in machine learning. Errors in the model's assumptions can lead to bias, causing it to overlook important relationships. The variance is an error that occurs when the model overfits and incorporates random noise from the training set. In conclusion, lets summarize the key points that have been discussed:

i. The training set is utilized to develop different models.
ii. The validation set is utilized to assess the models' ability to generalize to unseen data and make informed decisions between them.
iii. The test set is reserved and serves as an out-of-sample evaluation of the chosen model's accuracy upon completing the analysis (Ding et al., 2017).

In the example, the training set, validation set, and test set all contained an equal number of observations. In a typical machine learning application, a significant amount of data is usually available. The training set typically receives the majority of this data, around 60%, while the validation set and the test set each receive a smaller portion, ranging from 10% to 20%. It is crucial to highlight that the data sets in machine learning consist of significantly more observations compared to the baby data set we have utilized in this section. (It is clear that 10 observations are not enough to establish a reliable relationship.) Nevertheless, the baby data set offers an easy demonstration of the trade-off between bias and variance (Borg et al., 2018).

1.4. DATA CLEANING

Data cleaning plays a crucial role in machine learning, even though it may not be the most thrilling part of the process. Research suggests that a significant portion of a data scientist's time is dedicated to the crucial tasks of data collection and data cleaning. Large data sets often present challenges that require resolution (Krishnan et al., 2016). The quality of data cleaning plays a crucial role in determining the success or failure of machine learning endeavors.

The quality of the input data greatly impacts the results obtained from machine learning, just like in any other analysis. It is important to note that there are two distinct types of data: numerical and categorical. Numerical data primarily comprises of numbers. Categorical data refers to data that can be classified into various distinct categories. As an example, when predicting the price of a house, the data may classify driveways based on their material, such as asphalt, concrete, grass, and so on (Gudivada et al., 2017).

1.4.1. Inconsistent Recording

Inconsistent recording can occur in both numerical and categorical data. As an example, the square footage of a house, there are various ways to input the numerical data. It can be manually entered as 3,300, 3,300, 3,300 ft, or even 3,300+, among other possibilities (Chuck et al., 2017). Examining the data is crucial in order to identify any discrepancies and determine the most effective method for data cleansing. The categorical data may include different variations of the driveway material, such as "asphalt," "Asphalt," or even "aphalt." An effective strategy is to compile the various options provided for a specific attribute and combine them as necessary (Liu et al., 2016).

1.4.2. Unwanted Observations

When developing a model to predict house prices in a specific area, it is important to consider that some of the data may pertain to apartment prices or houses located outside the desired area. It is crucial to establish a method for identifying and eliminating this data prior to conducting any analysis (Whang et al., 2023).

1.4.3. Duplicate Observations

When data is combined from multiple sources or multiple individuals contribute to creating a dataset, it is possible to encounter duplicate observations. These factors can introduce biases into the results. Hence, it is crucial to use a search algorithm to detect and eliminate any instances of duplication to the greatest extent feasible (Corrales et al., 2018).

1.4.4. Outliers

When dealing with numerical data, outliers can be detected by plotting the data or looking for values that deviate significantly from the mean, typically by six standard deviations. Occasionally, it becomes evident that the outlier is simply a typographical error. As an example, when the square footage of a three-bedroom house is entered as 33,000, it is highly likely to be a typographical error and would more likely be 3,300. Nevertheless, it is advisable to eliminate outliers only when there is a valid justification for doing so (Neira-Rodado et al., 2020).

Abnormally large or small values for features or targets, if accurate, may potentially hold valuable insights. The influence of anomalies on the outcomes of machine learning is contingent upon the specific model used. Outliers can significantly impact regression models. Some models, like decision trees, are not as affected by outliers (Ilyas & Rekatsinas, 2022).

1.4.5. Missing Data

It is common to encounter missing data values in large data sets. One way to tackle this issue is by eliminating data that contains missing values in one or more features. However, this may not be ideal as it could lead to a decrease in the sample size and potentially introduce biases. When dealing with categorical data, an easy method is to introduce a new category called "Missing." When dealing with numerical data, a common strategy is to substitute missing values with the average or middle value of the available data (Chu et al., 2016).

As an example, where the square footage of a house is not provided, one can determine the median square footage of the available data to be 3,500. Consequently, we have the option to fill in the missing values with this value of 3,500. There are more advanced methods that can be used to address missing values, such as regressing the target against non-missing values and using the obtained results to fill in the missing values. There are situations where it is reasonable to assume that data is missing randomly, while in other cases, the fact that data is missing can actually provide valuable information. In certain situations, it may be advantageous to generate a fresh indicator variable that takes a value of zero when the data is available and one when it is absent (Wang et al., 2021).

1.5. APPLICATIONS OF MACHINE LEARNING

The idea of web page ranking will be familiar to most readers. The act of typing a search query into a search engine, which then returns webpages that are relevant to the query in the order that they are relevant. A sorted list of webpages is returned by the search engine after a query.

A search engine must "know" a variety of things in order to accomplish this goal, including the content of webpages, their link structure, how frequently users would click on suggested links in queries, and examples of queries combined with human ranked webpages. Automating the process of creating a high-quality search engine is becoming more and more dependent on machine learning as opposed to gut instinct and creative engineering (Schmidt et al., 2019).

Collaborative filtering is an application that is somewhat related. Online retailers like Amazon and rental video services like Netflix make considerable use of this data to persuade customers to buy more products (or rent more movies). The issue and the one pertaining to web page ranking are somewhat comparable. We wish to acquire a sorted list like before.

One notable distinction is the absence of an explicit query, requiring us to rely solely on the user's past purchase and viewing decisions to forecast their future habits. The crucial aspect to consider is the decisions made by similar users, which highlights the collaborative nature of the process. Having an automated system to address this issue would be highly beneficial, eliminating the need for guesswork and saving time (Vamathevan et al., 2019).

A similarly ambiguous issue is the automatic translation of papers. On one end of the spectrum, we could strive to achieve a complete comprehension of a text prior to translating it, using a well selected set of rules devised by a computational linguist who possesses extensive knowledge in both languages that we intend to translate. This activity is quite challenging, especially considering that the material may not always be grammatically ideal and the document understanding aspect is not simple.

Alternatively, individuals might utilize translated materials, such as the records of the Canadian parliament or other multilingual organizations (United Nations, European Union, Switzerland), as practical examples for acquiring translation skills between the two languages. One can utilize translation examples as a means to acquire translation skills. This machine learning approach shown significant success (Recknagel, 2001).

Face recognition is commonly used as a component in security applications, such as access control. Given a photograph or video recording of an individual, the task is to identify and recognize the identity of that person. In simple terms, the algorithm must categorize the faces into various predefined groups (such as Alice, Bob, Charlie, etc.,) or determine that it is an unfamiliar face.

Verification presents a challenge that is similar in nature, but conceptually distinct. The objective is to authenticate the individual's identity by confirming their claimed identity. It is important to note that, unlike before, this question can now be answered with a simple yes or no. In order to address variations in lighting conditions, facial expressions, the presence of spectacles, hairstyle, and other factors, it is advantageous to possess a system that can discern which characteristics are significant for the purpose of identifying an individual.

Learning can also be applied to address the challenge of named entity recognition. It involves the challenge of recognizing various elements, such as locations, job titles, personal names, activities, and more, within written materials. These steps play a vital role in the automated processing and comprehension of documents. Nowadays, certain modern e-mail clients, like Apple's Mail.app, come equipped with the capability to automatically detect addresses in emails and organize them in an address book (Langley & Simon, 1995).

Although systems that rely on hand-crafted rules can yield satisfactory results, it is much more efficient to automatically learn dependencies by using examples of marked-up documents, especially when using the system in multiple languages. As an example, the terms 'bush' and 'ri' are commonly associated with agriculture. However, in modern politics, they are often used to describe individuals affiliated with the Republican Party.

Other applications that utilize machine learning include speech recognition (converting audio sequences into text, like the system in Microsoft Vista), handwriting recognition (converting strokes into text, a common feature in PDAs), trackpads in computers (e.g., Synaptics, a major manufacturer of such pads, named after neural network synapses), failure detection in jet engines, avatar behavior in computer games (e.g., black and white), direct marketing (companies using past purchase behavior to estimate if you might make more purchases), and floor cleaning robots (like iRobot's Roomba).

The fundamental concept behind learning difficulties is the presence of a significant relationship between certain observations, denoted as x, and a desired response, denoted as y, for which an easy set of deterministic rules is not yet identified. Through the utilization of learning, one can deduce a systematic relationship between x and y (Lei et al., 2020).

In this section, one will address the issue of classification, as it will function as a typical difficulty throughout this book. It is a common occurrence in practical situations. For example, while conducting spam filtering, we seek a binary response indicating whether an email contains appropriate material or not.

It is important to consider that the significance of this matter varies depending on the user. For individuals who travel frequently, receiving emails from an airline regarding recent discounts could be considered valuable information. However, for many other recipients, this could be seen as more of an annoyance, especially if the email pertains to products that are only available overseas. Furthermore, the characteristics of annoying emails may evolve over time, for example, due to the emergence of new products such as Viagra, Cialis, Levitra, etc., the emergence of new methods for fraudulent activities like the Nigerian 419 scam which received modifications after the Iraq war, or the use of different data formats, such as spam that primarily consists of images.

In order to address these challenges, it is necessary to develop a system that can effectively learn and classify new e-mails. An apparently unrelated issue, such as cancer diagnosis, has a similar structure: determining the health status of a patient based on histological data, such as microarray analysis of their tissue. Once more, we are tasked with producing a binary response based on a collection of data points (Myszczynska et al., 2020) (Figure 1.8).

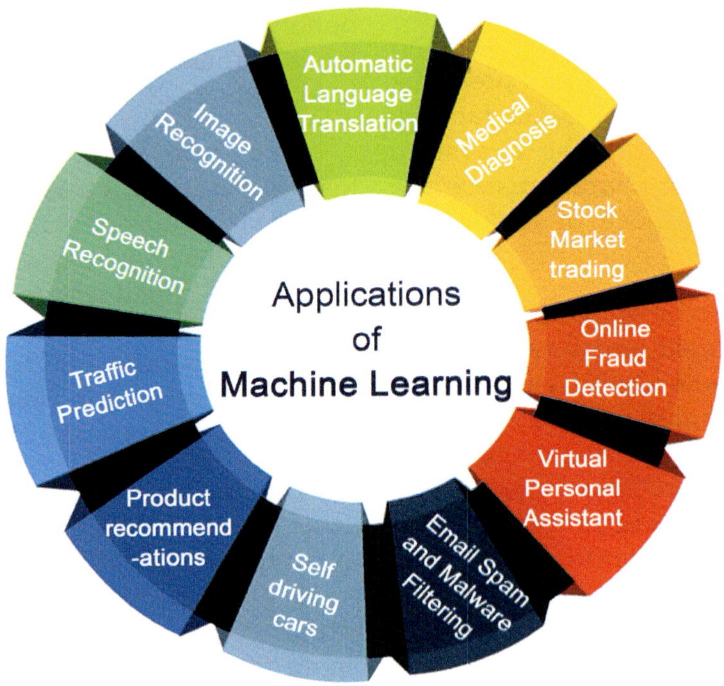

Figure 1.8. *Illustration of different applications of machine learning.*

Source: Shruti Singh, Creative Commons License.

ACTIVITY 1.1

- **Objective**: Gain hands-on experience with data cleaning and preprocessing techniques.
- Instructions:
  - Select a raw dataset with common data quality issues (e.g., missing values, inconsistencies)
  - Perform data cleaning steps such as handling missing values, correcting errors, and standardizing formats
  - Implement feature engineering techniques such as normalization, encoding categorical variables, and creating new features
- **Deliverables:** A clean and preprocessed dataset along with a detailed report on the data cleaning and preprocessing steps taken

SUMMARY

- Machine learning is a field within artificial intelligence that focuses on the process of learning from large sets of data. It involves the creation of algorithms to make predictions, cluster data, or devise a strategy for a sequence of decisions. In statistical analysis, the conventional approach has been to formulate a hypothesis before examining any data, and subsequently subjecting the hypothesis to rigorous testing using the available data. Machine learning sets itself apart. There is a lack of hypotheses. The model is derived solely from data.
- Cleaning up the data is crucial before applying any machine learning algorithms. Either numerical or categorical features make up the data. There might have been inconsistent data entry in either scenario. It is necessary to find and fix these discrepancies. It may be necessary to eliminate certain observations since they are unrelated to the current task. Duplicate observations can introduce bias into the data, so they should be examined for them. It is best to eliminate outliers that are obviously the product of input errors. Finally, it's important to handle missing data in a way that won't distort the outcomes. There are several uses for machine learning in many different sectors, including:

1. **Healthcare:** Predictive analytics for personalized treatment, illness diagnosis, and patient outcomes.
2. **Finance:** Algorithmic trading, fraud detection, and risk management.
3. **Retail:** Demand forecasting, customer segmentation, and recommendation systems.
4. **Manufacturing:** Quality control, predictive maintenance, and supply chain optimization.
5. **Transportation:** Route optimization, autonomous vehicles, and traffic prediction.

In conclusion, this chapter provides an overview of the basic principles of machine learning, including its concepts, model types, validation and testing processes, significance of data cleansing, and a variety of real-world applications.

REVIEW QUESTIONS

1. Explain two types of predictions that are made in supervised learning?
2. When is reinforcement learning appropriate?
3. Explain the role of the validation data set and the test data set?
4. List five different types of data cleaning?
5. What down some applications of machine learning in information security?

MULTIPLE CHOICE QUESTIONS

1. **What is the primary goal of machine learning?**
   a. To manually program each possible decision
   b. To enable computers to learn from data and make predictions
   c. To create hardware for computing tasks
   d. To develop software with predefined outputs
2. **Which type of machine learning involves labeled data to train models?**
   a. Supervised Learning
   b. Unsupervised Learning
   c. Reinforcement Learning
   d. Semi-supervised Learning
3. **Which machine learning technique is primarily used for clustering data?**
   a. Supervised Learning
   b. Unsupervised Learning
   c. Reinforcement Learning
   d. Supervised and Unsupervised Learning
4. **What is the purpose of cross-validation in machine learning?**
   a. To increase the dataset size
   b. To prevent overfitting and assess model stability
   c. To improve model accuracy on the test set
   d. To automate the data cleaning process
5. **Which of the following is an application of machine learning in healthcare?**
   a. Predictive analytics for patient outcomes
   b. Manual data entry
   c. Traditional statistical analysis
   d. Developing electronic health records

Answers to Multiple Questions

1. (b); 2. (a); 3. (b); 4. (b); 5. (a)

REFERENCES

1. Ayodele, T. O. (2010). Types of machine learning algorithms. *New Advances in Machine Learning, 3*(19–48), 5–1.
2. Badillo, S., Banfai, B., Birzele, F., Davydov, I. I., Hutchinson, L., Kam-Thong, T., & Zhang, J. D. (2020). An introduction to machine learning. *Clinical Pharmacology & Therapeutics, 107*(4), 871–885.

3. Borg, M., Englund, C., Wnuk, K., Duran, B., Levandowski, C., Gao, S., & Törnqvist, J. (2018). Safely entering the deep: A review of verification and validation for machine learning and a challenge elicitation in the automotive industry. *arXiv preprint arXiv:1812.05389,* 7(3), 875--880.

4. Burzykowski, T., Geubbelmans, M., Rousseau, A. J., & Valkenborg, D. (2023). Validation of machine learning algorithms. *American Journal of Orthodontics and Dentofacial Orthopedics, 164*(2), 295–297.

5. Cabitza, F., Campagner, A., Soares, F., de Guadiana-Romualdo, L. G., Challa, F., Sulejmani, A., & Carobene, A. (2021). The importance of being external: Methodological insights for the external validation of machine learning models in medicine. *Computer Methods and Programs in Biomedicine, 208*, 106288.

6. Carbonell, J. G., Michalski, R. S., & Mitchell, T. M. (1983). An overview of machine learning. *Machine Learning, 8*(5), 3–23.

7. Chatzimparmpas, A., Martins, R. M., Jusufi, I., & Kerren, A. (2020). A survey of surveys on the use of visualization for interpreting machine learning models. *Information Visualization, 19*(3), 207–233.

8. Chorev, S., Tannor, P., Israel, D. B., Bressler, N., Gabbay, I., Hutnik, N., & Rokach, L. (2022). Deepchecks: A library for testing and validating machine learning models and data. *Journal of Machine Learning Research, 23*(285), 1–6.

9. Chu, X., Ilyas, I. F., Krishnan, S., & Wang, J. (2016). Data cleaning: Overview and emerging challenges. In *Proceedings of the 2016 International Conference on Management of Data* (Vol. 2, pp. 2201–2206).

10. Chuck, C., Laskey, M., Krishnan, S., Joshi, R., Fox, R., & Goldberg, K. (2017). Statistical data cleaning for deep learning of automation tasks from demonstrations. In *2017 13th IEEE Conference on Automation Science and Engineering (CASE)*. IEEE. (Vol. 1, pp. 1142–1149).

11. Corrales, D. C., Corrales, J. C., & Ledezma, A. (2018). How to address the data quality issues in regression models: A guided process for data cleaning. *Symmetry, 10*(4), 99.

12. Das, K., & Behera, R. N. (2017). A survey on machine learning: Concept, algorithms, and applications. *International Journal of Innovative Research in Computer and Communication Engineering,* 5(2), 1301–1309.

13. Dietterich, T. G. (1990). Machine learning. *Annual Review of Computer Science, 4*(1), 255–306.

14. Ding, J., Hu, X. H., & Gudivada, V. (2017). A machine learning based framework for verification and validation of massive scale image data. *IEEE Transactions on Big Data,* 7(2), 451–467.

15. El Misilmani, H. M., & Naous, T. (2019). Machine learning in antenna design: An overview on machine learning concept and algorithms. In *2019 International Conference on High Performance Computing & Simulation (HPCS)*. IEEE. (Vol. 2, pp. 600–607).

16. El Naqa, I., & Murphy, M. J. (2015). What is machine learning? In *Machine Learning in Radiation Oncology* (pp. 3–11). Springer International Publishing.
17. El Naqa, I., Ruan, D., Valdes, G., Dekker, A., McNutt, T., Ge, Y., & Ten Haken, R. (2018). Machine learning and modeling: Data, validation, communication challenges. *Medical Physics, 45*(10), 834–840.
18. Ferdinandy, B., Gerencsér, L., Corrieri, L., Perez, P., Újváry, D., Csizmadia, G., & Miklósi, Á. (2020). Challenges of machine learning model validation using correlated behavior data: Evaluation of cross-validation strategies and accuracy measures. *PLOS ONE, 15*(7), e0236092.
19. Gudivada, V., Apon, A., & Ding, J. (2017). Data quality considerations for big data and machine learning: Going beyond data cleaning and transformations. *International Journal on Advances in Software, 10*(1), 1–20.
20. Ilyas, I. F., & Rekatsinas, T. (2022). Machine learning and data cleaning: Which serves the other? *ACM Journal of Data and Information Quality (JDIQ), 14*(3), 1–11.
21. Jacobs, M. (2018). The validation of machine-learning models for the stress testing of credit risk. *Journal of Risk Management in Financial Institutions, 11*(3), 218–243.
22. Jamal, S., Goyal, S., Grover, A., & Shanker, A. (2018). Machine learning: What, why, and how? In *Bioinformatics: Sequences, Structures, Phylogeny* (pp. 359–374). Springer International Publishing.
23. Janiesch, C., Zschech, P., & Heinrich, K. (2021). Machine learning and deep learning. *Electronic Markets, 31*(3), 685–695.
24. Jordan, M. I., & Mitchell, T. M. (2015). Machine learning: Trends, perspectives, and prospects. *Science, 349*(6245), 255–260.
25. Krishnan, S., Franklin, M. J., Goldberg, K., Wang, J., & Wu, E. (2016). Active clean: An interactive data cleaning framework for modern machine learning. In *Proceedings of the 2016 International Conference on Management of Data* (Vol. 2, pp. 2117–2120).
26. Kulesza, T., Amershi, S., Caruana, R., Fisher, D., & Charles, D. (2014). Structured labeling for facilitating concept evolution in machine learning. In *Proceedings of the SIGCHI Conference on Human Factors in Computing Systems* (Vol. 2, pp. 3075–3084).
27. Kuznetsov, S. O. (2001). Machine learning on the basis of formal concept analysis. *Automation and Remote Control, 62*, 1543–1564.
28. Kuznetsov, S. O. (2004). Machine learning and formal concept analysis. In *International Conference on Formal Concept Analysis* (Vol. 2, pp. 287–312). Berlin, Heidelberg: Springer Berlin Heidelberg.
29. Langley, P., & Simon, H. A. (1995). Applications of machine learning and rule induction. *Communications of the ACM, 38*(11), 54–64.
30. Lei, Y., Yang, B., Jiang, X., Jia, F., Li, N., & Nandi, A. K. (2020). Applications of machine learning to machine fault diagnosis: A review and roadmap. *Mechanical Systems and Signal Processing, 138*, 106587.
31. Lemm, S., Blankertz, B., Dickhaus, T., & Müller, K. R. (2011). Introduction to machine learning for brain imaging. *Neuroimage, 56*(2), 387–399.

32. Liu, H., Tk, A. K., Thomas, J. P., & Hou, X. (2016). Cleaning framework for big data: An interactive approach for data cleaning. In *2016 IEEE Second International Conference on Big Data Computing Service and Applications (BigDataService)* (Vol. 2, pp. 174–181). IEEE.
33. Maleki, F., Muthukrishnan, N., Ovens, K., Reinhold, C., & Forghani, R. (2020). Machine learning algorithm validation: From essentials to advanced applications and implications for regulatory certification and deployment. *Neuroimaging Clinics, 30*(4), 433–445.
34. Mitchell, T. (1997). Introduction to machine learning. *Machine Learning, 7*, 2–5.
35. Myszczynska, M. A., Ojamies, P. N., Lacoste, A. M., Neil, D., Saffari, A., Mead, R., & Ferraiuolo, L. (2020). Applications of machine learning to diagnosis and treatment of neurodegenerative diseases. *Nature Reviews Neurology, 16*(8), 440–456.
36. Neira-Rodado, D., Nugent, C., Cleland, I., Velasquez, J., & Viloria, A. (2020). Evaluating the impact of a two-stage multivariate data cleansing approach to improve the performance of machine learning classifiers: A case study in human activity recognition. *Sensors, 20*(7), 1858.
37. Polyzotis, N., Zinkevich, M., Roy, S., Breck, E., & Whang, S. (2019). Data validation for machine learning. *Proceedings of Machine Learning and Systems, 1*, 334–347.
38. Recknagel, F. (2001). Applications of machine learning to ecological modelling. *Ecological Modelling, 146*(1–3), 303–310.
39. Schmidt, J., Marques, M. R., Botti, S., & Marques, M. A. (2019). Recent advances and applications of machine learning in solid-state materials science. *npj Computational Materials, 5*(1), 83.
40. Simeone, O. (2018). A brief introduction to machine learning for engineers. *Foundations and Trends® in Signal Processing, 12*(3–4), 200–431.
41. Smola, A., & Vishwanathan, S. V. N. (2008). Introduction to machine learning. *Cambridge University, UK, 32*(34), 2008.
42. Song, C., Ristenpart, T., & Shmatikov, V. (2017). Machine learning models that remember too much. In *Proceedings of the 2017 ACM SIGSAC Conference on Computer and Communications Security* (Vol. 1, pp. 587–601).
43. Straub, J. (2021). Machine learning performance validation and training using a 'perfect' expert system. *MethodsX, 8*, 101477.
44. Suthaharan, S. (2016). Machine learning models and algorithms for big data classification. *Integr. Ser. Inf. Syst, 36*, 1–12.
45. Vabalas, A., Gowen, E., Poliakoff, E., & Casson, A. J. (2019). Machine learning algorithm validation with a limited sample size. *PLOS ONE, 14*(11), e0224365.
46. Vamathevan, J., Clark, D., Czodrowski, P., Dunham, I., Ferran, E., Lee, G., & Zhao, S. (2019). Applications of machine learning in drug discovery and development. *Nature Reviews Drug Discovery, 18*(6), 463–477.
47. Vishnukumar, H. J., Butting, B., Müller, C., & Sax, E. (2017). Machine learning and deep neural network—Artificial intelligence core for lab and real-world test and validation for ADAS and autonomous vehicles: AI for efficient and quality

test and validation. In *2017 Intelligent Systems Conference (IntelliSys)* (Vol. 2, pp. 714–721). IEEE.

48. Wang, H., Ma, C., & Zhou, L. (2009). A brief review of machine learning and its application. In *2009 International Conference on Information Engineering and Computer Science* (Vol. 1, pp. 1–4). IEEE.
49. Wang, Z., Tsai, C. F., & Lin, W. C. (2021). Data cleaning issues in class imbalanced datasets: Instance selection and missing values imputation for one-class classifiers. *Data Technologies and Applications, 55*(5), 771–787.
50. Wexler, J., Pushkarna, M., Bolukbasi, T., Wattenberg, M., Viégas, F., & Wilson, J. (2019). The what-if tool: Interactive probing of machine learning models. *IEEE Transactions on Visualization and Computer Graphics, 26*(1), 56–65.
51. Whang, S. E., Roh, Y., Song, H., & Lee, J. G. (2023). Data collection and quality challenges in deep learning: A data-centric AI perspective. *The VLDB Journal, 32*(4), 791–813.
52. Xie, X., Ho, J. W., Murphy, C., Kaiser, G., Xu, B., & Chen, T. Y. (2011). Testing and validating machine learning classifiers by metamorphic testing. *Journal of Systems and Software, 84*(4), 544–558.
53. Yang, Q., Liu, Y., Chen, T., & Tong, Y. (2019). Federated machine learning: Concept and applications. *ACM Transactions on Intelligent Systems and Technology (TIST), 10*(2), 1–19.

CHAPTER 2

Unsupervised Learning

LEARNING OBJECTIVES

After studying this chapter, you will be able to:

- Understand the fundamentals of unsupervised learning;
- Comprehend unsupervised learning models;
- Understand feature scaling and k-means clustering;
- Learn about dimensionality in unsupervised learning; and
- Comprehend the alternating clustering approaches.

KEY TERMS FROM THIS CHAPTER

Autoencoders
Dimensionality
Expectation maximization
Maximum likelihood
Clustering
Discriminative models
Feature scaling

UNIT INTRODUCTION

Unsupervised learning problems include working with data sets that do not have any labels or annotations. In addition to this broad statement, unsupervised learning is characterized by a less rigid definition compared to supervised, and it likewise lacks a robust theoretical foundation that aligns with the PAC learning theory. However, there is widespread anticipation that advancements in the theory and development of algorithms for unsupervised learning will be the primary source of future advancements in machine learning. This is because there are large collections of unlabeled data available, and the machine can learn without any supervision or feedback in a wide range of learning tasks. Some people regard unsupervised learning to be the crucial factor in developing broad artificial intelligence, rather than AI that is dedicated to a particular task (Morales et al., 2022).

Unsupervised learning algorithms generally seek to learn specific aspects of the underlying data-generating method. Unsupervised learning focuses on the examination of generative models, yet there are some conditions and limitations associated with this assertion. Many unsupervised learning models incorporate hidden or latent variables to elucidate the underlying structure of the data (Parasa et al., 2021).

The chapter commences by examining the practical uses of unsupervised learning and presenting a detailed explanation of the renowned K-means algorithm. Next, it discusses both directed as well as undirected generative probabilistic frameworks used in unsupervised learning. As will be explained in more detail, these models propose several sorts of statistical relationships between variables that are measured and those that are hidden (James et al., 2023).

Remember

Unsupervised learning identifies patterns or structures in data without predefined labels or outputs. It is commonly used for clustering, dimensionality reduction, and association rule learning.

2.1. CONCEPT OF UNSUPERVISED LEARNING

An all-encompassing and somewhat vague description of unsupervised learning assignments is as follows. From a frequentist perspective, a dataset D is provided that contains N independent and identically distributed (i.i.d.) unlabeled observations xn ∈ RD. It is assumed that these are independently and identically drawn from a distribution that is not known (Brydges et al., 2010).

$$D = \{X_N\}_{n=1}^{N} \underset{i.i.d}{\sim} p(x)$$

The objective is to acquire valuable characteristics of p(x), with the specific features of interest contingent upon the particular application. Unsupervised learning issues are commonly defined by the existence of concealed or latent variables. Prominent instances encompass the subsequent examples (Djukanovic et al., 1993).

i. **Density Estimation:** It is the process of directly learning an accurate estimate of the distribution p(x). This approximation can be used for various purposes such as plug-in estimators, designing compression methods, or detecting outliers (Tlusty et al., 2018).
ii. **Clustering:** It involves the assumption that there is an unseen label z_n assigned to every data point x_n. The objective is to determine the labels z_n for every point in the dataset D. For instance, one might want to group a collection D of textual documents based on their subjects, by representing the subjects as an unseen label z_n. In general, this task involves the grouping of documents that have similarities based on a specific measurement. At this juncture, it is crucial to underscore the differentiation between clustering and classification: The former method relies on a labeled set of training data and assesses its capacity to generalize by using an additional set of unlabeled examples. In contrast, the later method just uses a single set of unlabeled instances (Rojas & Rojas, 1996).
iii. **Dimensionality Reduction and Representation:** To reduce the dimensionality of the data points $x_n \in {}^D$, it is aimed to represent them in a lower-dimensional space. This enables the identification of distinct explanatory factors and facilitates the presentation and comprehension of data, such as in the case of text analysis using vector embedding (Kumar, 2009).

iv. **Feature Extraction:** It is the process of generating meaningful lower-dimensional inputs from data points x_n, which can be used for tasks like supervised learning. The features that have been obtained are not directly observable and hence are considered latent variables. For instance, in a deep neural network, the concealed layer is responsible for extracting features from the data, which are then utilized by the output layer (Chen & Lin, 1994).

v. **New Samples:** The objective is to train a model that can generate samples that closely follow the actual distribution p(x). For instance, in the field of digital graphics for cinematography or gaming, there may be a need to teach a software program capable of generating synthetic scenarios based on a provided description (Zhu et al., 2019).

Unsupervised learning is considered a less formalized area than supervised learning due to the wide range of problems and the challenge of establishing precise definitions, such as determining the authenticity of an artificially produced image (Iba & Langley, 1999).

2.1.1. Unsupervised Learning Models

This section will examine the various types of models which can be employed to address unsupervised learning difficulties (Figueiredo & Jain, 2002).

2.1.1.1. Directed Generative Models

In the context of mixture models, these models are a subset in which the pattern of distribution $p(x|\theta)$ of the data set is determined by a parametrized dependent distribution $p(x|z, \theta)$ that describes the relationship between the latent and observable variables, and a parametrized preceding distribution $p(z|\theta)$ that is connected to the latent variables z. For this reason, the distribution can be stated numerically in the case of discrete latent variables z (Basanisi et al., 2020):

$$p(x|\theta) = \sum_z p(z|\theta) p(x|z,\theta)$$

Causal models are appropriate for capturing the cause-effect linkages between z and x. Figure 2.1(a) displays a Bayesian Network that describes directed generative models. The next chapter will provide a comprehensive analysis of graphical models, including Bayesian networks (Abukmeil et al., 2021).

2.1.1.2. Undirected Generative Models

These models explicitly parameterize the joint distributions of the measured variables x and the variables that are hidden as $p(x, z|\theta)$. Consequently, the distribution is expressed correspondingly (Peis et al., 2023):

$$p(x|\theta) = \sum_z p(x|z,\theta)$$

2.1.1.3. Discriminative Models

Discriminative models aim to directly acquire a probability mapping $p(z|x, \theta)$ that encodes the relationship among the data point x and the representation z. The representation of this is denoted by the BN in Figure 2.1(c) (Xu et al., 2006).

2.1.1.4. Autoencoders

Autoencoders include a parametrized generative model, denoted as $p(x|z, \theta)$, which generates the data x based on z. The first one is referred to as an encoder, while the second one is called a decoder. Therefore, the latent variables are also known as the code. Instead of using more generic $p(x|z, \theta)$ and $p(z|x, \theta)$, the most common implementations utilize $x = G\theta(z)$ and $z = F\theta(x)$ (Wetzel, 2017).

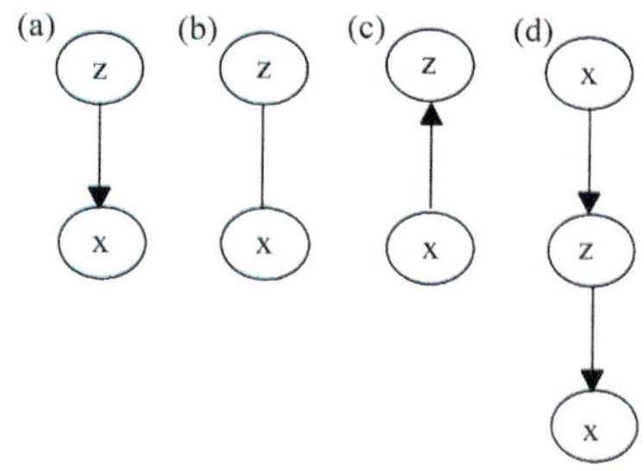

Figure 2.1. *Illustration of (a) directed generative models; (b) undirected generative models; (c) discriminative models; (d) autoencoders.*

Source: Osvaldo Simeone, Creative Commons License.

2.2. FEATURE SCALING

Before delving into clustering techniques, it is crucial to address the concept of feature scaling. This process is commonly known as data normalization or data standardization. It is an essential initial stage for most ML algorithms. Its goal is to guarantee that all features are weighted equally in an algorithm. Consider a scenario of grouping males based on two characteristics: their height in inches and their weight in pounds. The heights can vary between 60 and 80 inches, while the weights can range between 100 and 350 pounds. Feature scaling is necessary to ensure equal priority is given to each feature, as the range of heights (20 inches) is far smaller than the range of masses (250 pounds). An effective method for feature scaling involves computing the standard deviation and mean for each feature and then scaling the observations as follows (Raina et al., 2009):

$$Scaled\ Feature\ Value = \frac{V - \mu}{\sigma}$$

where; μ and σ represent the calculated average and standard deviation obtained from measurements on the attribute in question. This feature scaling technique is occasionally known as Z-score normalization or Z-score scaling. The scaled characteristics have a mean of zero and a standard deviation of one. To prioritize a certain feature's impact on cluster separation above other features, its scale can be adjusted so that the standard deviation exceeds one. Another method for feature scaling involves subtracting the least value of the feature and dividing it by the range (difference) between the highest and lowest values:

$$Scaled\ Feature\ Value = \frac{V - \min}{\max - \min}$$

where; "max" and "min" represent the highest and lowest values of the features. This process is commonly known as min-max scaling. The scaled value of features ranges from zero to one.

The Z-score approach is commonly favored for scaling as it is less influenced by outliers. However, min-max scaling may be appropriate when features are being measured on limited scales (Ozsahin et al., 2022).

2.3. K-MEANS CLUSTERING

This section will begin by examining the widely recognized K-means clustering algorithm. The objective is to highlight the mathematical framework known as the Expectation Maximization (EM) algorithm, which forms the conceptual foundation for numerous unsupervised learning techniques.

Given a data set D = {xn}Nn=1, the objective is to categorize each vector xn ∈ RD into one of K clusters. The encoding of cluster indices is achieved by using categorical variables zn using the process of one-hot encoding. Hence, the algorithm must identify patterns in the data to partition the dataset into K groups (Abbas et al., 2021).

Did you know?

The K-means clustering algorithm dates back to the 1950s and was first used in signal processing and image compression.

K-means is an algorithmic approach that aims to group data points that are close to each other based on their Euclidean distance. To achieve this objective, K–means allocates a specific "prototype" representative vector μ_k to all points within the same cluster. This is represented as the cluster representatives $\mu_{k:}$

$$\min_{\{z_n\},\{\mu k\}} \sum_{n=1}^{N} \sum_{k=1}^{K} z_{kn} d\left(x_n, \mu k\right),$$

The function d(x, μ) calculates the squared Euclidean distance, which is denoted as $\| x - \mu\|^2$. The utilization of a generic distance metric necessitates the adoption of the K-medoids algorithm, which will be expounded upon. Regarding this matter, it is worth mentioning that clustering can be used to discrete data if the distance metric, usually represented by a matrix of pairwise dissimilarities, is appropriately established. The K-means algorithm iteratively optimizes z_n and μ_k:

i. Reset cluster representatives as $\{\mu_k^{old}\}$.

ii. *E Step:* Representing fixed vectors $\{\mu_k^{old}\}$,work out the above equation on the cluster assignment $\{z_n\}$ (Balakrishnan et al., 1994):

$$z_{kn}^{new} = \begin{cases} 1 \; for \; k = \arg\min_j d\left(x_n, \mu_j^{old}\right) \\ 0 \qquad otherwise \end{cases}$$

Consequently, every training point is allocated to the cluster that has the nearest prototype. It is important to understand that this particular phase often involves calculating K distances for every data point x_n.

iii. *M Step:* Solve the equation above for the cluster representative {μk} with the vectors {zn} fixed. By setting the gradient concerning the objective function in the equation above to zero, impose the optimality condition,

$$z_{kn}^{new} = \frac{\sum_{n=1}^{N} z_{kn}^{new} x_n}{\sum_{n=1}^{N} z_{kn}^{new}}$$

iv. In case a convergence condition is not fulfilled, set $\{\mu_k^{old}\} \leftarrow \{\mu_k^{new}\}$ and go again to the E step (Cohn & Holm, 2021).

Considering that both the E step and the M step are responsible for minimizing the objective function in the equations presented above, alternately over z_n μ_k, it can be concluded that the value of the objective function does not decrease between iterations.

It is important to highlight the challenge of determining the number K of clusters before moving on to addressing more generic solutions. There is a first potential that clusters might be added or removed until particular heuristic criteria are satisfied. One example of this would be the "purity" of clusters. Hierarchical clustering is a second method that involves the construction of a tree, also known as a dendrogram, that has clustering solutions that have a growing number of clusters as one proceeds away from the root of the tree. Allowing K to be chosen automatically by the use of a non-parametric Bayesian technique through the utilization of a Dirichlet process prior comes as yet another alternative (Virupakshappa & Oruklu, 2019).

2.4. ML, ELBO, AND EM

The next section will elaborate on the two important technological tools that are often utilized in the process of addressing unsupervised learning issues. These tools are the ELBO method and the EM algorithm. The initial point of departure is the fundamental challenge of acquiring p(x|θ) using the data via machine learning. This model might be directed or undirected (Firdaus & Hassan, 2020).

2.4.1. Maximum Likelihood (ML)

ML tends to reduce a KL divergence between the chosen hypothesis in the model and the true distribution p(x), asymptotically in N. It is helpful to begin the discussion with ML learning because this criterion is well-appropriate for many of the unsupervised training tasks that were previously stated, such as estimating density or the creation of new samples (Hochreiter & Mozer, 2000).

A few observations are necessary before proceeding. First, selecting divergences that are particular to the application of interest rather than Kullback-Leibler (KL) is frequently helpful. Second, the machine seeks to obtain useful features z when representation learning is the goal. Lastly, it's frequently impractical to acquire ML solutions, especially for large models. However, comprehending the machine learning problem helps one assess the effects of the assumptions and reductions used to produce effective algorithms more accurately.

Next, take a probabilistic, either directed or undirected model, and concentrate on a data set with just one point of data (N = 1) to simplify the notation. All that is needed to extend the LL function to a data collection with any number N of points is to append an outer sum to the sample index. The maximum of the LL function can be expressed as the ML problem:

$$\max_{\theta} \ln p(x|\theta) = \ln \left(\sum_{z} p(x, z|\theta) \right)$$

where; z represents the latent or hidden variables and x represents the data. This issue needs to be compared to the supervised learning ML problem that arises when all x and z are observed, specifically (Manavalan & Donepudi, 2016):

$$\max_{\theta} In\, p\left(x, z \middle| \theta\right)$$

2.4.2. Evidence Lower Bound (ELBO)

Maximizing the ELBO is the foundation for several approaches to the machine learning challenge. Several variational inference algorithms including the EM algorithm are examples of these methods. The addition of an auxiliary distribution q(z) on the latent variables is a crucial step in the development of the ELBO. For reasons that will become evident later, this is known as the variational posterior or variational distribution. As shall be seen, an average across distribution q(z) is needed for the calculation of the ELBO and can be fixed irrespective of the parameters of the model.

- **Definition:** These are the ELBO L(q, θ) comparable forms for each given value x and any type of distribution q(z), depending on the latent variables z (which may or may not be dependent on x) (Mrabah et al., 2023):

$$\begin{aligned}\mathcal{L}(q,\theta) &= \mathrm{E}_{z\sim q(z)}\underbrace{[\ln p(x,\mathrm{z}|\theta) - \ln q(\mathrm{z})]}_{\text{learning signal}} \\ &= \underbrace{\mathrm{E}_{z\sim q(z)}[\ln p(x,\mathrm{z}|\theta)]}_{\text{negative energy}} + \underbrace{H(q)}_{\text{entropy}} \\ &= \underbrace{\mathrm{E}_{z\sim q(z)}[\ln p(x|\mathrm{z},\theta)]}_{\text{cross-entropy}} - \underbrace{\mathrm{KL}\left(q(z)||p(z|\theta)\right)}_{\text{variational regularization}} \\ &= -\,\mathrm{KL}\left(q(z)||p(x,z|\theta)\right) \\ &= \ln p(x|\theta) - \mathrm{KL}\left(q(z)||p(z|x,\theta)\right),\end{aligned}$$

wherein KL(p||q) is defined even in cases where q is not normalized, and where certain words are indicated using standard nomenclature that will be explained in the following sections.

The subsequent theorem defines the feature of ELBO (Chen et al., 2018).

- **Theorem:** ELBO is a lower bound that applies to the LL function on a global scale,

$$\ln p(x|\theta) \;\geq \mathcal{L}(q,\theta),$$

The condition for equality to occur at a value θ0 is that the distribution q(z) is equal to p(z|x, θ0). In addition, ELBO exhibits concavity in q(z) when θ is held constant.

- **Proof:** The initial portion of the theorem can be readily deduced from the structure, which can be reformulated as:

$$\ln p(x|\theta) = \mathcal{L}(q,\theta) + \mathrm{KL}\left(q(z)||p(z|x,\theta)\right),$$

and derived from Gibbs' inequality. It is worth mentioning that an alternative demonstration of the first half of the proposition can be presented using the significance sampling technique and Jensen's inequality:

$$\begin{aligned}\ln p(x|\theta) &= \ln\left(\sum_z p(x,z|\theta)\right) \\ &= \ln\left(\sum_z q(z)\frac{p(x,z|\theta)}{q(z)}\right) \\ &\geq \sum_z q(z)\ln\left(\frac{p(x,z|\theta)}{q(z)}\right) = \mathcal{L}(q,\theta),\end{aligned}$$

The initial equality is derived by using the importance sampling technique, which involves dividing and multiplying by q(z). The final step follows directly from Jensen's inequality (Duan et al., 2017).

2.4.3. Expectation Maximization (EM)

Many effective approaches for unsupervised learning utilizing directed as well as undirected generative models rely on:

i. Prepare the parameter vector θ old.
ii. *E Step:* To optimize the ELBO for the variational distributions q, given a fixed parameter vector θold,

solve the issue of maximizing L(q, θold). This optimization process will result in a new distribution:

$$q^{\text{new}}(z) = p(z|x, \theta^{\text{old}}).$$

i.. *M Step:* To maximize the ELBO over the parameter vector θ, solve the issue of maximizing L(q ^{new}, θ), where q ^{new}(z) is a fixed variational distribution. The convex issue can be reformulated as the maximizing of the negative energy:

$$\max_{\theta} Q(\theta, \theta^{\text{old}}) = \mathrm{E}_{z \sim p(z|x, \theta^{\text{old}})} [\ln p(x, z|\theta)]$$

ii. If the convergence requirement is not met, assign the value of θ ^{old} to θ ^{new} and go back to the E step (Bailey & Elkan, 1995).

The maximizing of the ELBO function L(q, θ) instead of the LL function is discussed subsequently.

As observed, this process of maximizing has the primary benefit that the ELBO exhibits concavity with respect to the parameters θ. Moreover, the lower bound condition guarantees that if the evidence lower bound (ELBO) is tightly constrained at a certain value θ0, then optimizing the ELBO will inevitably produce a log-likelihood (LL) value that is equal to or greater than p(x|θ0). The EM algorithm utilizes this fact to design a technique that is ensured to converge to a fixed point of the fundamental maximum likelihood problem (Pu et al., 2023).

For many relevant issues, the model p(x, z|θ) can be represented as the multiplication of a prior and a probability from the exponential group for directed models, or as a direct member of the exponentially family for undirected models. In these instances, the equation mentioned earlier, which is addressed in the M step, can be simplified to the appropriate supervised learning problem. However, it is important to note that the adequate stats average out across the posterior distribution of p(z|x, θ^{old}).

The EM algorithm is a specific case of the broader Majorization Minimization (MM) technique. Within this algorithmic class, at each iteration, a precise lower limit of the goal function is created based on the present iterate θ ^{old}. The given constraint, which should be straightforward for maximizing, is then optimized, resulting in the new value of θ called θ ^{new}. The procedure is depicted in Figure 2.2. It is evident that with each iteration, there is a guarantee that the target function will not decrease, thereby ensuring convergence to the local optimal value of the underlying problem (Covões & Hruschka, 2013).

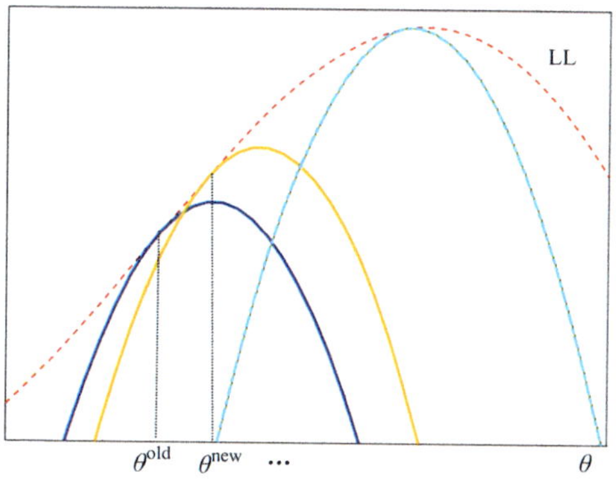

Figure 2.2. *Illustration of the EM algorithm. Dashed line is the LL function. Solid lines represent the ELBOs corresponding to first two steps of algorithm, while the dashed-dotted line is ELBO after a number of iterations.*

Source: John Hull, Creative Commons License.

The EM algorithm involves two steps:

i. Inferring the hidden variables z using the current model parameter θ in the E step, and

ii. Modifying the model θ to align with the data x and the inferred parameters z in the M step (Ruxanda & Smeureanu, 2012).

2.5. CURSE OF DIMENSIONALITY

As the number of characteristics rises, the k-means algorithm is impacted by a phenomenon called the "curse of dimensionality." The distances between observations are growing. Let's calculate the Euclidean separation between a point with all features equal to 1.0 and a point with all features equal to 0.0. The distance between features varies depending on the number of features. When there is one feature, the distance is 1.0. When there are two features, the distance is √2 or approximately 1.4. When there exist three features, the distance is √3 or approximately 1.7. When there are 100 features, the distance is 10 (Da & Grizzle, 2019).

Remember

The curse of dimensionality refers to the challenges of analyzing data in high-dimensional spaces, where data becomes sparse and distance metrics lose meaning. Dimensionality reduction techniques like PCA can help mitigate these issues.

Another issue arises when the number of characteristics increases, since the established distance metric may not effectively distinguish between data that are near compared to those that are distant. Consequently, the performance of the k-means algorithm is diminished. As a result, certain operators of the algorithm have been seeking alternate methods to estimate distance other than the Euclidean distance. The Euclidean separation between two observations, where the value of feature j in one observation is x_j and in the other observation is y_j, can be expressed (Cabannes et al., 2021):

$$\sqrt{\sum_{j=1}^{m} (x_j - y_j)^2}$$

One alternative is:

$$1 - \frac{\sum_{j=1}^{m} x_j y_j}{\sqrt{\sum_{j=1}^{m} x_j^2 \sum_{j=1}^{m} y_j^2}}$$

2.6. ALTERNATIVE CLUSTERING APPROACHES

The k-means technique is often used for clustering, however there are several options available. One method is agglomerative clustering with a hierarchical structure. This entails the subsequent procedures:

a. Begin by assigning each observation to its cluster.
b. Merge the two nearest groups.
c. Continue performing step 2 iteratively until all observations have been grouped into a single cluster.

This approach has the advantage of having hierarchical clusters, which make it possible to identify clusters inside clusters. Using the hierarchy, one may obtain exactly k clusters for any given value of k, which can range from one to the whole number of observations. This method's inclination to be computationally demanding is a downside, particularly when handling large amounts of data (Károly et al., 2018).

Several different metrics have been proposed to be used in step 2 to assess the proximity of two clusters, A and B. An observation in the A cluster and one in the B cluster have the same mean Euclidean separation of 1. As an alternative, one might use the smallest or largest of these distances. An additional metric computes the gain in inertia that results from the merger of the two clusters using Ward's methodology. Step 2 involves locating the two clusters with the lowest measure and merging them, regardless of the measure used.

Clusters are sometimes generated using assumed statistical distributions. Distribution-based clustering is the term used to describe this phenomenon most frequently. Assuming that the observations follow the probability distribution shown in Figure 2.3 and assuming there is just one characteristic for clarity. It makes sense to conclude that two normal distributions are combined to produce the findings. In this probability distribution, an observation has a probability of 1–p of being selected from a different standard distribution with an alternative standard deviation and mean and a probability of p of being taken from a normal distribution with a particular mean and standard deviation. When there are numerous characteristics and more than two distributions, an analogous work can be carried out (Pan et al., 2013).

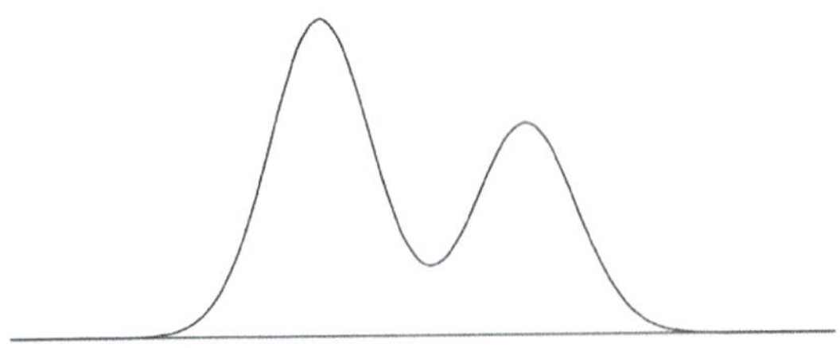

Figure 2.3. *Representation of probability distribution for data on a feature from which two normally distributed clusters could be separated.*

Source: Niti Mishra, Creative Commons License.

Density-based clustering is a method of grouping data points based on their proximity to each other. Initially, create a cluster consisting of eight closely related observations. Subsequently, introduce an additional observation to the cluster, which will be in close proximity to at least five of these observations. Following this, continue to add observations to the cluster that are close to at least five of the existing observations, and so forth. This can result in clusters that have significantly different forms compared to those evaluated by the k-means method. Figure 2.4 provides two illustrations. The k-means algorithm is unable to identify these clusters due to its utilization of cluster centers. The two clusters depicted in Figure 2.4a share identical centers, thereby making them indistinguishable by the k-means algorithm. Figure 2.4b demonstrates that the k-means algorithm may detect several clusters, however, it may not accurately identify the visually apparent groupings (Grira et al., 2004).

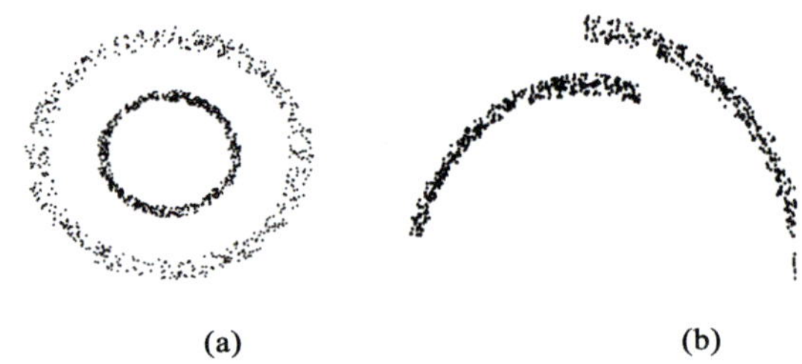

Figure 2.4. *Illustration of clusters which might be identified by a density-based clustering algorithm.*

Source: Jeff Li, Creative Commons License.

ACTIVITY 2.1

Suppose there are three features, A, B, and C. One observation has values 2, 3, and 4 for A, B, and C, respectively. Another has values 6, 8, and 7 for A, B, and C respectively.

Calculate the Euclidean distance between the two observations.

SUMMARY

- Unsupervised learning focuses on comprehending patterns inherent in data. Typically, this process entails searching for clusters, which are groups of related observations. Companies frequently employ unsupervised learning techniques to get insights into the many consumer segments they possess, enabling them to enhance their communication strategies. Feature scaling is typically required for the process of clustering. There are two primary methods for feature scaling. Z-score normalization is a method of scaling features so that their mean becomes zero and their standard deviation becomes one. Another approach is the min-max method, which involves scaling all characteristics to have values ranging from zero to one.
- A clustering algorithm necessitates the use of a distance metric. The Euclidean distance is the most often used measure in this context. The center of a cluster is determined by calculating the average feature values of all observations within the cluster. K-means is the most often used clustering technique. When considering a specific value of k (the number of clusters), the objective is to minimize inertia.
- This chapter has provided an overview of the fundamental principles of unsupervised learning. All the approaches being considered share a common feature, which is the existence of hidden or latent variables that aid in explaining the structure of the data. Machine learning was initially examined using the Expectation-Maximization (EM) algorithm, as well as its modifications, for both directed and undirected models.
- Several alternatives exist to the k-means method. One method is hierarchical clustering which begins by considering a scenario in which each individual observation is first assigned to its own separate cluster. Subsequently, gradually diminish the quantity of clusters by merging clusters that exhibit proximity to one another. Distribution-based clustering is assuming the data's distribution. Density-based clustering is a method that identifies areas in a dataset where there is a high concentration of data points, without considering specific cluster centers.

REVIEW QUESTIONS

What is unsupervised learning and how does it differ from supervised learning?

Why is feature scaling important in unsupervised learning? Explain two methods for feature scaling?

What is the objective of the K-means clustering algorithm?

How does hierarchical clustering work? What are its advantages and disadvantages relative to k-means?

How does the curse of dimensionality affect clustering algorithms?

MULTIPLE CHOICE QUESTIONS

1. **What is the main goal of unsupervised learning?**
   a. To predict output labels based on input features
   b. To classify data into predefined categories
   c. To identify hidden patterns or structures in data without predefined labels
   d. To reduce the dimensionality of the dataset
2. **Which of the following algorithms is used for clustering in unsupervised learning?**
   a. Linear regression
   b. K-means
   c. Decision trees
   d. Logistic regression
3. **What is feature scaling, and why is it important in unsupervised learning?**
   a. It is the process of removing irrelevant features.
   b. It is the process of normalizing the range of features to ensure each feature contributes equally.
   c. It is the process of increasing the dimensionality of the dataset.
   d. It is the process of labeling data points.
4. **What challenge does the curse of dimensionality present in unsupervised learning?**
   a. It makes data points closer to each other.
   b. It makes data points more meaningful.
   c. It makes the volume of the space increase exponentially, leading to sparse data.
   d. It reduces the number of features available.

Answers to Multiple Questions

1. (c); 2. (b); 3. (b); 4. (c)

REFERENCES

1. Abbas, A., Prayitno, P., Nurkim, N., Prumanto, D., Dewadi, F. M., Hidayati, N., & Windarto, A. P. (2021). Implementation of clustering unsupervised learning using K-Means mapping techniques. In *IOP Conference Series: Materials Science and Engineering* (Vol. 1088, pp. 12004). IOP Publishing.
2. Abukmeil, M., Ferrari, S., Genovese, A., Piuri, V., & Scotti, F. (2021). A survey of unsupervised generative models for exploratory data analysis and representation learning. *ACM Computing Surveys (CSUR), 54*(5), 1–40.
3. Bailey, T. L., & Elkan, C. (1995). Unsupervised learning of multiple motifs in biopolymers using expectation maximization. *Machine Learning, 21*, 51–80.
4. Balakrishnan, P. V., Cooper, M. C., Jacob, V. S., & Lewis, P. A. (1994). A study of the classification capabilities of neural networks using unsupervised learning: A comparison with K-means clustering. *Psychometrika, 59*, 509–525.
5. Basanisi, R., Brovelli, A., Cartoni, E., & Baldassarre, G. (2020). A generative spiking neural-network model of goal-directed behavior and one-step planning. *PLOS Computational Biology, 16*(12), e1007579.
6. Brydges, R., Dubrowski, A., & Regehr, G. (2010). A new concept of unsupervised learning: Directed self-guided learning in the health professions. *Academic Medicine, 85*(10), S49–S55.
7. Cabannes, V., Pillaud-Vivien, L., Bach, F., & Rudi, A. (2021). Overcoming the curse of dimensionality with Laplacian regularization in semi-supervised learning. *Advances in Neural Information Processing Systems, 34*, 30439–30451.
8. Chen, H., & Lin, R. W. (1994). An on-line unsupervised learning machine for adaptive feature extraction. *IEEE Transactions on Circuits and Systems II: Analog and Digital Signal Processing, 41*(2), 87–98.
9. Chen, L., Tao, C., Zhang, R., Henao, R., & Duke, L. C. (2018). Variational inference and model selection with generalized evidence bounds. In *International Conference on Machine Learning* (Vol. 2, pp. 893–902). PMLR.
10. Cohn, R., & Holm, E. (2021). Unsupervised machine learning via transfer learning and K-means clustering to classify materials image data. *Integrating Materials and Manufacturing Innovation, 10*(2), 231–244.
11. Covões, T. F., & Hruschka, E. R. (2013). Unsupervised learning of Gaussian mixture models: Evolutionary create and eliminate for expectation maximization algorithm. In *2013 IEEE Congress on Evolutionary Computation* (Vol. 2, pp. 3206–3213). IEEE.
12. Da, X., & Grizzle, J. (2019). Combining trajectory optimization, supervised machine learning, and model structure for mitigating the curse of dimensionality in the control of bipedal robots. *The International Journal of Robotics Research, 38*(9), 1063–1097.
13. Djukanovic, M., Babic, B., Sobajic, D. J., & Pao, Y. H. (1993). Unsupervised/supervised learning concept for 24-hour load forecasting. In *IEE Proceedings C (Generation, Transmission and Distribution)* (Vol. 140, pp. 311–318). IET Digital Library.

14. Duan, H., Yang, L., Fang, J., & Li, H. (2017). Fast inverse-free sparse Bayesian learning via relaxed evidence lower bound maximization. *IEEE Signal Processing Letters, 24*(6), 774–778.
15. Figueiredo, M. A. T., & Jain, A. K. (2002). Unsupervised learning of finite mixture models. *IEEE Transactions on Pattern Analysis and Machine Intelligence, 24*(3), 381–396.
16. Firdaus, H., & Hassan, S. I. (2020). Unsupervised learning on healthcare survey data with particle swarm optimization. *Machine Learning with Health Care Perspective: Machine Learning and Healthcare, 2*(1), 57–89.
17. Grira, N., Crucianu, M., & Boujemaa, N. (2004). Unsupervised and semi-supervised clustering: A brief survey. *A Review of Machine Learning Techniques for Processing Multimedia Content, 1*(2004), 9–16.
18. Hochreiter, S., & Mozer, M. C. (2000). Beyond maximum likelihood and density estimation: A sample-based criterion for unsupervised learning of complex models. *Advances in Neural Information Processing Systems, 13*, 987–990.
19. Iba, W., & Langley, P. (1999). Unsupervised learning of probabilistic concept hierarchies. In *Advanced Course on Artificial Intelligence* (Vol. 2, pp. 39–70). Berlin, Heidelberg: Springer Berlin Heidelberg.
20. James, G., Witten, D., Hastie, T., Tibshirani, R., & Taylor, J. (2023). Unsupervised learning. In *An Introduction to Statistical Learning: With Applications in Python* (Vol. 1, pp. 503–556). Cham: Springer International Publishing.
21. Károly, A. I., Fullér, R., & Galambos, P. (2018). Unsupervised clustering for deep learning: A tutorial survey. *Acta Polytechnica Hungarica, 15*(8), 29–53.
22. Kumar, A. C. (2009). Analysis of unsupervised dimensionality reduction techniques. *Computer Science and Information Systems, 6*(2), 217–227.
23. Manavalan, M., & Donepudi, P. K. (2016). A sample-based criterion for unsupervised learning of complex models beyond maximum likelihood and density estimation. *ABC Journal of Advanced Research, 5*(2), 123–130.
24. Morales, E. F., & Escalante, H. J. (2022). A brief introduction to supervised, unsupervised, and reinforcement learning. In *Biosignal Processing and Classification Using Computational Learning and Intelligence* (Vol. 1, pp. 111–129). Academic Press.
25. Mrabah, N., Bouguessa, M., & Ksantini, R. (2023). Beyond the evidence lower bound: Dual variational graph auto-encoders for node clustering. In *Proceedings of the 2023 SIAM International Conference on Data Mining (SDM)* (Vol. 2, pp. 100–108). Society for Industrial and Applied Mathematics.
26. Ozsahin, D. U., Mustapha, M. T., Mubarak, A. S., Ameen, Z. S., & Uzun, B. (2022). Impact of feature scaling on machine learning models for the diagnosis of diabetes. In *2022 International Conference on Artificial Intelligence in Everything (AIE)* (Vol. 2, pp. 87–94). IEEE.
27. Pan, W., Shen, X., & Liu, B. (2013). Cluster analysis: Unsupervised learning via supervised learning with a non-convex penalty. *Journal of Machine Learning Research, 14*(7), 879.

28. Parasa, N. A., Namgiri, J. V., Mohanty, S. N., & Dash, J. K. (2021). Introduction to unsupervised learning in bioinformatics. In *Data Analytics in Bioinformatics: A Machine Learning Perspective* (Vol. 4, pp. 35–49).

29. Peis, I., Olmos, P. M., & Artés-Rodríguez, A. (2023). Unsupervised learning of global factors in deep generative models. *Pattern Recognition, 134*, 109130.

30. Pu, Y., Sun, J., Tang, N., & Xu, Z. (2023). Deep expectation-maximization network for unsupervised image segmentation and clustering. *Image and Vision Computing, 135*, 104717.

31. Raina, R., Madhavan, A., & Ng, A. Y. (2009). Large-scale deep unsupervised learning using graphics processors. In *Proceedings of the 26th Annual International Conference on Machine Learning* (Vol. 2, pp. 873–880).

32. Rojas, R., & Rojas, R. (1996). Unsupervised learning and clustering algorithms. In *Neural Networks: A Systematic Introduction* (Vol. 2, pp. 99–121).

33. Ruxanda, G., & Smeureanu, I. (2012). Unsupervised learning with expected maximization algorithm. *Economic Computation and Economic Cybernetics Studies and Research, 46*(1), 17–44.

34. Tlusty, T., Amit, G., & Ben-Ari, R. (2018). Unsupervised clustering of mammograms for outlier detection and breast density estimation. In *2018 24th International Conference on Pattern Recognition (ICPR)* (Vol. 2, pp. 3808–3813). IEEE.

35. Virupakshappa, K., & Oruklu, E. (2019). Unsupervised machine learning for ultrasonic flaw detection using Gaussian mixture modeling, K-means clustering, and mean shift clustering. In *2019 IEEE International Ultrasonics Symposium (IUS)* (Vol. 2, pp. 647–649). IEEE.

36. Wetzel, S. J. (2017). Unsupervised learning of phase transitions: From principal component analysis to variational autoencoders. *Physical Review E, 96*(2), 022140.

37. Xu, L., Wilkinson, D., Southey, F., & Schuurmans, D. (2006). Discriminative unsupervised learning of structured predictors. In *Proceedings of the 23rd International Conference on Machine Learning* (Vol. 2, pp. 1057–1064).

38. Zhu, L., Zhang, C., Zhang, C., Zhang, Z., Nie, X., Zhou, X., & Wang, X. (2019). Forming a new small sample deep learning model to predict total organic carbon content by combining unsupervised learning with semi-supervised learning. *Applied Soft Computing, 83*, 105596.

CHAPTER 3

Supervised Learning: Linear Regression

LEARNING OBJECTIVES

After studying this chapter, you will be able to:

- Understand the principles of linear regression;
- Comprehend the difference between simple linear regression and multiple linear regression;
- Understand the concept of regularization; and
- Comprehend the technique of regression such as ridge, lasso, and elastic net regression.

KEY TERMS FROM THIS CHAPTER

Decision Criteria

Elastic Net Regression

Lasso Regression

Ridge Regression

Dummy Variable Trap

Gradient Descent Algorithm

Polynomial Regression

UNIT INTRODUCTION

Statisticians have employed linear regression for a considerable period. Carl Friedrich Gauss, a renowned mathematician, is attributed with initially proposing the least squares methodology that formed the foundation of linear regression in the year 1800. In the field of machine learning, it is not necessary to make assumptions about linear correlations. (Many of the technologies introduced later in this book result in non-linear models.) However, despite this fact, linear regression continues to be a significant technique in the field of machine learning. It is frequently one of the initial instruments employed by analysts in supervised learning (Sharma et al., 2020).

Vanilla linear regression is a method that aims to minimize the mean squared error (MSE) when predicting the value of a target variable based on one or more features. Many readers will find this familiar. This chapter explores the integration of categorical variables, which are non-numerical features, into linear regression models to enable prediction. The article also covers Ridge, Lasso, and Elastic Net regression, which are very valuable when making predictions based on a significant number of features. Next, the text proceeds to elucidate logistic regression, which is a methodology employed to address scenarios where the goal is to acquire knowledge about classifying data. Lastly, it discusses the k-nearest-neighbor approach, which serves as a straightforward alternative to linear and logistic regression (Josephine et al., 2021).

3.1. LINEAR REGRESSION: ONE FEATURE

Assume the basic scenario in which the prediction of the target variable Y is based on a single feature X. In linear regression, the assumption of a linear relationship between variables is made, which means that the model follows a straight line (Hasan et al., 2015):

$$Y = a + bX + \varepsilon$$

Where; 'a' and 'b' represent constants and 'ε' represents the error term. Let X_i and Y_i $(1 < i \leq n)$ represent the values of X and Y for the ith observation in the training set. The optimal values of variables a and b are determined as the ones that minimize the mean squared error (mse) for the observations in the training set (Chen et al., 2017). This implies that the values for variables a and b are selected in such a way that

$$\frac{1}{n}\sum_{i=1}^{n}(Y_i - a - bX_i)^2$$

is minimized. Calculus can be used to find the minimum. Denoting the averages of the observations on X and Y by X^- and Y^-

$$b = \frac{\sum_{i=1}^{n} X_i Y_i - n\bar{X}\bar{Y}}{\sum_{i=1}^{n} X_i^2 - n\bar{X}^2}$$

$$a = \bar{Y} - b\bar{X}$$

The model demonstrates an instance of linear regression using a single attribute. This is derived from the training data set presented in Table 3.1. In this scenario n = 10, X^- = 43, and Y^- = 216,500 (Guo et al., 2021). Also,

$$\sum_{i=1}^{10} X_i Y_i = 100{,}385{,}000$$

$$\sum_{i=1}^{10} X_i^2 = 20{,}454$$

So that

$$b = \frac{100{,}385{,}000 - 10 \times 43 \times 216{,}500}{20{,}454 - 10 \times 43^2} = 3{,}827.3$$

$$a = 216{,}500 - 3827.3 \times 43 = 51{,}160.4$$

and the model is

$$Y = 51{,}160.4 + 3{,}827.3X$$

The model is:

Y= 51,160.4 + 3,827.3X

At times when the parameter a is equal to zero (Wu & Yang, 2015),

$$b = \frac{\sum_{i=1}^{n} X_i Y_i}{\sum_{i=1}^{n} X_i^2}$$

Did you know?

Linear regression is one of the oldest and most widely used regression techniques in statistics and machine learning, dating back to the early 19th century.

Table 3.1. *Representation of Training Data Set: Salaries for a Random Sample of 10 People*

Age	Salary	
25 years	$ 135,000	
55 years	$ 260,000	
27 years	$ 105,000	
35 years	$ 220,000	
60 years	$ 240,000	
65 years	$ 265,000	
45 years	$ 270,000	
40 years	$ 300,000	
50 years	$ 265,000	
30 years	$ 105,000	
40 years	$ 300,000	

Source: Peter Hull, Creative Commons License.

3.2. LINEAR REGRESSION: MULTIPLE FEATURES

When many features are employed to predict a target, the model can be expressed as:

$$Y = a + b_1X_1 + b_2X_2 + \cdots + b_mX_m + \varepsilon$$

The aim is represented by the variable Y, whereas the features used to predict Y are designated as X_j ($1 \leq j \leq m$). The symbol ε represents the prediction error, as mentioned above. The parameters a and b_j ($1 \leq j \leq m$) are chosen to minimize the mean squared error over the training dataset. In linear regression, the goal is to find the optimal values of the coefficients a and b_j that minimize (Zhu et al., 2010):

$$\frac{1}{n}\sum_{i=1}^{n}(Y_i - a - b_1X_{i1} - b_2X_{i2} - \cdots - b_mX_{im})^2$$

Y_i represents the value of the target variable for observation i, while X_{ij} represents the value of the jth feature for observation i. In the field of machine learning, the parameter "a" is commonly known as the bias, whereas the coefficients "b_j" are commonly known as the weights. Calculus can be employed to ascertain the criteria for a minimum. This results in a system of simultaneous equations used to determine the values of a and b_j. Matrix algebra can be used to solve these equations (Nimon & Oswald, 2013).

3.2.1. Gradient Descent Algorithm

The gradient descent approach is a viable alternative to matrix algebra, which is necessary for some studies discussed in subsequent sections of this chapter. This is an iterative search algorithm designed to locate the smallest value. Visualize graphing the equation as a function of variables a and b_j (where j ranges from 1 to m) in a space with m + 1 dimensions. This function can be conceptualized as a valley, and the objective is to locate the lowest point of the valley. Calculus may be employed to ascertain the trajectory of the most rapid descent down the valley, regardless of the location inside it. This involves determining the optimal adjustments for both the variables a and b_j to descend as swiftly as feasible. The gradient descent algorithm operates in the following manner (Perkins et al., 2003):

i. Select initial values for the variables a and b_j.

ii. Determine the trajectory of the most rapid descent.

iii. Proceed down the line of greatest descent.

iv. Recalculate the trajectory of maximum descent.

v. Proceed with another stride, and repeat the process (Handoyo et al., 2022).

3.2.2. Polynomial Regressions

These are regressions in which there is just one feature, denoted as X, and X_j is assigned the same value as X_j, resulting in the model:

$$Y = a + b_1 X + b_2 X_2 + \cdots + b_m X_m + \varepsilon$$

Analysis revealed that the model with a value of m = 5 performs accurately on the training set but fails to generalize effectively to the validation set. The quadratic model with m = 2 was selected due to its superior fit compared to the linear model, while yet maintaining a high level of generalization.

Occasionally, regression analysis involves the utilization of both products and powers of features. An instance where the target is being forecasted based on two features is (Ajona et al., 2022):

$$Y = a + b_1 X_1 + b_2 X_1^2 + b_3 X_2 + b_4 X_2^2 + b_5 X_1 X_2 + \varepsilon$$

3.2.3. Regression Statistics

Several statistical measures can be derived from a linear regression analysis, and they can be valuable if the conditions specified previously are reasonably met. The R-squared statistic, ranging from zero to one, quantifies the fraction of the target's variance that can be accounted for by the features.

Remember

In linear regression, coefficients indicate the change in the dependent variable for a unit change in the corresponding independent variable, holding other variables constant.

$$1 - \frac{\text{Variance of the errors } \varepsilon}{\text{Variance of the observations on the target } Y}$$

R-squared is equal to the coefficient of correlation squared when there is just one feature. Regarding the data presented in Table 3.1, the R-squared value for the linear model is 0.54, whereas for the quadratic model, it is 0.80 (Kavitha et al., 2016).

3.3. CATEGORICAL FEATURES

The predictive model may incorporate both categorical and numerical data as features. A categorical variable is a variable that may be divided into separate and distinct categories. For example, the purchasers of a product can be categorized as either male or female. Women who buy a particular beauty product can be categorized according to their hair color, which can be described as blonde, red, brown, or black (Kampezidou et al., 2024).

A frequently employed approach for handling categorical data involves generating a binary variable for each category. This variable is a binary value that is equal to one if the feature corresponds to the category and zero if it does not. This process is widely acknowledged as one-hot encoding. By classifying individuals into distinct categories of male or female, two binary variables can be established. For males, the initial binary variable would be allocated a value of one, while the subsequent binary variable would be assigned a value of zero. For females, the first binary variable would be allocated a value of zero, while the next binary variable would be assigned a value of one. In the hair color example, there would be four binary variables, also known as dummy variables. Each observation would be assigned a binary value of one for the relevant variable and a binary value of zero for the other three variables (Sen et al., 2020).

3.3.1. The Dummy Variable Trap

When utilizing one-hot encoding to represent one or more categorical variables and include a constant (bias) factor in the regression, there is no unique optimal linear regression solution. This occurrence is widely recognized as the dummy variable trap (Khashei et al., 2012).

Assume that the equation above has been derived to predict the value of a target variable Y:

$$Y = a + b_1X_1 + b_2X_2 + \ldots + b_mX_m + \varepsilon$$

Furthermore, it is important to note that the initial set of features, X_1, X_2,..., X_k (where k is less than or equal to m), are binary variables generated through the process of one-hot encoding a specific categorical variable. Consider the outcome of adding a constant C to the bias, a, and subtracting C from each of the weights $\boxtimes_1$, $\boxtimes_2$,..., $\boxtimes_{\boxtimes}$. Due to the inherent nature of one-hot encoding, X_j must be equal to 0 for $1 \le j \le k$, except for a specific value of j where X_j equals 1. Consequently, by subtracting the value of C from each of $b_1, b_2, \ldots, b_k$, the predicted value of Y is precisely reduced by C. When C is added to a, the predicted value of Y increases by C. The projected value of Y remains unchanged when these two modifications are implemented. This is true for all values of C (Han et al., 2014).

Fortunately, regularization, a technique aimed at simplifying models and preventing over-fitting, also addresses the issue of the dummy variable trap problem by identifying the optimal regression equation. This equation involves weights with small magnitudes (Yoo et al., 2012).

3.4. REGULARIZATION

Machine learning generally involves a multitude of features, some of which may exhibit correlation. This can result in overfitting and models that are needlessly intricate. Regularization is a commonly used approach to address this issue. The following three parts will provide three regularization algorithms and demonstrate their application using the data provided in Table 3.1 (Chen et al., 2019).

3.5. RIDGE REGRESSION

Ridge regression, also known as Tikhonov regression, is a regularization method that involves modifying the objective function to be minimized (Seok, 2013):

$$\frac{1}{n}\sum_{i=1}^{n}(Y_i - a - b_1X_{i1} - b_2X_{i2} - \cdots - b_mX_{im})^2 + \lambda\sum_{j=1}^{m} b_j^2 \qquad (3.3)$$

Ridge regression incorporates the parameter λb_j^2 into the mean squared error for each feature j. This modification serves to incentivize the model to minimize the values of the weights b_j. L2 regularization is another term for ridge regression (Chang et al., 2017).

Examine a scenario with two features, X_1 and X_2, that are strongly associated. These features have been scaled in such a way that their average value is zero and their variability is one. Assume that the linear model with the best fit, derived by minimizing the objective function, is:

$Y = a + 1000X_1 - 980X_2$

Because the features are close substitutes, simpler models are used such as:

$Y = a + bX_1$ or...$Y = a + bX_2$

When the value of b is approximately 20, it is more likely to result in better generalization. Ridge regression, by imposing a penalty on coefficients with large positive or negative values, would identify one of these models (Tutz & Binder, 2007). The Ridge regression model, as defined in equation (3.3), is specifically designed for estimating model parameters based on the training set exclusively. After determining the model parameters, it is recommended to utilize equation (3.2) for making predictions. It is advisable to employ a validation set to assess the generalization performance of equation (3.2). The chosen model's accuracy should be measured using equation (3.2) on the test set

(Nouretdinov et al., 2001). The parameter λ is considered a hyperparameter as it is utilized in the training process of the model, but it is not included in the model itself for predicting Y. The selection of a value for λ is crucial. If λ is a large amount, then all the b_j would be set to zero. (The resulting model would be uninteresting since it would consistently predict a value equal to a for Y.) Practically, it is advantageous to experiment with multiple options for λ and evaluate the performance of the resulting models on a validation set to assess their generalizability (Patwary et al., 2022). It was previously stated that the objective function of standard linear regression, as shown in equation (3.2), can be minimized analytically through the utilization of matrix algebra. An analytical approach can be used to minimize the objective function of Ridge regression, as shown in equation (3.3). The gradient descent approach discussed in Section 3.2 is another option. As an illustration of regularization, the model in which a polynomial of degree five was applied to the training data set in Table 3.1 will be used. Chapter 1 provides evidence that the model exhibits overfitting on the training set. Observing how regularization deals with this will provide valuable insights (Zhang et al., 2018).

Initially, it is important to perform feature scaling. This example consists of five distinct aspects. These are X, X^2, X^3, X^4, and X^5, where X is the age in years. Each of these items must be proportionally adjusted in size. (Note that scaling only the X-axis is not enough.) Z-score normalization shall be implied. Table 3.2 displays the values of the characteristics along with their corresponding means and standard deviations. The magnitude of the numbers in the table underscores the significance of scaling. Table 3.3 displays the scaled characteristics. The optimal linear regression model is obtained when the characteristics are scaled according to the values provided in Table 3.3, and the salary Y is measured in thousands of dollars (Kärkkäinen, 2019):

$$Y = 216.5 - 32{,}622.6X + 135{,}402.7X^2 - 215{,}493.1X^3 + 155{,}314.6X^4 - 42{,}558.8X^5 \quad (3.4)$$

Table 3.2. *Representation of Feature Values. X Equals the Age of Individuals in the Training Set*

Instance	X	X^2	X^3	X^4	X^5
1	25	625	15,625	390,625	9,765,625
2	65	4,225	274,625	17,850,625	1,160,290,625
3	27	729	19,683	531,441	14,348,907
4	55	3,025	166,375	9,150,625	503,284,375
5	60	3,600	216,000	12,960,000	777,600,000
6	40	1,600	64,000	2,560,000	102,400,000
7	45	2,025	91,125	4,100,625	184,528,125
8	30	900	27,000	810,000	24,300,000
9	50	2,500	125,000	6,250,000	312,500,000
10	35	1,225	42,875	1,500,625	52,521,875
S.D.	14.1	1,259	89,653	5,975,341	389,179,640
Mean	43.2	2,045	104,231	5,610,457	314,153,953

Source: John Hull, Creative Commons License.

Table 3.3. *Values of Features in Table 3.2 After Scaling*

Instance	X	X^2	X^3	X^4	X^5
1	−1.148	−1.046	−0.943	−0.850	−0.770
2	0.836	1	1	1	0
3	0.128	−0.016	−0.146	−0.253	−0.333
4	−0.581	−0.652	−0.684	−0.688	−0.672
5	−1.290	−1.128	−0.988	−0.874	−0.782
6	1.545	2	2	2	2
7	0.482	0	0	0	−0.004
8	−0.227	−0.354	−0.449	−0.511	−0.544
9	1.191	1	1	1	1
10	−0.936	−0.910	−0.861	−0.803	−0.745

Source: John Hull, Creative Commons License.

It is now possible to utilize Ridge regression. Table 3.4 displays the bias, denoted as "a," and the weights, denoted as "b_j," for two distinct values of λ. By setting λ= 0, the regression result in equation (3.4) would be simplified to a basic and straightforward form (Tsigler & Bartlett, 2023). Transitioning from λ = 0 to λ = 0.02 has a significant impact on the weights, causing a substantial decrease by several orders of magnitude. When λ is increased from 0.02 to 1.0, the weights are decreased even more. Figures 3.1, 3.2, and 3.3 display the projected wage based on age for the forecasts made with λ values of 0, 0.02, and 0.1. It is evident that as the value of λ increases, the model's complexity decreases. The model with λ = 0.02 has a high degree of similarity to the quadratic model (Stock et al., 2018).

Table 3.4. *Variation of Bias and Weights for Different Values of λ for Ridge Regression*

λ	a	b_1	b_2	b_3	b_4	b_5
0.1	216.5	56.5	28.1	3.7	−15.1	−28.4
0.02	216.5	97.8	36.6	−8.5	−35.0	−44.6

Source: Emilio Barone, Creative Commons License.

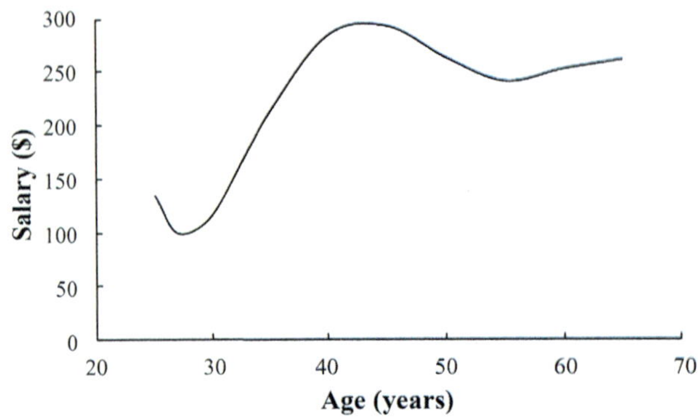

Figure 3.1. *Prediction of salary ($'000s), no regularization (λ= 0).*

Source: Jay Cao, Creative Commons License.

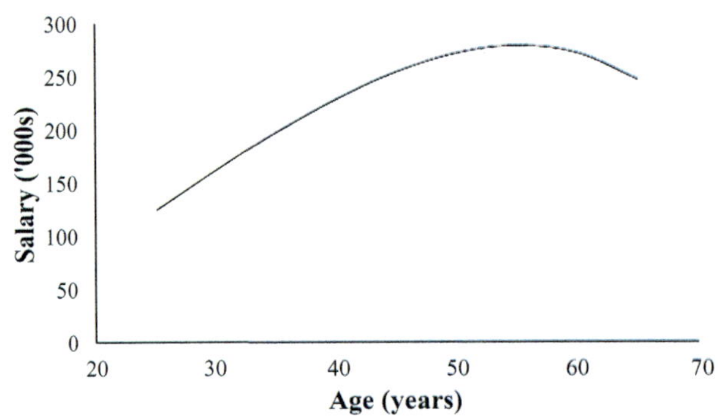

Figure 3.2. *Prediction of salary ($'000s) when Ridge regression is used with λ= 0.02.*

Source: Jeff Li, Creative Commons License.

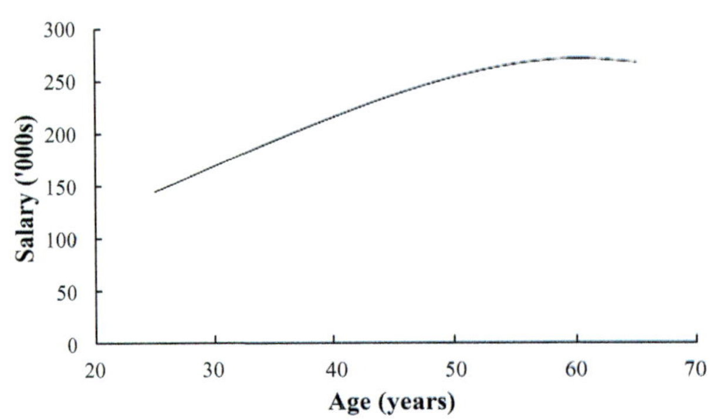

Figure 3.3. *Prediction of salary when Ridge regression is used with λ=0.1.*

Source: Niti Mishra, Creative Commons License.

3.6. LASSO REGRESSION

Lasso is an abbreviation for the term "Least absolute shrinkage and selection operator." In the Ridge method, a scalar multiple of the sum of the weights squared was incorporated into the goal function. In Lasso, a scalar multiple of the total sum of the absolute weights is incorporated. The result is the subsequent objective function (Afrin et al., 2021):

$$\frac{1}{n}\sum_{i=1}^{n}(Y_i - a - b_1X_{i1} - b_2X_{i2} - \cdots - b_mX_{im})^2 + \lambda\sum_{j=1}^{m}|b_j|$$

An analytical minimization of this function is not possible, so a method similar to the previously mentioned gradient descent process must be employed. Lasso regression is commonly known as L1 regularization. In the preceding section, it was demonstrated that Ridge regression diminishes the weights allocated to characteristics to streamline the model. The simplified model typically exhibits superior generalization compared to the unregularized model. Lasso regression offers the ability to streamline the model. This is achieved by assigning a weight of zero to insignificant traits. Lasso is capable of selecting a small subset of features from a vast pool to create an effective prediction model (Huang et al., 2020). Table 3.5 displays the outcomes of employing Lasso in the example, where a fifth-order polynomial is utilized to forecast an individual's pay based on their age. The table demonstrates that Lasso effectively assigns a weight of zero to certain attributes. It is anticipated that the values of b_5, b_4, and potentially b_3 will be zero, resulting in the simplification of the model to a quadratic or cubic model. Contrary to what is being suggested, this is not the case. At λ= 0.02, Lasso exclusively eliminates the value of b_3; at λ= 0.1, Lasso eliminates the values of b_2 and b_4; at λ= 1, Lasso eliminates the values of b_2, b_3, and b_5 (Emmert-Streib & Dehmer, 2019).

Table 3.5. *Variation of Bias and Weights for Different Values of λ for Lasso regression.*

λ	a	b_1	b_2	b_3	b_4	b_5
1	216.5	147.4	0	0	−99.3	0
0.1	216.5	355.4	0	−494.8	0	196.5
0.02	216.5	−646.4	2,046.60	0	−3,351.0	2,007.90

Source: Jacky Chen, Creative Commons License.

Figures 3.4, 3.5, and 3.6 display the prediction models generated for λ values of 0.02, 0.1, and 1. They are less complex than the fifth-degree polynomial model described in equation (3.4) and have significantly smaller coefficients. Similar to ridge regression, the complexity of the models decreases when the value of λ is increased. The model depicted in Figure 3.6 bears a striking resemblance to the quadratic model (Roy et al., 2015).

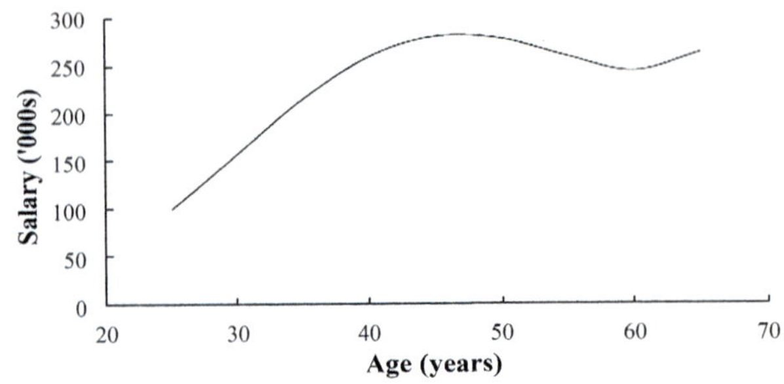

Figure 3.4. *Prediction of salary when Lasso regression is used with λ= 0.02. Salary is measured in $'000s.*

Source: Jun Yuan, Creative Commons License.

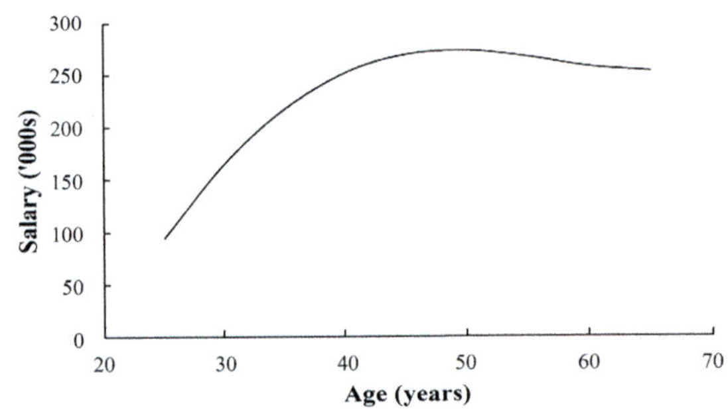

Figure 3.5. *Prediction of salary when Lasso regression is used with λ = 0.1. Salary is measured in $'000s.*

Source: Eddie Mizzi, Creative Commons License.

Figure 3.6. *Prediction of salary when Lasso regression is used with λ=1. Salary is measured in $'000s.*

Source: Raymond Kan, Creative Commons License.

3.7. ELASTIC NET REGRESSION

Elastic Net regression combines the characteristics of Ridge and Lasso regression. The objective function consists of two terms: one is the product of a constant and the sum of squared weights, and the other is the product of a separate constant and the sum of absolute values of the weights (Ryan & Culp, 2015).

$$\frac{1}{n}\sum_{i=1}^{n}(Y_i - a - b_1X_{1i} - b_2X_{2i} - \cdots - b_mX_{mi})^2 + \lambda_1\sum_{j=1}^{m}b_j^2 + \lambda_2\sum_{j=1}^{m}|b_j|$$

While using Lasso, certain weights are diminished to zero, while others may be significantly amplified. In Ridge regression, the weights are characterized by their modest magnitude, but they are not completely diminished to zero. The concept behind Elastic Net is that optimal results can potentially be achieved by setting certain weights to zero while decreasing the magnitude of the remaining weights. To demonstrate this in the example of a fifth-order polynomial, values λ1 = 0.02 and λ2 = 1 are assigned. The derived model for forecasting pay ($'000s), Y, based on age (years), X, is as follows (Hans, 2011):

$$Y = 216.5 + 96.7X + 21.1X^2 - 26.0X^4 - 45.5X^5$$

The structure of this model closely resembles that of the Lasso model with a lambda value of 0.02, as shown in Table 3.5. However, the non-zero weights in this model are significantly less. Figure 3.7 displays the model. Once again, it is observed that the outcome closely resembles the quadratic model that was established for this particular instance (Soomro et al., 2016).

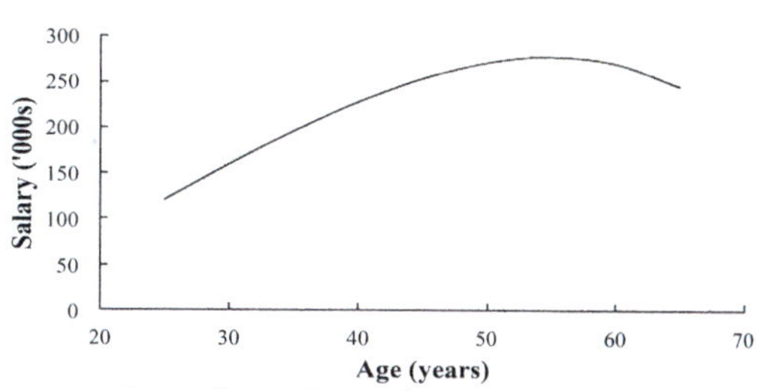

Figure 3.7. *Prediction of salary when Elastic Net regression is used with λ_1= 0.2 and λ_2= 1.0.*

Source: Peter Hull, Creative Commons License.

3.8. RESULTS FOR HOUSE PRICE DATA

Local authorities in numerous countries must forecast the market prices of houses to ascertain property taxes. They can accomplish this by establishing a correlation between the documented sale prices of houses and specific attributes such as the number of bedrooms, the quantity of bathrooms, and the geographical location of the property. The dataset that will be utilized comprises data on houses that were sold in Iowa over four years (Fory⊠, 2022).

Before commencing, the significance of the information about the necessity of partitioning all accessible data into three distinct components: a training set, a validation set, and a test set is stressed. The training set is utilized to ascertain parameters for experimental models. The validation set is utilized to assess the level of generalization of the models derived from the training set to novel data. The test set is utilized as a conclusive evaluation of the precision of the selected model. Following the process of data cleaning, a total of 2,908 observations were obtained (Matey et al., 2022).

The complete dataset has approximately 80 characteristics, consisting of both numerical and category variables. To demonstrate the regression approaches that have been covered in this chapter, a total of 23 distinct features will be utilized. The items are enumerated in Table 3.6. There are 21 numerical variables and two category variables. One of the categorical attributes pertains to the quality of the basement, as determined by the height of the ceiling. The classifications are (Rana et al., 2020):

i. Excellent (>100 inches)
ii. Good (90 to 99 inches)
iii. Typical (80 to 89 inches)
iv. Fair (70 to 79 inches)
v. Poor (< 70 inches)
vi. No basement

This is an instance of a categorical variable that exhibits inherent ordering. A novel variable was introduced, assigning the values 5, 4, 3, 2, 1, and 0 to the six respective categories (Banerjee & Dutta, 2017).

The additional category element indicates the precise position of the house inside one of the 25 communities. Considering the real estate brokers' emphasis on the significance of location, it was deemed crucial to incorporate this function. Consequently, 25 placeholder variables were implemented. The binary variable takes the value of one if the house is located in the specified neighborhood, and zero otherwise. The model consisted of a total of 47 features, including 21 numerical features, 1 feature representing basement condition, and 25 features representing location (Mora-Garcia et al., 2022).

Table 3.6. *Features for Estimating House Prices and Weights Using a Linear Regression Model on Scaled Data with no Regularization*

Feature	Weights for simple linear regression
Lot area (ft^2)	0.08
Overall quality (scale: 1-10)	0.21
Overall condition (scale: 1-10)	0.1
Built year	0.16
Remodel year	0.03
Finished basement (ft^2)	0.09
Unfinished basement (ft^2)	−0.03
Total basement (ft^2)	0.14
First floor (ft^2)	0.15
Second floor (ft^2)	0.13
Living area (ft^2)	0.16
Total full bathrooms	−0.02
Total half bathrooms	0.02
Total bedrooms	−0.08
Total above grade rooms	0.08
Fireplaces	0.03
Parking spaces inside garage	0.04
Garage area (ft^2)	0.05
Wood deck (ft^2)	0.02
Open porch (ft^2)	0.03
Enclosed porch (ft^2)	0.01
Neighborhood (25 features)	−0.05 to 0.12
Quality of basement	0.01

Source: Niti Mishra, Creative Commons License.

There exist correlations among the characteristics presented in Table 3.6. For instance, the total basement area is calculated by adding together the portions that are finished and the unfinished areas. Features such as the square footage of the living area, the number of bedrooms, and the number of bathrooms are directly associated with the size of the house and are thus highly likely to be correlated. Ridge and Lasso regression are capable of addressing these types of problems.

The Z-score approach was used to scale the features and dummy variables using the training set data. In addition, the goal values (i.e., the house prices) are standardized using the Z-score approach and the observations from the training set (Vineeth et al., 2018).

The utilization of a basic linear regression model yields the outcomes presented in Table 3.6. The training set exhibits a mean squared error of 0.114 for the prediction of housing prices. Given that the observations on the price have been adjusted to have a variance of 1, it can be concluded that 88.6% of the volatility in house prices in the training set is accounted for by the regression model.

Based on the data analyzed, it is evident that this regression model demonstrates strong generalization capabilities. The validation set had a slightly greater mean squared error of 0.117 compared to the training set. Nevertheless, the absence of regularization in linear regression yields peculiar outcomes due to the interdependencies among characteristics. It is illogical that the weights assigned to the number of full bathrooms and number of bedrooms are negative (Thamarai & Malarvizhi, 2020). Ridge regression was applied using various values of the hyperparameter, λ. Figure 3.8 demonstrates the effect of this on the prediction errors for the validation set. As anticipated, the margin of error in the forecast grows proportionally with the increase in λ. Values of λ ranging from 0 to 0.1 can be reasonably evaluated, as the rise in prediction errors is minimal within this range. Nevertheless, it appears that the enhancement in the model is somewhat minimal for these specific values of λ. The mean magnitude of the weights drops from around 0.049 to approximately 0.046 as the value of λ grows from 0 to 0.1. Even with an increase in λ to 0.6, the average absolute value of the weights decreases significantly to only 0.039.

Lasso regression yields more intriguing outcomes. Figure 3.9 illustrates the relationship between the error in the validation set and the incrementally increasing value of Lasso's λ, starting from zero.

For values of λ that are small, the error is lower than when λ is equal to 0. However, when λ goes beyond around 0.02, the error begins to rise. A λ value of 0.04 may be appealing.

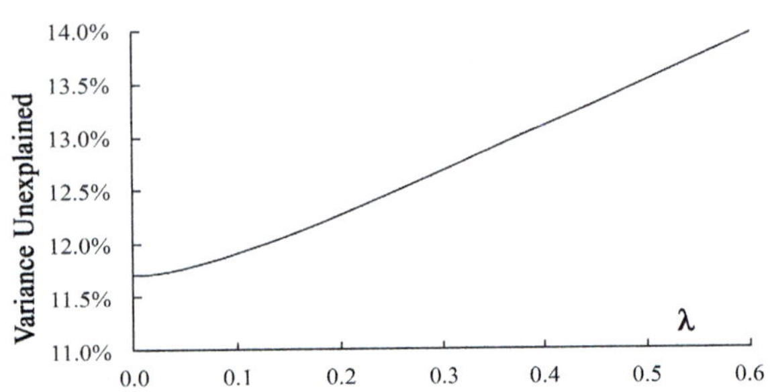

Figure 3.8. *Illustration of ridge regression results showing the mean squared error as a percent of the total squared error in the observations for the validation set.*

Source: Jeff Li, Creative Commons License.

The decrease in precision is negligible. The validation set's mean squared error accounts for just 12.0% of the total variance in the data, which is somewhat higher than the 11.7% when λ is set to 0, resulting in no regularization. However, at a value of λ equal to 0.04, 25 of the weights have a value of zero, and the average value of the weights is decreased to 0.034 (Bansal et al., 2021).

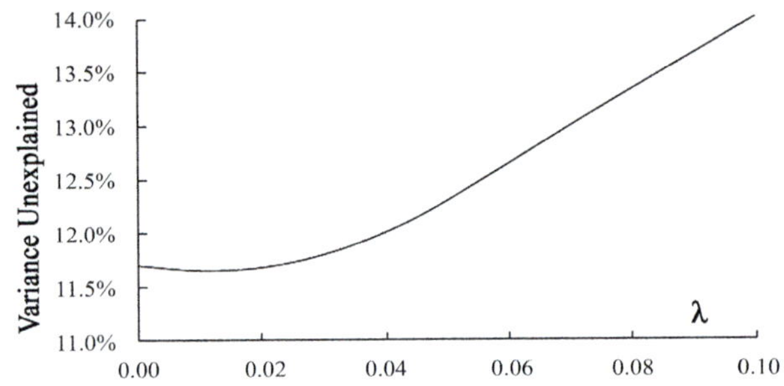

Figure 3.9. *Lasso results for validation set for different values of λ.*

Source: Jay Cao, Creative Commons License.

If an increase in the percentage mean squared error to around 14% is tolerable, a value of 0.1 can be assigned to λ. As a consequence, 30 of the weights are reduced to zero.

The weights that are not equal to zero are displayed in Table 3.7. The weights for the wood deck and open porch were negligible, measuring less than 0.005. Although they were not exactly zero, they are not included in the table.

Tables 3.6 and 3.7 demonstrate that the most significant predictors are overall quality and total living area. An important aspect is that the nonsensical negative weights in Table 3.6 have been removed (He & He, 2021).

Table 3.7. *Non-Zero Features in the Lasso Model and Their Weights (After Scaling) When λ=0.1*

Feature	Weight
Area of lot (ft^2)	0.04
Overall quality (1-10)	0.3
Built year	0.05
Remodel year	0.06
Finished basement (ft^2)	0.12
Total basement (ft^2)	0.1
1st floor (ft^2)	0.03
Living space area (ft^2)	0.3
Total fireplaces	0.02
Parking spaces inside garage	0.03
Area of garage (ft^2)	0.07
Neighborhoods (3 out of 25 non-zero)	0.01, 0.02, and 0.08
Quality of basement	0.02

Source: Raymond Kan, Creative Commons License.

When analyzing the data, Elastic Net did not yield any enhancement compared to Lasso. Given the circumstances, it is probable that an analyst would choose one of the Lasso models in this scenario. After selecting the model, it is important to evaluate its correctness by utilizing the test set. Choosing Lasso with a regularization parameter (λ) of 0.04 results in a mean squared error of 12.5% for the test data set, indicating that 87.5% of the volatility in house prices is accounted for. When selecting Lasso with a regularization parameter (λ) of 0.1, the mean squared error for the test data set is 14.7%. This implies that 85.3% of the volatility in house prices is accounted for (Verma et al., 2022).

3.9. DECISION CRITERIA

After developing the model to estimate the likelihood of a positive result, it becomes crucial to select a criterion for determining whether a new observation should be classed as positive. There is a strong inclination to optimize a basic accuracy metric, which is the proportion of correctly identified data. However, this approach is not consistently effective (Geurts et al., 2009).

Assume the objective is to identify instances of credit card fraud based on factors such as the frequency of charges per day, the nature of purchases, and other relevant characteristics. By assuming that all transactions are legitimate, an accuracy of 99% can be achieved if just 1% of transactions are fraudulent (Painsky, 2023).

The issue at hand is the presence of a disparity in class distribution. There are two categories:

i. Transaction goods
ii. Transaction fraud

The first category is far larger than the second. If the classes were of similar magnitude (or about equal in magnitude), using the aforementioned accuracy metric would be suitable. Regrettably, the majority of the classes are uneven (Mohamed, 2017).

An approach to address this issue is to generate a balanced training dataset by selectively reducing the number of observations from the dominant class. As an illustration, in the aforementioned scenario, an analyst may create a training set by gathering information about 100,000 deceitful transactions and combining it with a random selection of 100,000 legitimate transactions (Hastie et al., 2009).

Logistic regression commonly does not employ a balanced training set in practice. It is crucial to consider the classification's objective. The cost of misclassifying a new observation as positive when it is negative is often different from the cost of misclassifying it as negative when it is positive. Therefore, it is erroneous to make decisions solely based on whether Q is larger than or less than 0.5. A criterion for Q that deviates from 0.5 would probably be more suitable (Akinsola et al., 2019).

ACTIVITY 3.1.

- **Objective:** To implement and visualize simple linear regression using a dataset
- **Instructions:**
  - Select a dataset with a single independent variable (feature) and a continuous dependent variable (target)
  - Load and preprocess the dataset, handling any missing values or outliers
  - Implement simple linear regression using Python (using libraries like NumPy, pandas, and scikit-learn) or R
  - Visualize the dataset, the fitted regression line, and the predictions
  - Evaluate the model's performance using appropriate metrics such as mean squared error (MSE) or R-squared

SUMMARY

- Linear regression is a well-established machine-learning approach. For a significant period, it has been of utmost importance in empirical research. Data scientists have embraced it as a tool for making predictions. Machine learning applications frequently contain numerous features, some of which exhibit a strong correlation. Linear regression may yield a result that assigns a significantly positive coefficient to one feature and a significantly negative coefficient to another linked feature.
- Ridge regression is a method that can be used to decrease the magnitude of weights in a regression model. Another method is Lasso regression. This has the consequence of diminishing the significance of insignificant variables to zero. Elastic Net regression combines the principles of Ridge and Lasso regression to simultaneously achieve the benefits of both methods, namely, reducing the size of coefficients and eliminating irrelevant variables. In linear regression, categorical variables can be incorporated by generating dummy variables, where each category is represented by a separate variable. The binary variable for an observation is assigned a value of one if the observation belongs to the category, and zero otherwise. Logistic regression, similar to ordinary linear regression, has been employed in empirical research for a considerable period. It has emerged as a crucial categorization tool for data scientists. Usually, there are two categories. One is labeled as "positive"; the other is labeled as "negative." The sigmoid function, which has an S-shaped curve, is employed to determine the likelihood of an observation belonging to the positive class. An iterative search algorithm is employed to discover a linear function of the feature

values that, when inserted into the sigmoid function, optimally assigns a high probability to positive outcomes and a low probability to negative outcomes. A confusion matrix provides a concise summary of the outcomes obtained by applying logistic regression to the test data set.

- It is important to understand that machine learning models are not capable of making flawless predictions. The crucial criterion is whether their forecasts are equal to or superior to the forecasts produced by a humans. The widespread adoption of machine learning models across several domains suggests that they are successfully meeting this criterion.

REVIEW QUESTIONS

1. What is the objective function in a "plain vanilla" linear regression?
2. Explain the meaning of the term "regularization." What is the difference between L1 and L2 regularization?
3. What is the main advantage of (a) Ridge regression and (b) Lasso Regression?
4. What is the objective function in a logistic regression?
5. Explain what is meant by the dummy variable trap?

MULTIPLE CHOICE QUESTIONS

1. What is the goal of linear regression?

a. To classify data into different categories

b. To predict continuous values based on input features

c. To cluster data points

d. To reduce dimensionality

2. What is the purpose of regularization in regression models?

a. To increase the complexity of the model

b. To prevent overfitting by penalizing large coefficients

c. To ensure the model perfectly fits the training data

d. To reduce the number of features

3. Which of the following is true about ridge regression?

a. It uses L1 regularization

b. It can shrink some coefficients to zero

c. It adds a penalty equal to the sum of the squared coefficients

d. It is used primarily for feature selection

4. What is the elastic net regression a combination of?

a. Simple linear regression and logistic regression

b. L1 and L2 regularization

c. Polynomial regression and ridge regression

d. Multiple linear regression and k-means clustering

Answers to Multiple Choice Questions

1. (b); 2. (b); 3. (c); 4. (b)

REFERENCES

1. Afrin, S., Shamrat, F. J. M., Nibir, T. I., Muntasim, M. F., Moharram, M. S., Imran, M. M., & Abdulla, M. (2021). Supervised machine learning based liver disease prediction approach with LASSO feature selection. *Bulletin of Electrical Engineering and Informatics, 10*(6), 3369–3376.
2. Ajona, M., Vasanthi, P., & Vijayan, D. S. (2022). Application of multiple linear and polynomial regression in the sustainable biodegradation process of crude oil. *Sustainable Energy Technologies and Assessments, 54*, 102797.
3. Akinsola, J. E. T., Awodele, O., Kuyoro, S. O., & Kasali, F. A. (2019). Performance evaluation of supervised machine learning algorithms using multi-criteria decision-making techniques. In *Proceedings of the International Conference on Information Technology in Education and Development (ITED)* (Vol. 2, pp. 17–34).
4. Banerjee, D., & Dutta, S. (2017). Predicting the housing price direction using machine learning techniques. In *2017 IEEE International Conference on Power, Control, Signals and Instrumentation Engineering (ICPCSI)* (Vol. 1, pp. 2998–3000). IEEE.
5. Bansal, U., Narang, A., Sachdeva, A., Kashyap, I., & Panda, S. P. (2021). Empirical analysis of regression techniques by house price and salary prediction. In *IOP Conference Series: Materials Science and Engineering* (Vol. 1022, pp. 12110). IOP Publishing.
6. Chang, X., Lin, S. B., & Zhou, D. X. (2017). Distributed semi-supervised learning with kernel ridge regression. *Journal of Machine Learning Research, 18*(46), 1–22.
7. Chen, J., de Hoogh, K., Gulliver, J., Hoffmann, B., Hertel, O., Ketzel, M., & Hoek, G. (2019). A comparison of linear regression, regularization, and machine learning algorithms to develop Europe-wide spatial models of fine particles and nitrogen dioxide. *Environment International, 130*, 104934.
8. Chen, Y., Shao, Y., Yan, J., Yuan, T. F., Qu, Y., Lee, E., & Wang, S. (2017). A feature-free 30-disease pathological brain detection system by linear regression classifier. *CNS & Neurological Disorders–Drug Targets, 16*(1), 5–10.
9. Emmert-Streib, F., & Dehmer, M. (2019). High-dimensional LASSO-based computational regression models: Regularization, shrinkage, and selection. *Machine Learning and Knowledge Extraction, 1*(1), 359–383.
10. Foryś, I. (2022). Machine learning in house price analysis: Regression models versus neural networks. *Procedia Computer Science, 207*, 435–445.

11. Geurts, P., Irrthum, A., & Wehenkel, L. (2009). Supervised learning with decision tree-based methods in computational and systems biology. *Molecular Biosystems, 5*(12), 1593–1605.
12. Guo, Y., Wang, W., & Wang, X. (2021). A robust linear regression feature selection method for data sets with unknown noise. *IEEE Transactions on Knowledge and Data Engineering, 35*(1), 31–44.
13. Han, J., Zhang, D., Cheng, G., Guo, L., & Ren, J. (2014). Object detection in optical remote sensing images based on weakly supervised learning and high-level feature learning. *IEEE Transactions on Geoscience and Remote Sensing, 53*(6), 3325–3337.
14. Handoyo, S., Pradianti, N., Nugroho, W. H., & Akri, Y. J. (2022). A heuristic feature selection in logistic regression modeling with newton Raphson and gradient descent algorithm. *International Journal of Advanced Computer Science and Applications, 13*(3), 872–875.
15. Hans, C. (2011). Elastic net regression modeling with the orthant normal prior. *Journal of the American Statistical Association, 106*(496), 1383–1393.
16. Hasan, M. A., Hasan, M. K., & Mottalib, M. A. (2015). Linear regression–based feature selection for microarray data classification. *International Journal of Data Mining and Bioinformatics, 11*(2), 167–179.
17. Hastie, T., Tibshirani, R., Friedman, J., Hastie, T., Tibshirani, R., & Friedman, J. (2009). Overview of supervised learning. In *The Elements of Statistical Learning: Data Mining, Inference, and Prediction* (7th ed., Vol. 3, pp. 9–41). Springer.
18. He, K., & He, C. (2021). Housing price analysis using linear regression and logistic regression: A comprehensive explanation using Melbourne real estate data. In *2021 IEEE International Conference on Computing (ICOCO)* (Vol. 2, pp. 241–246).
19. Huang, J. C., Tsai, Y. C., Wu, P. Y., Lien, Y. H., Chien, C. Y., Kuo, C. F., & Kuo, C. H. (2020). Predictive modeling of blood pressure during hemodialysis: A comparison of linear model, random forest, support vector regression, XGBoost, LASSO regression and ensemble method. *Computer Methods and Programs in Biomedicine, 195*, 105536.
20. Josephine, P. K., Prakash, V. S., & Divya, K. S. (2021). Supervised learning algorithms: A comparison. *Kristu Jayanti Journal of Computational Sciences (KJCS), 7*(3), 01–12.
21. Kampezidou, S. I., Tikayat Ray, A., Bhat, A. P., Pinon Fischer, O. J., & Mavris, D. N. (2024). Fundamental components and principles of supervised machine learning workflows with numerical and categorical data. *Eng, 5*(1), 384–416.
22. Kärkkäinen, T. (2019). Extreme minimal learning machine: Ridge regression with distance-based basis. *Neurocomputing, 342*, 33–48.
23. Kavitha, S., Varuna, S., & Ramya, R. (2016). A comparative analysis on linear regression and support vector regression. In *2016 Online International Conference on Green Engineering and Technologies (IC-GET)* (Vol. 2, pp. 1–5). IEEE.
24. Khashei, M., Hamadani, A. Z., & Bijari, M. (2012). A novel hybrid classification model of artificial neural networks and multiple linear regression models. *Expert Systems with Applications, 39*(3), 2606–2620.

25. Matey, V., Chauhan, N., Mahale, A., Bhistannavar, V., & Shitole, A. (2022). Real estate price prediction using supervised learning. In *2022 IEEE Pune Section International Conference (PuneCon)* (Vol. 2, pp. 1–5). IEEE.

26. Mohamed, A. E. (2017). Comparative study of four supervised machine learning techniques for classification. *International Journal of Applied, 7*(2), 1–15.

27. Mora-Garcia, R. T., Cespedes-Lopez, M. F., & Perez-Sanchez, V. R. (2022). Housing price prediction using machine learning algorithms in COVID-19 times. *Land, 11*(11), 2100.

28. Nimon, K. F., & Oswald, F. L. (2013). Understanding the results of multiple linear regression: Beyond standardized regression coefficients. *Organizational Research Methods, 16*(4), 650–674.

29. Nouretdinov, I., Melluish, T., & Vovk, V. (2001). Ridge regression confidence machine. In *ICML* (Vol. 2, pp. 385–392).

30. Painsky, A. (2023). Quality assessment and evaluation criteria in supervised learning. In *Machine Learning for Data Science Handbook: Data Mining and Knowledge Discovery Handbook* (pp. 171–195).

31. Patwary, M. J., Karim, M. J., Hamim, S. I., Sifath, M., Bhuiyan, M. A. S., & Miraz, M. H. (2022). Stock price prediction using semi-supervised ridge regression. In *International Conference for Emerging Technologies in Computing* (Vol. 2, pp. 118–128). Springer Nature Switzerland.

32. Perkins, S., Lacker, K., & Theiler, J. (2003). Grafting: Fast, incremental feature selection by gradient descent in function space. *The Journal of Machine Learning Research, 3*, 1333–1356.

33. Rana, V. S., Mondal, J., Sharma, A., & Kashyap, I. (2020). House price prediction using optimal regression techniques. In *2020 2nd International Conference on Advances in Computing, Communication Control and Networking (ICACCCN)* (Vol. 2, pp. 203–208). IEEE.

34. Roy, S. S., Mittal, D., Basu, A., & Abraham, A. (2015). Stock market forecasting using LASSO linear regression model. In *Afro-European Conference for Industrial Advancement: Proceedings of the First International Afro-European Conference for Industrial Advancement AECIA 2014* (Vol. 2, pp. 371–381). Springer International Publishing.

35. Ryan, K. J., & Culp, M. V. (2015). On semi-supervised linear regression in covariate shift problems. *The Journal of Machine Learning Research, 16*(1), 3183–3217.

36. Sen, P. C., Hajra, M., & Ghosh, M. (2020). Supervised classification algorithms in machine learning: A survey and review. In *Emerging Technology in Modelling and Graphics0Proceedings of IEM Graph 2018* (Vol. 2, pp. 99–111). Springer Singapore.

37. Seok, K. (2013). A study on semi-supervised kernel ridge regression estimation. *Journal of the Korean Data and Information Science Society, 24*(2), 341–353.

38. Sharma, R., Sharma, K., & Khanna, A. (2020). Study of supervised learning and unsupervised learning. *International Journal for Research in Applied Science and Engineering Technology, 8*(6), 588–593.

39. Soomro, B. N., Xiao, L., Huang, L., Soomro, S. H., & Molaei, M. (2016). Bilayer elastic net regression model for supervised spectral-spatial hyperspectral image classification. *IEEE Journal of Selected Topics in Applied Earth Observations and Remote Sensing, 9*(9), 4102–4116.
40. Stock, M., Pahikkala, T., Airola, A., De Baets, B., & Waegeman, W. (2018). A comparative study of pairwise learning methods based on kernel ridge regression. *Neural Computation, 30*(8), 2245–2283.
41. Thamarai, M., & Malarvizhi, S. P. (2020). House price prediction modeling using machine learning. *International Journal of Information Engineering & Electronic Business, 12*(2), 87–90.
42. Tsigler, A., & Bartlett, P. L. (2023). Benign overfitting in ridge regression. *Journal of Machine Learning Research, 24*(123), 1–76.
43. Tutz, G., & Binder, H. (2007). Boosting ridge regression. *Computational Statistics & Data Analysis, 51*(12), 6044–6059.
44. Verma, A., Nagar, C., Singhi, N., Dongariya, N., & Sethi, N. (2022). Predicting house price in India using linear regression machine learning algorithms. In *2022 3rd International Conference on Intelligent Engineering and Management (ICIEM)* (Vol. 2, pp. 917–924). IEEE.
45. Vineeth, N., Ayyappa, M., & Bharathi, B. (2018). House price prediction using machine learning algorithms. In *Soft Computing Systems: Second International Conference, ICSCS 2018, Kollam, India, April 19–20, 2018, Revised Selected Papers* (Vol. 1, pp. 425–433). Springer Singapore.
46. Wu, J., & Yang, H. (2015). Linear regression-based efficient SVM learning for large-scale classification. *IEEE Transactions on Neural Networks and Learning Systems, 26*(10), 2357–2369.
47. Yoo, S., Im, J., & Wagner, J. E. (2012). Variable selection for hedonic model using machine learning approaches: A case study in Onondaga County, NY. *Landscape and Urban Planning, 107*(3), 293–306.
48. Zhang, S., Cheng, D., Hu, R., & Deng, Z. (2018). Supervised feature selection algorithm via discriminative ridge regression. *World Wide Web, 21*, 1545–1562.
49. Zhu, L., O'Dwyer, J. P., Chang, V. S., Granda, C. B., & Holtzapple, M. T. (2010). Multiple linear regression model for predicting biomass digestibility from structural features. *Bioresource Technology, 101*(13), 4971–4979.

CHAPTER

4 Decision Trees

LEARNING OBJECTIVES

After studying this chapter, you will be able to:

- Understand the purpose of decision trees in machine learning;
- Comprehend the difference between classification trees and regression trees;
- Understand the concept and importance of pruning in decision trees;
- Comprehend the process of converting decision paths from decision trees into if-then rules; and
- Understand the concept of multivariate trees and how they differ from univariate trees.

KEY TERMS FROM THIS CHAPTER

Classification trees
Multivariate trees
Regression trees
Entropy
Pruning
Univariate trees

UNIT INTRODUCTION

The process of parametric estimation begins with the development of a model that incorporates the entire input space, followed by the learning of the model's parameters through the utilization of all of the training data that is accessible (McSherry, 1999). Following this, the same model and parameter configuration are used for each and every test input. Based on a distance measure such as the Euclidean norm, the input space is divided into local areas in the context of nonparametric estimation. This is done in order to facilitate the estimation process (Tang, 2020). It is the matching local model that is utilized for each input. This model is built by the training data that is contained inside that region. The process of determining the local data that should be used to define the local model is a time-consuming and costly endeavor in nonparametric models. The computation of the distances between the input that is provided and all of the training samples has a temporal complexity of O(N), which allows for this to be accomplished (Apté & Weiss, 1997).

A decision tree stands for a hierarchical framework that is utilized in the process of supervised learning. The local region is identified using a series of recursive splits, which enables a more efficient process with fewer steps. This allows for a more efficient process overall. Internal decision nodes and terminal leaves are the two components that make up a decision tree (see picture 4.1 for more information) (Ali et al., 2012). In order to determine which branches are present, each decision node m is responsible for carrying out a test function $f_m(x)$ that generates discrete outcomes. After receiving input, a test is carried out at each node, and the outcome of the test is used to determine which branch should be followed after the input. This process starts at the root and is carried out in an iterative manner until it reaches a leaf node. At that point, the value that is engraved in the leaf is used as the output (Myles et al., 2004).

Each function $f_m(x)$ creates a discriminant in the d-dimensional input space, dividing it into smaller portions that are further subdivided while moving from the root downwards. This process continues until the discriminant is completely established. $f_m(.)$ is a fundamental function that, when expressed as a tree, simplifies a complicated function into a series of straightforward options. This is accomplished by decomposing the function into trees. A number of different decision tree approaches make a variety of assumptions regarding the models for $f_m(.)$, and the model class is what dictates the shape of the regions and the form of the discriminant (Thomas et al., 2020). Every single terminal node is equipped with an outcome label, which, in the case of classification tasks, stands for the class code, and in the case of regression tasks, is a numerical value. The term "leaf node" refers to a component that delineates a certain region inside the input space. Instances that are contained within this region produce the same output. The discriminants that are encoded in the internal nodes along the path from the root node to the leaf node are what determine the boundaries of the regions (Murthy et al., 1994).

The decision-making process is organized in a hierarchical fashion, which makes it possible to quickly identify the particular area that represents an input. In the event that the decisions are of a binary type, for example, then in an ideal scenario, each alternative would eliminate 50% of the scenarios. If there are b regions, then in the best-case scenario, the appropriate area can be determined by utilizing log b decisions rather than any other method (Kotsiantis, 2013). The interpretability of the decision tree is an additional advantage brought about by its use. It is possible to convert the tree into a set of IF-THEN rules that are easily understandable, as will be seen in the following section. As a result of this rationale, decision trees are highly favored and are sometimes prioritized over alternatives that are more exact but may be more difficult to understand (Heath et al., 1993). At the outset, concentrate on univariate trees, which are characterized by the utilization of a single input variable for the evaluation of a decision node. Various ways are investigated in which these trees can be formed for the goals of classification as well as regression. Subsequently, the scope of this idea is broadened to include multivariate trees, in which every input can be exploited within an internal node (Matheus & Rendell, 1989).

Did you know?

Decision trees have their roots in the 1960s, originally used in operations research and statistics before becoming popular in machine learning.

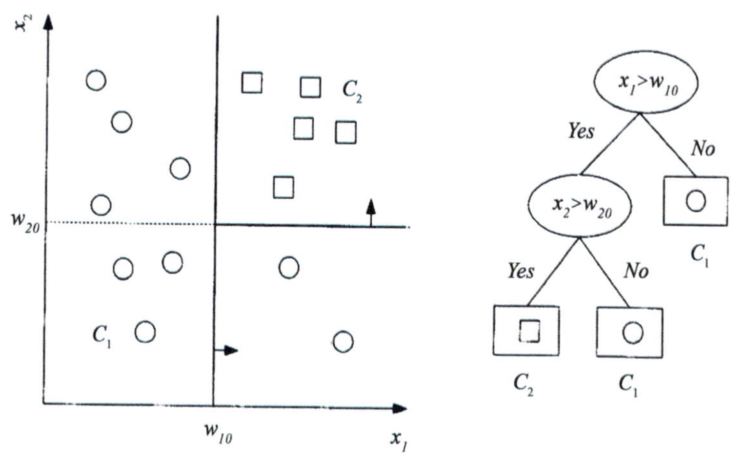

Figure 4.1. *Example of a dataset and the corresponding decision tree.*

Source: Ethem Alpaydm, Creative Commons License.

4.1. UNIVARIATE TREES

In a univariate tree, each internal node utilizes just a single input dimension for the test. If the given input dimension, x_j, is in nature discrete and may take one of the n potential values, the decision node examines the value of x_j and selects the appropriate branch, resulting in an n-way split. For instance, if there is an attribute called "color" with the potential values of {red, blue, green}, subsequently a node representing that property will have three branches, each matching one of the three potential attribute values. A decision node consists of distinct branches, and if a numeric input is provided, it has to be discretized. If x_j is a numeric value that is ordered, then the test is a comparison (De'Ath, 2002).

$$f_m(x): x_j \geq w_{m0}$$

Where; w_{mo} is a threshold value that has been appropriately selected. A binary split is performed by the decision node, which splits the input space into two regions: $R_m = \{x \backslash x_j < w_{mo}\}$ and $L_m = \{x \backslash x_j \geq w_{mo}\}$. Moving from the root towards a leaf, each decision node in the route divides into two by using different characteristics and creating splits that are perpendicular to each other. The leaf nodes delineate hyperrectangles inside the input space (refer to Figure 4.1) (Naima et al., 2012).

Tree induction refers to the process of creating a tree structure based on a set of training data. Given a training set, there are several trees that can encode it without any errors. To simplify, the objective is to discover the shortest tree among them, where the size of the tree is determined by the number of nodes and the level of difficulty of the decision nodes. The problem of locating the shortest tree is classified as NP-complete, as demonstrated by Quinlan in 1986 (Yıldız, 2015). Consequently, local search algorithms are employed that rely on heuristics to generate trees that are both acceptable in size and can be obtained within a reasonable timeframe. Tree learning algorithms exhibit a greedy behavior, as they iteratively search for the optimal split at each step, beginning at the root and utilizing the whole training data. This process divides the training data into two or more subsets, based on whether the selected property is numerical or discrete. Subsequently, this proceeds to recursively divide the data into smaller subsets, each according to a certain criterion, until further division is unnecessary. At this juncture, a leaf node is generated and assigned a label (Li et al., 2005).

4.1.1. Classification Trees

A split is considered pure if, following the split, all instances that choose a branch in all branches fall under the same class. For a given node m, N_m represents the count of training cases that reach that node. The root node, denoted as , represents the class C_i, where N_m is the total number of instances and $\Sigma i, = N_m$. If a scenario reaches node m, the estimated probability of class C_i is (Rivera-Lopez et al., 2022):

$$\hat{P}(C_i \mid x, m) \equiv p_m^i = \frac{N_m^i}{N_m}$$

A node m is considered pure if all values , for every i, are either 0 or 1. The value is 0 when neither of the instances that reach node m belong to class C_i, and it is 1 if all of these examples belong to C_i. If the split is pure, there is no need for additional splitting. Instead, one may create a leaf node and assign it the label of the class for which is equal to 1. An alternative method for quantifying impurity is through the use of entropy, as proposed by Quinlan in 1986 (see Figure 4.2) (De Ville, 2013):

$$\mathrm{I}_m = -\sum_{i=1}^{K} p_m^i \log_2 p_m^i$$

The value of 0log0=0. Entropy, in the context of information theory, represents the smallest amount of bits required to encode the correctness of classifying a specific occurrence. In a binary classification issue, where the probability of class 1 (p^1) is 1 and the probability of class 2 (p^2) is 0, all samples belong to class C_1. In this case, there is no need to provide any information, and the entropy is 0. Given that $p^1 = p^2 = 0.5$, in order to indicate one of the two possibilities, one must transmit a single bit, resulting in an entropy of 1 (Patel & Prajapati, 2018). Within the spectrum of these two extremes, one may create codes and utilize less than one unit of information per message by employing shorter codes for the more probable category and longer codes for the less probable category. When there are more than two classes (K > 2), the same explanation applies and the maximum entropy is equal to the logarithm of K when pi is equal to 1/K. However, entropy is not the only conceivable metric (Bulac & Bulac, 2016):

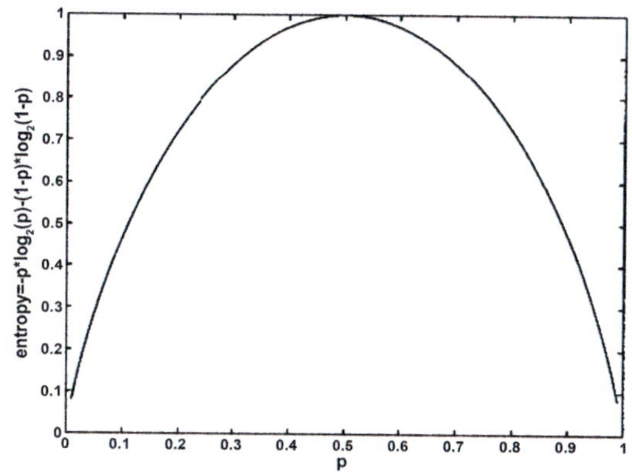

Figure 4.2. *Illustration of entropy function for a two-class problem.*

Source: Micheal Jordan, Creative Commons License.

These concepts may be extended to situations where there are more than two classes, and the mistake of misclassifying can be extended to finding the least risk based on a particular loss function. Studies have indicated that there is no substantial disparity among these three parameters (Bertsimas & Dunn, 2017).

If node m is not natural, then each case should be divided to reduce impurity, since there are several potential characteristics on which division might be based. Multiple split places are available for a numeric characteristic. When searching for the optimal split, the goal is to reduce impurity after splitting in order to create the most compact tree. If the subsets obtained after splitting are more homogeneous, there will be a reduced need for subsequent splits, if any at all. Undoubtedly, this solution is locally optimum, but there is no assurance that the most minimal decision tree will be discovered (Schmid, 2010).

If the test at node m yields outcome j, the estimated probability of C_i is:

$$\hat{P}(C_i \mid x, m, j) \equiv p^i_{mj} = \frac{N^i_{mj}}{N_{mj}}$$

The impurity afterward the split is:

$$I'_m = -\sum_{j=1}^{n} \frac{N_{mj}}{N_m} \sum_{i=1}^{K} p^i_{mj} \log_2 p^i_{mj}$$

In order to compute for a numeric attribute, it is necessary to have knowledge of w_{m0} for the corresponding node. There are N_m - 1 potential w_{m0} values between N_m data points. It is unnecessary to test every single point, which may potentially be infinite in number. Instead, it suffices to test at specific intervals, such as the midpoint between points (Sharma & Kumar, 2016). It is important to note that the optimal division is consistently found amongst neighboring data points that belong to distinct categories.

```
GenerateTree(𝒳)
    If NodeEntropy(𝒳)< θ_I /* equation 9.3 */
      Create leaf labelled by majority class in 𝒳
      Return
    i ← SplitAttribute(𝒳)
    For each branch of x_i
      Find 𝒳_i falling in branch
      GenerateTree(𝒳_i)

SplitAttribute(𝒳)
    MinEnt← MAX
    For all attributes i = 1,...,d
        If x_i is discrete with n values
          Split 𝒳 into 𝒳_1,...,𝒳_n by x_i
          e ← SplitEntropy(𝒳_1,...,𝒳_n) /* equation 9.8 */
          If e<MinEnt MinEnt ← e; bestf ← i
        Else /* x_i is numeric */
          For all possible splits
              Split 𝒳 into 𝒳_1,𝒳_2 on x_i
              e←SplitEntropy(𝒳_1,𝒳_2)
              If e<MinEnt MinEnt ← e; bestf ← i
    Return bestf
```

Figure 4.3. *Representation of classification tree construction.*

Source: Fikret Gurden, Creative Commons License.

Remember

Decision trees are capable of handling both numerical and categorical data, which makes them adaptable to various sorts of datasets.

Therefore, they are tested and the one with the highest level of purity is selected to represent the attribute's purity. For a discrete characteristic, there is no need for iteration. For both discrete and numeric qualities, as well as for numeric attributes at all split points, the impurity is computed and the one with the lowest entropy is selected. Next, the process of tree creation proceeds recursively and concurrently for any branches that are not pure, until all branches become pure (Zhou & Zhou, 2021). The algorithm's pseudocode is provided in Figure 4.3 (Song & Ying, 2015).

An issue arises when the splitting process gives preference to characteristics that have a large number of values. With a larger number of values, the number of branches also increases, resulting in a potentially lower level of impurity. For instance, consider the training index t as a characteristic, the impurity measure will select it since it results in an impurity of 0 for each branch, even though it may not be a logical or meaningful feature (Kwok & Carter, 1990). Various techniques have been suggested to impose penalties on these characteristics and to achieve a balance between the reduction in impurity and the number of branches. In the presence of noise, if one continues to build the tree until it becomes completely pure, there is a risk of overfitting. For instance, take a scenario where there is a mislabeled instance within a bunch of properly classified examples (Buntine, 2020). In order to mitigate this issue of overfitting, the building of the tree stops when the nodes reach a level of purity that meets a certain threshold, meaning that a subset of the data is not divided any further if ⊠ <θ_i. This indicates that it is not necessary for to be exactly 0 or 1, but it should be sufficiently near, with a threshold θ_p. Under such circumstances, a leaf node is generated and assigned the label of the class with the greatest value (Rokach & Maimon, 2010).

θ_I (or θ_p) represents the complexity parameter, similar to the variables h or k used in nonparametric estimation. When the size of the trees is small, there is a high level of variation and the tree develops to a big size in order to properly represent the training set. Conversely, when the size of the trees is large, the level of variation is reduced and a smaller tree is sufficient to roughly represent the training set, although it may have a significant bias. The optimal value is contingent upon the expenses associated with misclassification, and also the expenditures related to memory and computation (Biggs et al., 1991).

4.2.2. Regression Trees

It is possible to construct a regression tree in a manner that is analogous to that of a classification tree; the sole distinction lies in the fact that the impurity measurement that is utilized for classification is replaced with a measurement that is appropriate for regression (Westreich et al., 2010). Let X_m be the subset of X that makes it to the given node m. This subset is referred to as X_m. To put it another way, X_m is the collection of all x € X that satisfy the conditions in the decision nodes that are located along the path that leads from the root to the node m. Constructing a definition that is both explicit and exact (De'ath & Fabricius, 2000):

$$b_m(x) = \begin{cases} 1 \ \text{if } x \in X_m : x \text{ reaches node } m \\ 0 \ \text{otherwise} \end{cases}$$

$$E_m = \frac{1}{N_m} \sum_t (r^t - g_m)^2 b_m(x^t)$$

$$\text{where } N_m = |X_m| = \sum_t b_m(x^t).$$

In a node,

$$g_m = \frac{\sum_t b_m(x^t) r^t}{\sum_t b_m(x^t)}$$

The equation above relates to the variance at m. If the error at a node is within an acceptable range, namely $E_m < \theta_r$, a leaf node is generated to store the g_m value. This results in a piecewise constant estimate that exhibits discontinuities at the edges of the leaves (Elith et al., 2008).

If the mistake is deemed undesirable, the data reaching m is divided into smaller parts in order to minimize the total error across all branches. In the process of classification, examine each node and search for the attribute that results in the lowest error. Proceed to repeat this process recursively (Loh, 2014).

Consider X_{mj}, as the subset of X_m,

$$b_{mj}(x) = \begin{cases} 1 \;\; if\; x \in X_m : x\, reaches\, node\, m\, and\, takes\, branch\; j \\ 0 \qquad otherwise \end{cases}$$

In branch j of m, g_{mj} exists as,

$$g_{mj} = \frac{\sum_t b_{mj}(x^t) r^t}{\sum_t b_m j(x^t)}$$

and the error is,

$$E'_m = \frac{1}{N_m} \sum_j \sum_t (r^t - g_{mj})^2 b_{mj}(x^t)$$

Mean square error is (Khemphila & Boonjing, 2010),

$$E_m = \max_j \max_t | r^t - g_{mj} | b_m(x^t)$$

Through the utilization of a particular approach, it can be guaranteed that the inaccuracy in any given case will never be above a threshold that has been established beforehand. The complexity parameter is what establishes the acceptable error level for the system. When the complexity parameter is low, it results in the production of large trees, which in turn raises the risk of overfitting (Sutton, 2005). A large complexity value, on the other hand, results in underfitting and excessive smoothing of the data. Figure 4.4 provides a visual representation of the information below. Instead of generating an average at a leaf node that reflects a constant fit, one could alternatively do a linear regression fit over all of the instances that are allocated to the leaf node. This would be analogous to the process of converting from a running mean to a line in nonparametric regression (Timofeev, 2004):

$$g_m(x) = w_m^T x + w_{m0}$$

The estimate in a leaf is influenced by the variable x, resulting in the production of smaller trees. However, this comes at the cost of more computation (Xu et al., 2005).

4.2. PRUNING

This concept highlights that making decisions based on a limited number of cases leads to variability and, consequently, errors in generalization. Terminating the process of tree building before it reaches its maximum capacity is referred to as pre-pruning the tree (Esposito et al., 1999).

Post-pruning is an alternative method to obtain less complex trees, and it is generally more effective than pre-pruning. As previously seen, the process of tree growth follows a greedy approach. At each stage, a choice is made to build a decision node and proceed forward without backtracking or exploring alternate options. Post-pruning is the sole case in which the attempt to identify and remove unneeded subtrees is made (Appel et al., 2013). During the process of post-pruning, the tree is expanded until all of its leaves are pure and the training error is reduced to zero. Next, identify subtrees that contribute to overfitting and subsequently remove them through pruning (Almuallim, 1996). Reserve a pruning set from the original labeled set, which is not utilized throughout the training process. Each subtree is substituted with a leaf node that is marked with the training examples covered by the subtree, based on whether it is for classification or regression (Shah & Sastry, 1999).

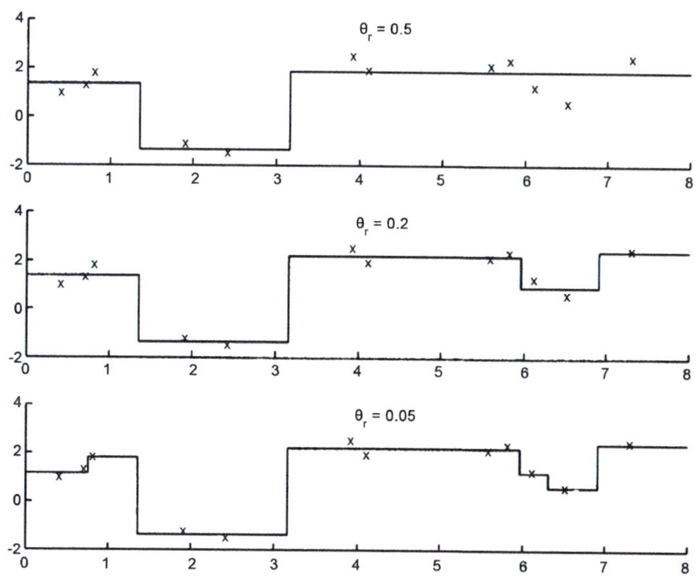

Figure 4.4. *Representation of regression tree smooths from various values of θ_r.*

Source: Fikret Gurden, Creative Commons License.

If the subtree on the pruning set has a higher complexity than the subtree pruned and the leaf node is retained, as the added intricacy of the subtree is not warranted. Otherwise, the subtree alone is retained. For instance, within the tree seen in Figure 4.5, there exists a subtree that starts with the criterion x < 6.31 (Mingers, 1989).

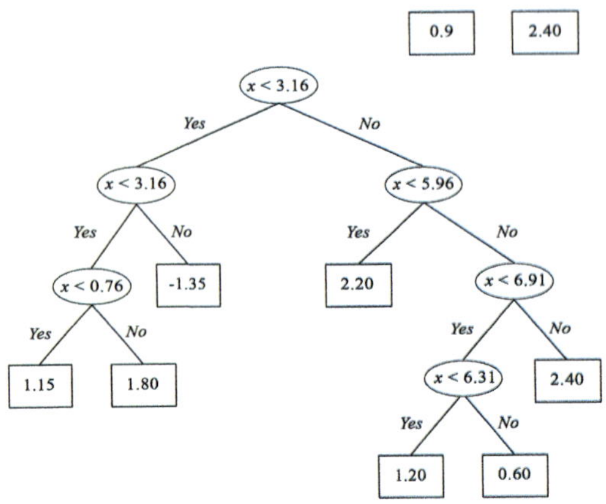

Figure 4.5. *Illustration of regression tree implementing the smooths of figure 4.4 for value of* θ_r.

Source: Ethem Alpaydm, Creative Commons License.

4.3. RULE EXTRACTION FROM TREES

The univariate tree exclusively utilizes the essential variables, and it is possible that certain features may remain unused once the tree is constructed. It might be stated that traits that are closer to the root are more significant on a global scale (Bologna, 2021). Figure 4.6 illustrates a decision tree that utilizes variables x_1, x_2, and x_4, while excluding x_3. Feature extraction may be accomplished using a decision tree. Construct a tree and subsequently choose only the characteristics employed by the tree as inputs for another learning technique (Barakat & Bradley, 2010).

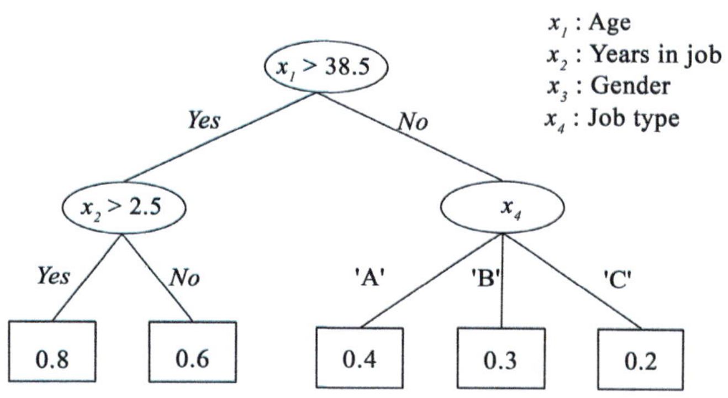

Figure 4.6. *Example of a (hypothetical) decision tree. Each path from the root to a leaf can be written down as a conjunctive rule, composed of conditions defined by the decision nodes on the path.*

Source: Taner Bilgic, Creative Commons License.

Every route from the root to a leaf represents a combination of tests, as all of those requirements must be met in order to reach the leaf. The collection of these pathways may be expressed as a rule base, consisting of a set of IF-THEN rules. For instance, the decision tree seen in Figure 4.6 may be expressed as the subsequent collection of rules (Pal & Chakraborty, 2001):

i. R1: If the age is more than 38.5 and the job years are greater than 2.5, then the value of y is 0.8.

ii. R2: If the age is greater than 38.5 and the job years are less than or equal to 2.5, then the value of y is 0.6.

iii. R3: If the age is less than or equal to 38.5 and the work type is 'A', then the value of y is 0.4.

iv. R4: If the age is less than or equal to 38.5 and the job type is 'B', then the value of y is 0.3.

v. R5: If the age is less than or equal to 38.5 and the job type is 'C', then the value of y is 0.2 (Bologna & Hayashi, 2018).

Because it is easily understandable and enables specialists to check the model that is created from data, a rule base of this nature makes it possible to extract information. The percentage of training data that is incorporated into a rule is referred to as rule support, and it is feasible to quantify this percentage for every rule inside the system.

When it comes to the key characteristics of the dataset, the rules are a direct depiction of them. Displayed here are the basic characteristics as well as the split locations. In this hypothetical scenario, for instance, observe that persons who are 38 years old or younger are distinct from those who are 39 years old or older in respect to the set purpose. This is because the age difference between the two groups is 38 years. One of the defining characteristics of the latter group is the kind of work that is being performed, whereas the most important differentiating characteristic of the former group is the length of time that they have been employed. Within the framework of a classification tree, it is feasible for a number of leaves to be assigned the same class label. If several conjunctive expressions that belong to different paths occur, it is possible to combine them into a disjunction, also known as an OR. Each patch is the region that is determined by a single leaf, and the class region is a composite of numerous patches that make up the class region. For example, the class C_1 that can be seen in picture 4.1 is represented as (Obregon & Jung, 2023):

Remember

Decision trees mimic human decision-making processes. The way humans make choices based on certain conditions is similar to how decision trees split data.

$$IF(x \leq w_{10})\,OR\,((x_1 > w_{10})\,AND(x_2 > w_{20}))\,THEN\; C_1$$

It is feasible to prune rules for the sake of simplicity. Pruning a subtree involves removing terms from many rules simultaneously. It is perhaps feasible to remove a phrase from one rule without affecting any other rules. For instance, in the aforementioned set of rules, if one observes that individuals with job-type = 'A' consistently have outcomes near 0.4, irrespective of their age, rule R3 may be eliminated:

$$R3':IF\,(job-type='A')\,THEN\;y=0.4$$

It should be noted that after the guidelines are pruned, it may no longer be feasible to reconstruct them in the form of a tree (Mi & Huang, 2008).

4.4. LEARNING RULES FROM DATA

As previously demonstrated, a method for obtaining IF-THEN rules involves training a decision tree and subsequently transforming it into rules. Another approach is to acquire knowledge of the rules firsthand. Rule induction operates in a manner similar to tree induction, but with a few key differences. Rule induction employs a depth-first search strategy, generating one path (rule) at a time. In contrast, tree induction uses a breadth-first approach, generating all pathways simultaneously (Hong et al., 2002).

An instance is derived from a previous algorithm called Irep (Fiirnkrantz and Widmer 1994). Consider a scenario involving two classes, distinguishing between positive and negative examples. Subsequently, extend the analysis to encompass situations with more than two classes, denoted as K > 2. Rules are included to elucidate positive instances. If an instance does not fall under any rule, it is categorized as negative. When a rule matches, it can either be valid (true positive) or result in a false positive (Nayebi et al., 2020).

Assume a rule called R, and R′ represents the candidate rule that is obtained by adding a condition. The term "change in gain" is defined as:

$$Gain(R',R) = s.\left(\log_2 \frac{N_+^{'}}{N^{i}} - \log_2 \frac{N_+}{N}\right)$$

Where; N represents the total number of occurrences that are encompassed by R, whereas N represents the number of true positives inside those instances. The terms N' and have analogous definitions in the context of R. After a rule has been established, it is trimmed by removing criteria in reverse sequence in order to identify the rule that optimizes the rule value metric (Widmer, 2003):

$$rvm(R) = \frac{p-n}{p+n}$$

Let p represent the number of true positives and n represent the number of false positives on the pruning set.

After a rule has been developed and refined, all positive and negative training instances that the rule covers are eliminated from the training set. If there are any positive instances remaining, the process of rule induction will continue. If there is enough noise, there is the option to terminate the process prematurely, namely when a rule fails to adequately account for a sufficient number of cases. The minimal description length (MDL) method is employed to quantify the value of a regulation, as proposed by Quinlan in 1995 (Sacchi et al., 2007).

Ripper's complexity is $O(N\log^2 N)$, where N is the size of the training set. This technique is suitable for handling huge training sets, as mentioned by Dietterich in 1997. The rules acquired are propositional rules. First-order rules with variables in conditions, known as predicates, are more expressive. A predicate is a function that evaluates the value of its input and produces a boolean result, either true or false. Predicates enable the establishment of relationships between attribute values, a task that propositions are unable to accomplish (Apolloni et al., 2004).

If there is a father (y) and the person is female (y), then the person is the daughter (x) of the father (y).

Inductive logic programming is the process of getting these rules from data. These rules can be considered as scripts in a programming syntax such as Prolog, and the inductive logic programming process is the act of acquiring them. A good illustration of an algorithm is Foil, which was first presented by Quinlan in the year 1990 (An, 2003).

Binding is the process of assigning a value to a variable. Binding is also known as assignment. In order for a rule to be regarded as a match, it must be possible to establish a series of links between the variables that are included in the training set. There is a process that is comparable to that of learning propositional rules when it comes to learning first-order procedures (Evans & Grefenstette, 2018). Specifically, it is made up of an outer loop that is responsible for adding rules, and an inner loop that is responsible for adding conditions to each rule. After each iteration of the loop, any items that are deemed unneeded are eliminated. The difference is in the inner loop, which is when one investigates a single predicate to include (rather than a proposition) and evaluates the enhancement in the execution of the rule (Sánchez et al., 2009).

4.5. MULTIVARIATE TREES

A univariate tree utilizes a single input dimension for each split. Within a multivariate tree, each input dimension may be utilized at a decision node, resulting in a higher level of generality. A binary linear multimodal node is defined when every input is numeric (Brodley & Utgoff, 1995):

$$f_m(x): w_m^T x + w_{m0} > 0$$

Because the linear multivariate node computes a weighted sum, discrete qualities ought to be represented by binary numeric variables (0/1 dummy variables). A hyperplane with a random orientation is defined by the equation that is presented (see picture 4.7 for further explanation). The polyhedra in the input space are divided by each node that is located along a path that extends from the root to a leaf (Larsen & Speckman, 2004). There is a one-of-a-kind circumstance known as the univariate node with a numeric characteristic, in which all of the w_{mj} values, except one, are equal to 0. Therefore, the univariate numeric node establishes a linear discriminant that is perpendicular to the x_j axis, crossing it at w_{m0}, and running parallel to all other x_i. As a result, it is clear that in a univariate node, there are d potential orientations (w_m) and N_m, — 1 potential threshold (—w_{mo}), which makes it possible to conduct an exhaustive search (Miller et al., 2016):

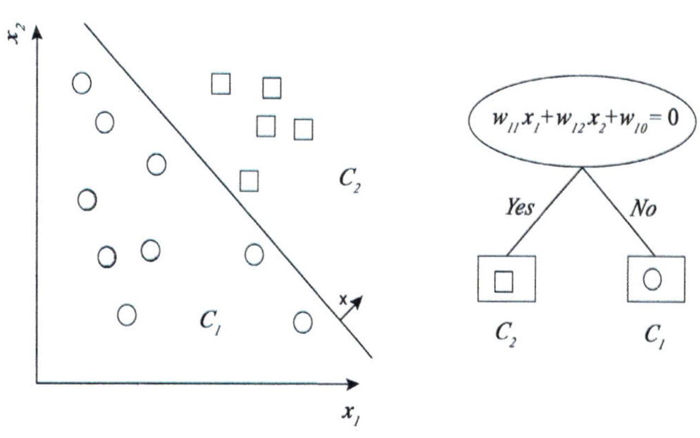

Figure 4.7. *Example of a linear multivariate decision tree.*

Source: Taner Bilgic, Creative Commons License.

Transitioning from a univariate node into a linear multivariate node enhances the node's flexibility. Enhanced flexibility can be achieved by employing a nonlinear multivariate node. For instance, considering a quadratic equation (Gama, 2004),

$$f_m(x): x^T W_m x + w_m^T x + w_{m0} > 0$$

Another possibility is a sphere node,

$$f_m(x): \| x - c_m \| \leq \alpha_m$$

with c_m as its center point and α_m as its radius (Cañete-Sifuentes et al., 2021). Several techniques have been developed for the purpose of developing multivariate decision trees in categorization. The oldest variant of the CART algorithm is the multivariate version, which adjusts the weights w_{mj} individually in order to reduce impurity. The CART algorithm includes a preprocessing stage that aims to minimize dimensionality by selecting a subset of features and so simplifying the structure of the node (Segal & Xiao, 2011). The OCI algorithm, developed by Murthy et. al. in 1994, is an extension of the CART method. An alternative approach is to assume that all classes follow a Gaussian distribution with a shared covariance matrix. This allows for the use of linear discriminants to separate each class from the others. When there are K classes, each node in this scenario has K branches, and each branch has the discriminant that distinguishes one class from the rest. Brodley and Utgoff provided a technique in 1995 in which the linear discriminants undergo training to minimize the classification error. Bshouty & Mansour (2002) suggest a heuristic method for dividing K > 2 classes into two larger groups, which allows for the learning of binary multivariate trees. Loh and Shih in 1997 employed 2-means clustering to partition data into two distinct groups. Yildiz and Alpaydin in the year 2000 employed Latent Dirichlet Allocation (LDA) to determine the discriminant after the classes have been divided into two groups (Pande et al., 2017). A classifier selects a hypothesis within its hypothesis class to approximate the unknown true discriminant. When employing univariate nodes, the estimation relies on piecewise, axis-aligned hyperplanes. By employing linear multivariate nodes, one has the ability to utilize arbitrary hyperplanes, resulting in a more accurate approximation with a reduced number of nodes (Sok et al., 2016). However, in cases when the fundamental discriminant is curved, nonlinear nodes prove to be more effective. The branching factor determines the variety of discriminants that a node defines, thereby having a comparable impact. A binary decision node with two branches serves as a discriminant that divides the input space into two distinct regions. An n-way node divides into n-halves (Bshouty & Mansour, 1995). Hence, there exists a correlation between the intricacy of a node, the number of branches, and the size of the tree. By using uncomplicated nodes and limited branching factors, it is possible to create extensive trees (Korting, 2006). However, trees with univariate binary nodes, for instance, are easier to understand and comprehend. Interpreting linear multivariate nodes poses further difficulty. As one descends the tree and has fewer data, more intricate nodes need additional data and are susceptible to overfitting (Quan & Valdez, 2018). When the nodes are intricate and the tree is diminutive, one also forfeits the fundamental concept of the tree, which is to break down the problem into a collection of uncomplicated problems. Ultimately, it is possible to construct an intricate classifier at the root that effectively distinguishes all classes from one another. However, this would deviate from the structure of a tree (Zhu et al., 2020).

ACTIVITY 4.1

- **Objective:** Understand the process of constructing a decision tree from a dataset
- **Instructions:**

i. Form small groups.
ii. Select a publicly available dataset (e.g., the Iris dataset).
iii. Use a decision tree algorithm (e.g., ID3, CART) to construct a decision tree for classification or regression tasks.
iv. Visualize the decision tree using a tool like Scikit-Learn in Python or Weka.
v. Discuss the criteria used for splitting nodes and the structure of the tree.
vi. Present your decision tree and findings to the class.

SUMMARY

- This chapter offers a comprehensive examination of decision trees, a key technique in machine learning employed for regression and classification applications. Decision trees provide inherent intuitiveness, are readily interpretable, and have the capability to handle data that is both categorized and numerical. Classification trees are utilized for the purpose of forecasting a categorical result. The construction of the tree involves dividing the dataset into smaller groups by utilizing the feature that yields the most information gain or the lowest Gini impurity. Regression trees are utilized for the purpose of forecasting continuous outcomes. The construction of the tree follows a similar approach to classification trees, but it uses mean squared error or mean absolute error as the standard for determining how to divide the tree.
- Pruning involves eliminating tree components that do not contribute significantly to forecasting goal variables. This aids in mitigating overfitting and enhancing the model's capacity to generalize. Rule extraction is the process of transforming the decision routes of a tree into a collection of if-then rules. These guidelines are easily comprehensible and may be employed to grasp the model's decision-making process. Every route from the main node to a terminal node symbolizes a rule. The process of learning rules from data entails constructing models that directly acquire the if-then rules from the dataset, without the need to construct a complete decision tree. This approach is especially beneficial for datasets in which the correlation between attributes and outcomes can be easily articulated using rules. Multivariate trees enable the partitioning of data based on a mixture of factors, rather than relying on a single attribute at each node. This allows for the creation of more intricate decision boundaries and the ability to record the interplay between different elements. Nevertheless, the interpretation of multivariate trees is more intricate and may need more processing resources.

REVIEW QUESTIONS

1. What are the main differences between classification trees and regression trees?
2. What is the purpose of pruning in decision trees?
3. Describe the process of learning rules directly from data without constructing a full decision tree?
4. How are decision rules extracted from a decision tree?
5. What distinguishes multivariate trees from univariate trees?

MULTIPLE CHOICE QUESTIONS

1. What is the primary criterion for splitting nodes in a classification tree?

a. Mean Squared Error (MSE)

b. Mean Absolute Error (MAE)

c. Information Gain or Gini Impurity
d. Root Mean Squared Error (RMSE)

2. Which of the following best describes the process of pruning in decision trees?
a. Adding more branches to the tree
b. Removing branches that have little importance
c. Splitting nodes based on multiple features
d. Converting the decision tree into a set of rules

3. How are decision rules typically extracted from a decision tree?
a. By following paths from the root to leaf nodes
b. By performing pre-pruning
c. By splitting nodes based on multiple features
d. By calculating the mean absolute error (MAE)

4. Which algorithm is commonly used for learning rules directly from data?
a. K-means clustering
b. Apriori algorithm
c. ID3 algorithm
d. Linear regression

5. What is a common challenge associated with using decision trees?
a. They cannot handle categorical data
b. They tend to overfit the training data
c. They are difficult to interpret
d. They require a large amount of data

Answers to Multiple Questions

1. (c); 2. (b); 3. (a); 4. (b); 5. (b)

REFERENCES

1. Ali, J., Khan, R., Ahmad, N., & Maqsood, I. (2012). Random forests and decision trees. *International Journal of Computer Science Issues (IJCSI), 9*(5), 272.
2. Almuallim, H. (1996). An efficient algorithm for optimal pruning of decision trees. *Artificial Intelligence, 83*(2), 347–362.
3. An, A. (2003). Learning classification rules from data. *Computers & Mathematics with Applications, 45*(4–5), 737–748.
4. Apolloni, B., Esposito, A., Malchiodi, D., Orovas, C., Palmas, G., & Taylor, J. G. (2004). A general framework for learning rules from data. *IEEE Transactions on Neural Networks, 15*(6), 1333–1349.

5. Appel, R., Fuchs, T., Dollár, P., & Perona, P. (2013). Quickly boosting decision trees: Pruning underachieving features early. In *International Conference on Machine Learning* (Vol. 1, pp. 594–602). PMLR.

6. Apté, C., & Weiss, S. (1997). Data mining with decision trees and decision rules. *Future Generation Computer Systems, 13*(2–3), 197–210.

7. Barakat, N., & Bradley, A. P. (2010). Rule extraction from support vector machines: A review. *Neurocomputing, 74*(1–3), 178–190.

8. Bertsimas, D., & Dunn, J. (2017). Optimal classification trees. *Machine Learning, 106*, 1039–1082.

9. Biggs, D., De Ville, B., & Suen, E. (1991). A method of choosing multiway partitions for classification and decision trees. *Journal of Applied Statistics, 18*(1), 49–62.

10. Bologna, G. (2021). A rule extraction technique applied to ensembles of neural networks, random forests, and gradient-boosted trees. *Algorithms, 14*(12), 339.

11. Bologna, G., & Hayashi, Y. (2018). A comparison study on rule extraction from neural network ensembles, boosted shallow trees, and SVMs. *Applied Computational Intelligence and Soft Computing, 2018*(1), 4084850.

12. Brodley, C. E., & Utgoff, P. E. (1995). Multivariate decision trees. *Machine Learning, 19*, 45–77.

13. Bshouty, N. H., & Mansour, Y. (1995). Simple learning algorithms for decision trees and multivariate polynomials. In *Proceedings of IEEE 36th Annual Foundations of Computer Science* (Vol. 1, pp. 304–311). IEEE.

14. Bshouty, N. H., & Mansour, Y. (2002). Simple learning algorithms for decision trees and multivariate polynomials. *SIAM Journal on Computing, 31*(6), 1909–1925.

15. Bulac, C., & Bulac, A. (2016). Decision trees. In *Advanced Solutions in Power Systems: HVDC, FACTS, and Artificial Intelligence* (pp. 819–844).

16. Buntine, W. (2020). Learning classification trees. In *Artificial Intelligence Frontiers in Statistics* (Vol. 1, pp. 182–201). Chapman and Hall/CRC.

17. Cañete-Sifuentes, L., Monroy, R., & Medina-Pérez, M. A. (2021). A review and experimental comparison of multivariate decision trees. *IEEE Access, 9*, 110451–110479.

18. De Ville, B. (2013). Decision trees. *Wiley Interdisciplinary Reviews: Computational Statistics, 5*(6), 448–455.

19. De'Ath, G. (2002). Multivariate regression trees: A new technique for modeling species–environment relationships. *Ecology, 83*(4), 1105–1117.

20. De'ath, G., & Fabricius, K. E. (2000). Classification and regression trees: A powerful yet simple technique for ecological data analysis. *Ecology, 81*(11), 3178–3192.

21. Elith, J., Leathwick, J. R., & Hastie, T. (2008). A working guide to boosted regression trees. *Journal of Animal Ecology, 77*(4), 802–813.

22. Esposito, F., Malerba, D., Semeraro, G., & Tamma, V. (1999). The effects of pruning methods on the predictive accuracy of induced decision trees. *Applied Stochastic Models in Business and Industry, 15*(4), 277–299.

23. Evans, R., & Grefenstette, E. (2018). Learning explanatory rules from noisy data. *Journal of Artificial Intelligence Research, 61*, 1–64.

24. Gama, J. (2004). Functional trees. *Machine Learning, 55*, 219–250.

25. Heath, D., Kasif, S., & Salzberg, S. (1993). Induction of oblique decision trees. In *IJCAI* (Vol. 1993, pp. 1002–1007).

26. Hong, T. P., Tseng, L. H., & Wang, S. L. (2002). Learning rules from incomplete training examples by rough sets. *Expert Systems with Applications, 22*(4), 285–293.

27. Khemphila, A., & Boonjing, V. (2010). Comparing performances of logistic regression, decision trees, and neural networks for classifying heart disease patients. In *2010 International Conference on Computer Information Systems and Industrial Management Applications (CISIM)* (Vol. 1, pp. 193–198). IEEE.

28. Korting, T. S. (2006). C4.5 algorithm and multivariate decision trees. *Image Processing Division, National Institute for Space Research–INPE Sao Jose dos Campos–SP, Brazil, 22*, 852–855.

29. Kotsiantis, S. B. (2013). Decision trees: A recent overview. *Artificial Intelligence Review, 39*, 261–283.

30. Kwok, S. W., & Carter, C. (1990). Multiple decision trees. In *Machine Intelligence and Pattern Recognition* (Vol. 9, pp. 327–335). North-Holland.

31. Larsen, D. R., & Speckman, P. L. (2004). Multivariate regression trees for analysis of abundance data. *Biometrics, 60*(2), 543–549.

32. Li, Y., Dong, M., & Kothari, R. (2005). Classifiability-based omnivariate decision trees. *IEEE Transactions on Neural Networks, 16*(6), 1547–1560.

33. Loh, W. Y. (2014). Fifty years of classification and regression trees. *International Statistical Review, 82*(3), 329–348.

34. Matheus, C. J., & Rendell, L. A. (1989). Constructive induction on decision trees. In *IJCAI* (Vol. 89, pp. 645–650).

35. McSherry, D. (1999). Strategic induction of decision trees. *Knowledge-Based Systems, 12*(5–6), 269–275.

36. Mi, H., & Huang, L. (2008). Forest-based translation rule extraction. In *Proceedings of the 2008 Conference on Empirical Methods in Natural Language Processing* (Vol. 1, pp. 206–214).

37. Miller, P. J., Lubke, G. H., McArtor, D. B., & Bergeman, C. S. (2016). Finding structure in data using multivariate tree boosting. *Psychological Methods, 21*(4), 583.

38. Mingers, J. (1989). An empirical comparison of pruning methods for decision tree induction. *Machine Learning, 4*, 227–243.

39. Murthy, S. K., Kasif, S., & Salzberg, S. (1994). A system for induction of oblique decision trees. *Journal of Artificial Intelligence Research, 2*, 1–32.

40. Myles, A. J., Feudale, R. N., Liu, Y., Woody, N. A., & Brown, S. D. (2004). An introduction to decision tree modeling. *Journal of Chemometrics: A Journal of the Chemometrics Society, 18*(6), 275–285.

41. Naima, A. I. T., Msanda, F., & El Mousadik, A. (2012). Univariate and multivariate analysis of agronomical traits of preselected argan trees. *Notulae Botanicae Horti Agrobotanici Cluj-Napoca, 40*(2), 308–316.
42. Nayebi, A., Srivastava, S., Ganguli, S., & Yamins, D. L. (2020). Identifying learning rules from neural network observables. *Advances in Neural Information Processing Systems, 33*, 2639–2650.
43. Obregon, J., & Jung, J. Y. (2023). RuleCOSI+: Rule extraction for interpreting classification tree ensembles. *Information Fusion, 89*, 355–381.
44. Pal, N. R., & Chakraborty, S. (2001). Fuzzy rule extraction from ID3-type decision trees for real data. *IEEE Transactions on Systems, Man, and Cybernetics, Part B (Cybernetics), 31*(5), 745–754.
45. Pande, A., Li, L., Rajeswaran, J., Ehrlinger, J., Kogalur, U. B., Blackstone, E. H., & Ishwaran, H. (2017). Boosted multivariate trees for longitudinal data. *Machine Learning, 106*, 277–305.
46. Patel, H. H., & Prajapati, P. (2018). Study and analysis of decision tree-based classification algorithms. *International Journal of Computer Sciences and Engineering, 6*(10), 74–78.
47. Quan, Z., & Valdez, E. A. (2018). Predictive analytics of insurance claims using multivariate decision trees. *Dependence Modeling, 6*(1), 377–407.
48. Rivera-Lopez, R., Canul-Reich, J., Mezura-Montes, E., & Cruz-Chávez, M. A. (2022). Induction of decision trees as classification models through metaheuristics. *Swarm and Evolutionary Computation, 69*, 101006.
49. Rokach, L., & Maimon, O. (2010). Classification trees. In *Data Mining and Knowledge Discovery Handbook* (pp. 149–174). Springer.
50. Sacchi, L., Larizza, C., Combi, C., & Bellazzi, R. (2007). Data mining with temporal abstractions: Learning rules from time series. *Data Mining and Knowledge Discovery, 15*, 217–247.
51. Sánchez, L., Couso, I., & Casillas, J. (2009). Genetic learning of fuzzy rules based on low-quality data. *Fuzzy Sets and Systems, 160*(17), 2524–2552.
52. Schmid, H. (2010). Decision trees. In *The Handbook of Computational Linguistics and Natural Language Processing* (pp. 180–196). Wiley-Blackwell.
53. Segal, M., & Xiao, Y. (2011). Multivariate random forests. *Wiley Interdisciplinary Reviews: Data Mining and Knowledge Discovery, 1*(1), 80–87.
54. Shah, S., & Sastry, P. S. (1999). New algorithms for learning and pruning oblique decision trees. *IEEE Transactions on Systems, Man, and Cybernetics, Part C (Applications and Reviews), 29*(4), 494–505.
55. Sharma, H., & Kumar, S. (2016). A survey on decision tree algorithms of classification in data mining. *International Journal of Science and Research (IJSR), 5*(4), 2094–2097.
56. Sok, H. K., Ooi, M. P. L., Kuang, Y. C., & Demidenko, S. (2016). Multivariate alternating decision trees. *Pattern Recognition, 50*, 195–209.
57. Song, Y. Y., & Ying, L. U. (2015). Decision tree methods: Applications for classification

and prediction. *Shanghai Archives of Psychiatry, 27*(2), 130–135.

58. Sutton, C. D. (2005). Classification and regression trees, bagging, and boosting. In *Handbook of Statistics* (Vol. 24, pp. 303–329). Elsevier.
59. Tang, M. (2020). A simple introduction to programming and statistics with decision trees in R. *Teaching Statistics, 42*(2), 36–40.
60. Thomas, T., Vijayaraghavan, P. A., & Emmanuel, S. (2020). Applications of decision trees. In *Machine Learning Approaches in Cyber Security Analytics* (Vol. 4, pp. 157–174).
61. Timofeev, R. (2004). Classification and regression trees (CART) theory and applications. *Humboldt University, Berlin, 4*, 54–58.
62. Westreich, D., Lessler, J., & Funk, M. J. (2010). Propensity score estimation: Neural networks, support vector machines, decision trees (CART), and meta-classifiers as alternatives to logistic regression. *Journal of Clinical Epidemiology, 63*(8), 826–833.
63. Widmer, G. (2003). Discovering simple rules in complex data: A meta-learning algorithm and some surprising musical discoveries. *Artificial Intelligence, 146*(2), 129–148.
64. Xu, M., Watanachaturaporn, P., Varshney, P. K., & Arora, M. K. (2005). Decision tree regression for soft classification of remote sensing data. *Remote Sensing of Environment, 97*(3), 322–336.
65. Yıldız, O. T. (2015). VC-dimension of univariate decision trees. *IEEE Transactions on Neural Networks and Learning Systems, 26*(2), 378–387.
66. Zhou, Z. H. (2021). Decision trees. *Machine Learning, 5*, 79–102.
67. Zhu, H., Murali, P., Phan, D., Nguyen, L., & Kalagnanam, J. (2020). A scalable MIP-based method for learning optimal multivariate decision trees. *Advances in Neural Information Processing Systems, 33*, 1771–1781.

CHAPTER 5

Artificial Neural Networks

LEARNING OBJECTIVES

After studying this chapter, you will be able to:

- Comprehend the role and significance of artificial neural networks in modern machine learning and artificial intelligence;
- Understand the basic principles of artificial neural network design;
- Learn about the basic network structures;
- Comprehend the perceptron model along with its capabilities;
- Identify how the Adaline model differs from the Perceptron model; and
- Explore diverse applications of artificial neural networks.

KEY TERMS FROM THIS CHAPTER

Artificial neural network
Classification
Function approximation
Pattern association
Vector quantization
Adaline
Clustering
Perceptron
Optimization

UNIT INTRODUCTION

Artificial Neural Networks (ANNs) are a crucial element of artificial intelligence, designed to mimic the neural architecture of the human brain. They have fundamentally transformed the approach to solving intricate problems, leading to substantial progress in diverse domains such as natural language processing, computer vision, and robotics. This chapter will offer a thorough examination of Artificial Neural Networks (ANNs), encompassing its fundamental principles of construction, fundamental architecture, and wide-ranging applications (Grossi & Buscema, 2007).

ANNs are now essential components in machine learning due to their capacity to acquire knowledge from data and extrapolate from instances. Due to their adaptability, they are capable of handling a diverse set of tasks that conventional algorithms find challenging, including pattern identification, picture and speech recognition, and forecasting. Creating a proficient neural network requires the application of certain fundamental ideas. Neurons and synapses are the fundamental components of ANNs. Neurons handle input processing, while synapses, also known as weights, adapt to enhance the learning process (Dongare et al., 2012). Activation functions are essential for incorporating non-linearity into the network and are vital for representing intricate interactions. Some often used activation functions include the tanh, sigmoid, and ReLU functions. The arrangement of neurons in layers (input, concealed, and output) in the network architecture dictates the information flow and the learning capacity of the network. Training computations, such as backpropagation and descent of gradients, optimize the weights of the network by reducing the total error. Comprehending these principles is crucial for creating networks that can efficiently acquire knowledge and make generalizations based on data. Various network architectures are designed to suit particular categories of challenges. Feedforward neural networks, also known as multilayer perceptrons, are the most basic type of neural networks. They operate by passing data in a single way, from the input layer to the output layer. These networks are particularly well-suited for tasks involving classification and regression that are relatively simple and direct (Uhrig, 1995).

Perceptron is an essential part of artificial neural networks (ANNs) and acts as an initial step towards understanding more intricate neural networks. The perceptron accepts input features, each with a weight, and employs a function for activation to ascertain whether it fires, usually employing a step function to binary classification. The output of the perceptron is the ultimate decision or prediction. Gaining a comprehensive understanding of the fundamental principles of the perceptron is essential for establishing the foundation of more sophisticated neural network models (Zhang, 2016). The Adaline model, also known as the Adaptive Linear Neuron, enhances the perceptron by incorporating continuous output and employing a distinct learning mechanism. Adaline, unlike the perceptron, has a function with a linear activation instead of a binary output, which makes it well-suited for regression applications (Krenker et al., 2011).

Artificial Neural Networks possess a diverse range of applications across several areas. The mentioned applications encompass classification, vector quantization, clustering, pattern organization, forecasting, function approximations, and control. Classification is the process of organizing data into predetermined categories, such as identifying spam in emails or diagnosing illnesses. Clustering is a technique that groups data points that are similar to each other. It is commonly used in segmenting consumers and picture compression. Vector quantization is a technique that decreases the number of dimensions in data while maintaining its structure. It is commonly employed in data compression. Pattern association is essential for tasks such as handwriting recognition. Function approximations are mathematical techniques used to calculate unknown functions that transfer input to output. They are commonly employed in automation and financial simulation. Forecasting is a method used to anticipate future data points by analyzing historical patterns. It is commonly used in predicting stock market trends and forecasting meteorological conditions. Control applications enhance the performance of dynamic systems, including controlled robotics and computerized trading systems (Priddy & Keller, 2005).

Did you know?

The first artificial neuron, the Perceptron, was introduced by Frank Rosenblatt in 1957. It was designed to recognize patterns and learn from data inputs.

5.1. ROLE OF ARTIFICIAL NEURAL NETWORKS

ANNs are computational networks that aim to mimic, in a simplified way, the networks of neurons in the central nervous system of humans or animals. This simulation is a comprehensive cell-by-cell simulation. It draws upon the neurophysiological understanding of the biological neurons and networks of these neurons. Therefore, it distinguishes itself from traditional computing devices, whether they are digital or analog, that aim to substitute, improve, or accelerate human brain calculation without considering the arrangement of the computing components and their interconnection. However, it is important to note that the simulation provided by the neural networks is somewhat crude (Paturi et al., 2022).

Why should one consider artificial neural networks as more than just a simulation exercise? It is necessary to pose this question, particularly because, from a computational standpoint, a traditional digital computer is capable of performing all the tasks that an ANN can accomplish (Goel et al., 2023).

The answer resides in two crucial components. The neural network is a computer architecture and algorithmization architecture that simulates a biological neural network. It differs from conventional computers in its novelty and unique approach. It enables the utilization of basic computational operations such as addition, multiplication, and basic logic elements to address intricate, mathematically ambiguous problems, nonlinear problems, or stochastic situations. A typical algorithm utilizes intricate sets of equations and applies exclusively to a certain problem. The artificial neural network (ANN) will possess both computational and algorithmic simplicity, as well as a self-organizing capability that enables it to address a diverse array of issues (Passos et al., 2006).

For instance, when a mouse skillfully evades a cat, it does not engage in solving differential equations related to trajectories, nor does it utilize intricate pattern recognition algorithms. The brain of this organism is rather uncomplicated, yet it utilizes a small number of core neuronal cells that adhere to the structure found in more complex species, including humans. The solution proposed by the ANN will similarly strive for a similar level of simplicity, although it may not be exactly the same. According to Albert Einstein, a solution or model should be as straightforward and as feasible to effectively address the given problem (Estahbanati & Bouduhi, 2002).

Another distinguishing and possibly advantageous property of Artificial Neural Networks (ANNs) is their high level of parallelism, specifically in terms of element-wise parallelism, which sets them apart from traditional computers. A traditional digital computer operates in a sequential manner. If a single transistor, among the multitude of millions, malfunctions, the entire machine ceases to function. Within the adult human nervous system, hundreds of neurons undergo apoptosis annually, however, overall brain function remains unaffected, unless there is a significant loss of cells in specific critical areas, such as after big strokes (Kavzoglu & Mather, 2002). The insensitivity to the destruction of a few cells in biological neural networks is a result of their high parallel structure, which differs from the sequential design of ordinary computers. ANNs also exhibit the same redundancy feature. However, because the majority of ANNs are currently simulated on traditional digital computers, the characteristic of being unaffected by component failure is not applicable. This includes the development of integrated circuits that contain hundreds, and in some cases, even 1,000 ANN neurons on just one chip (Dayhoff & DeLeo, 2001). Overall, the enthusiasm surrounding ANNs cannot be restricted solely to their increased similarity to the human brain. The level of self-organizing capacity can be integrated into traditional digital computers through complex artificial intelligence algorithms. The primary advantage of ANNs is their ability to mimic biological neural networks, enabling them to solve complex problems that are non-analytical, nonlinear, nonstationary, and stochastic. ANNs achieve this by employing low-level programming techniques and self-organizing capabilities, which can be applied to a diverse range of problems without the need for re-programming or other program modifications. The lack of susceptibility to partial hardware breakdowns is an additional appealing feature, but it is only applicable when specialized artificial neural network hardware is utilized (Asadollahfardi & Asadollahfardi, 2015). The emergence of Artificial Neural Networks (ANN) is increasingly acknowledged as a means to enhance comprehension of streamlining programming and algorithmic design for specific purposes and a diverse array of objectives. It should highlight the most basic algorithm without undermining the importance of complex logic and mathematics, which will always play a dominant role in mathematical comprehension and serve as a systematic foundation for eventually narrowing down to precise details (Montesinos López et al., 2022). Clearly, when attempting to solve a system of differential equations, employing an Artificial Neural Network (ANN) would be inappropriate, just as it would be illogical to expect a mouse or a cat to solve them. However, issues about recognition, filtering, and control are well-suited for Artificial Neural Networks (ANNs). As is customary, it is unreasonable to expect any tool or discipline to be capable of accomplishing everything. Currently, artificial neural networks (ANNs) are in their early stages of development. Their inception occurred in the 1950s, although significant public interest in them emerged in the early 1980s. In conclusion, artificial neural networks (ANNs) warrant earnest consideration. The days when they were dismissed as a gimmick or a mere mental exercise are definitely in the past. It is important to examine hybrid architectures that combine artificial neural networks (ANN) with serial computers to take advantage of the strengths of both systems when it is suitable to do so (Kumar & Thakur, 2012).

Did you know?

Neural networks are used to create art! Generative Adversarial Networks (GANs) can generate realistic images, music, and even paintings by learning from a dataset of examples.

5.2. BASIC PRINCIPLES OF ANN DESIGN

The fundamental tenets of ANNs were initially established by McCulloch and Pitts in 1943, based on five underlying assumptions, outlined as follows:

i. The behavior of a neuron in an artificial neural network (ANN) is binary, meaning it either fires or does not fire.
ii. In order for a single neuron to be excited, a specific number of synapses, which is greater than 1, must be stimulated within a specific time frame of neuronal addition.
iii. The sole notable latency inside the brain network is the synaptic delay.
iv. The function of any inhibiting synapse completely blocks the stimulation of the neurons at that particular moment.
v .The interconnection network's structure remains constant over time (Dedecker et al., 2004).

Based on the aforementioned assumption (i), it can be inferred that the neuron functions as a binary entity. While these principles may be the earliest systematic ones in history, they may not all pertain to the current state-of-the-art in ANN construction. This rule can be elucidated by the subsequent illustration: Assume that cell S stimulates the production of saliva and is activated by cell F, which is in turn activated by the visual perception of food. Furthermore, assume that cell L, which is stimulated by the sound of a bell, forms a connection with cell S but is unable to independently trigger S to discharge (Ding & Yue, 2004). Now, with the repetitive activation of cell F, while cell L is simultaneously being activated, cell L will eventually develop the ability to activate cell S without the need for cell F. This will occur as a result of the eventual augmentation in the magnitude of the input from cell L into cell S. In the example of the Hebbian rule mentioned above, cells L and S serve as substitutes for cells A and B, respectively. Furthermore, it is not necessary to utilize the Hebbian rule in every artificial neural network (ANN) architecture. However, it is commonly and indirectly employed in designs (Guillod et al., 2020). Nevertheless, the utilization of values at the input level to each neuron of an artificial neural network (ANN), and the adjustment of these weights based on a specific technique is a universal characteristic of all ANNs. It occurs in every biological neuron. In the latter scenario, changes in weights occur via intricate biochemical mechanisms at the dendrite end of the brain cell, namely at the synaptic junction, and within the molecular frameworks of the chemical signals that traverse that junction. It is also affected by further metabolic alterations occurring in the vicinity of the cell's membrane, but outside of it (Zupan, 1994).

Remember

Backpropagation and gradient descent are essential for training ANNs, allowing the network to learn by adjusting weights to minimize error.

5.3. BASIC NETWORK STRUCTURES

The network structures can be classified into a number of different groups:

i. The Perceptron, invented by psychologist Frank Rosenblatt, is one of the earliest artificial neural networks in history.

ii. The Artron is a Statistical Switch-based Artificial Neural Network (ANN).

iii. The Adaline is also known as the Adaptive Linear Neuron. The artificial neuron is commonly referred to as the ALC (adaptive linear combiner), with the ALC being its main constituent. It is a solitary neuron, as opposed to a network of neurons.

iv. The Madaline (Many Adaline) is a variant of the Adaline algorithm. This formulation is an artificial neural network (ANN) based on the Adaline model mentioned earlier (Basheer & Hajmeer, 2000).

The principles of the four neurons mentioned above, particularly the Perceptron, serve as fundamental components in many subsequent advances in Artificial Neural Networks (ANN).

Three subsequent foundational networks are:

i. The Back-Propagation network is a type of neural network. An artificial neural network (ANN) based on a multi-layer Perceptron, provides a sophisticated approach to learning hidden layers (Bielecki & Bielecki, 2019).

ii. The Hopfield Network is a type of artificial neural network. This network exhibits significant differences from the previous four artificial neural networks, particularly in its recurrent characteristic of feedback across neurons. Therefore, while some of its concepts have not been integrated into ANNs derived from the previous four ANNs, it can be considered as a distinct class of ANN.

iii. The Counter-Propagation Network employs Kohonen's Self-Organizing Mapping to enable unsupervised learning, meaning there is no external guidance or "teacher" involved (Anderson & McNeill, 1992).

Other networks, such as ART, Cognitron, LAMSTAR, and others, incorporate specific components from these basic networks or utilize them as foundational parts. This is typically done in conjunction with other decision-making elements, whether they be statistical or deterministic, and with higher-level controllers (Yegnanarayana, 1994).

5.4. THE PERCEPTRON'S INPUT-OUTPUT PRINCIPLES

The Perceptron, potentially the oldest artificial neuron conceived, serves as the fundamental component of almost all Artificial Neural Networks (ANNs). The Artron is a contender for the title of the earliest artificial neuron. However, the Perceptron and its closely associated Adaline are more broad and important in the later development of Artificial Neural Networks (ANN) compared to this particular model (Barrow, 1996). The only notable contribution of this model is the invention of the probabilistic switch. It is sufficient to state that the basic structure of this model is a crude yet straightforward representation of a biological neuron, as shown in Figure 5.1 below. It adheres to the input/output relationships (Rumelhart et al., 1994):

$$Z = \sum wixi \qquad (5.1)$$

$$y = fN(z) \qquad (5.2)$$

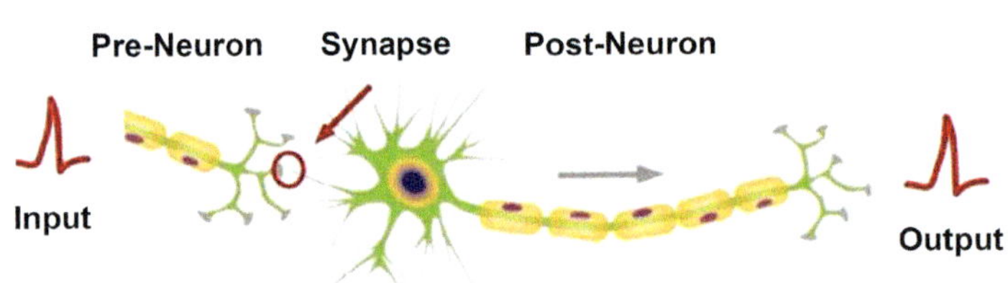

Figure 5.1. *Representation of a biological neuron's input output structure.*

Source: Qilin Hua, Creative Commons License.

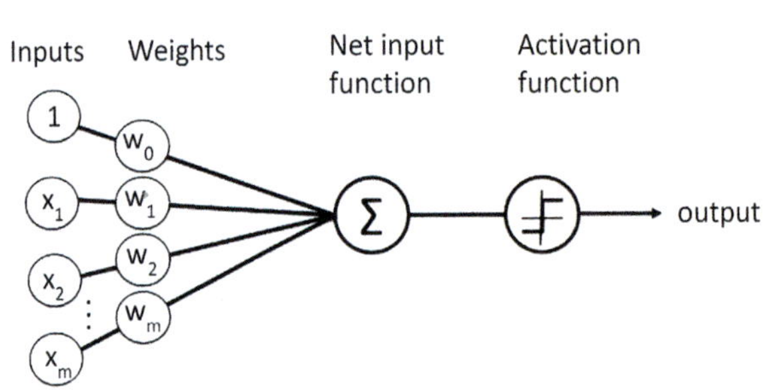

Figure 5.2. *Representation of a perceptron's input/output structure.*

Source: Mayank Banoula, Creative Commons License.

The neuron's output denoted as y in Figure 5.1, is obtained by applying a nonlinear operator, denoted as f_N, to the summation output of the weights at the inputs, denoted as w_i and x_i, where z represents the node. The operator 2 is a non-linear operator that will be addressed at a later point. It is used to calculate the output of the neuron, denoted as y, as shown in Figure 5.2 (Buscema et al., 2018).

5.5. THE ADALINE (ALC)

The Adaline, short for Adaptive Linear Neuron, shares the basic components of a bipolar Perceptron, as described in Section 5.1. It utilizes a form of weight training known as least error square (LS). The system adheres to the input/node relationships (Nguyen et al., 2018):

$$z = w_o + \sum_{i=1}^{n} w_i x_i$$

Where; w_o is a term related to bias that is determined during the training technique described below. The Adaline output, denoted as y, is obtained by using a basic threshold element as the nonlinear operator:

y = sign(z)

as in Figure 5.3 (Muralikrishnan & Mohanty, 2019),

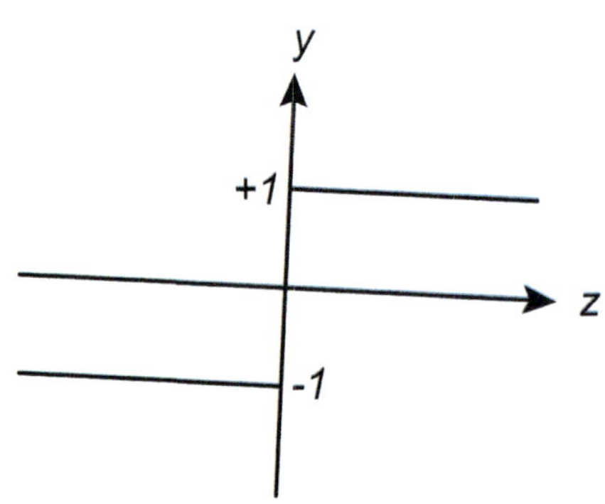

Figure 5.3. *Illustration of activation function nonlinearity.*

Source: Daniel Graupe, Creative Commons License.

$w_o = 0$

$$z = \sum_{i} w_i x_i$$

5.5.1. LMS Training of ALC

Training an Artificial Neural Network (ANN) involves the process of adjusting its weights. The training of the Adaline focuses on adjusting the weights of the ALC, which is the linear summation component shared by all Adaline/Perceptron neurons. This training adheres to the subsequent process:

Provided L training sets x_1 through x_L and corresponding outputs d_1 through d_L (Kumar et al., 2019):

$$J(\mathrm{w}) \triangleq E\left[e_k^2\right] \cong \frac{1}{L}\sum_{k=1}^{L} e_k^2$$

$$\mathrm{w} \triangleq [w_1 \cdots w_n]_L^T$$

The symbol "E" represents an expectation, while "e_k" represents the training error at the kth set.,

$$e_k \triangleq d_k - z_k$$

z_k is the neuron's real output.

Following this representation,

$$E\left[e_k^2\right] = E\left[d_k^2\right] + \mathrm{w}^T E\left[\mathrm{x}_k \mathrm{x}_k^T\right]\mathrm{w} - 2\mathrm{w}^T E[d_k \mathrm{x}_k]$$

with

$$E[\mathrm{xx}^T] \triangleq R$$

$$E[d\mathrm{x}] = \mathrm{p}$$

To give the gradient ∇J such that:

$$\nabla J = \frac{\partial J(\mathrm{w})}{\partial \mathrm{w}} = 2R\mathrm{w} - 2\mathrm{p}$$

Therefore, the most favorable configuration of w in the LMS algorithm, which results in the lowest cost J(w), is as follows (Teodorescu & Bonciu, 1997):

$$\nabla J = \frac{\partial J}{\partial \mathrm{w}} = 0$$

Or,

$$\mathrm{w}^{LMS} = R^{-1}\mathrm{p}$$

The LMS technique described above utilizes an expectation approach, but the training data is restricted to just a handful of L sets. As a result, the sample averages may not accurately predict the genuine expectations used in the LMS procedure. Achieving convergence to the true estimation requires a large number of L sets. A possible alternative to using small-sample averages of L sets is to apply a Steepest Descent training approach for ALC (Khan et al., 2020).

5.5.2. Steepest Descent Training of ALC

The steepest descent approach to train an ALC neuron does not address the limitations of small sample averages, as previously described in connection to the LMS procedure. However, it aims to generate weight-setting estimates for subsequent training sets, commencing with an initial estimate of L = n + 1, where n represents the number of inputs. It is crucial to note that to obtain n weights, this process is essential (Kermani et al., 2005):

$$L > n + 1$$

The steepest descent procedure, also known as a gradient search procedure, can be summarized as follows:

Representing the weights vector configuration at the wth iteration as w(m), then

$$\mathrm{w}(m+1) = \mathrm{w}(m) + \Delta\mathrm{w}(m)$$

Or:

$$\Delta w(m) = \mu \nabla J_{w(m)}$$

And,

$$\nabla J = \left[\frac{\partial J}{\partial w_1} \cdots \frac{\partial J}{\partial w_n}\right]^T$$

Updating w(m) follows the following steps (Chen, 1996):

i. For the mth training set, apply the input vector x_m and the output vector d_m.

ii. Find out e^2_m where;

$$e_m^2 = [d_m - w_{(m)}^T x(m)]^2$$
$$= d_m^2 - 2d_m w^T(m)x(m) + w^T(m)x(m)x^T(m)w(m)$$

iii. Evaluate

$$\nabla J = \frac{\partial e_m^2}{\partial w_{(m)}} = 2x(m)w^T(m)x(m) - 2d_m x(m)$$
$$= -2\left[d(m) - w^T(m)x(m)\right]x(m) = -2e_m x(m)$$

Approximation to ΔJ is achieved by using e^2_m as an approximate to J,

$$\nabla J \cong -2e_m x(m)$$

iv. Now update w(m + 1) above,

$$w(m+1) = w(m) - 2\mu e_m x(m)$$

This is termed as the Delta Rule of ANN. In this scenario, μ is selected to fulfill (Dehuri et al., 2012):

$$\frac{1}{\lambda_{max}} > \mu > 0$$

where;

$$\lambda_{max} = \max[\lambda(R)]$$

Let ʎ (R) represent an eigenvalue of R in the equation given above. Alternatively, one could contemplate the Droretzky theorem of stochastic approximation as a means of determining μ, in order to achieve the desired outcome:

$$\mu = \frac{\mu_0}{m}$$

By selecting a suitable value for μ_0, such as μ_0 = 1, one can ensure that w(m) converges to the true value of was m approaches infinity. This convergence occurs in the theoretical limit, however it may not be practicable to achieve in reality (Faris et al., 2016).

5.6. APPLICATIONS OF ARTIFICIAL NEURAL NETWORKS

The interaction of brain networks is necessary for almost every non-mechanical task carried out by animals. Perception, acknowledgment, recollection, deliberate thought, dreams, and sensorimotor control are only a few examples of cognitive processes. The motivation for the advancement of ANNs stems from the aspiration to replicate certain tasks through simulation. This section outlines the rationale for investigating neural networks based on their applicability to various computational tasks. For every task, performance metrics are developed that may be utilized to assess the level of achievement of a neural network in carrying out the task (Li & Ma, 2010).

Broadly speaking, the tasks carried out utilizing neural networks can be categorized as either necessitating supervised or unsupervised training. In the context of supervised learning, an instructor is present to provide feedback on the system's performance, either by indicating correctness, specifying a desired response, validating the acceptability of the system's outputs, or quantifying the level of error in the system's performance. In contrast to unsupervised learning, which lacks a teacher and relies on heuristic guidance from the system's examination of data samples or the environment. An instance of supervised learning can be seen in "classification" problems, while "clustering" serves as a case study of unsupervised learning (Baxt, 1995).

5.6.1. Classification

Classification, which involves assigning every item to a specific "class" from a set of predetermined groupings, is crucial in several fields like as image and speech recognition, as well as the social sciences. Given is a "training set" that contains sample patterns representing all classes, together with the corresponding class membership data for each pattern. By utilizing the training collection, rules are derived for categorizing instances into each class and a classifier is constructed. This classifier can subsequently be employed to assign new patterns to their corresponding classes based on these rules.

Neural networks are employed for the purpose of categorizing samples, meaning they are able to associate input patterns with distinct classes. For example, each output node represents a single class. A class is assigned to an input pattern if the ith output node produces a greater value than the other output nodes whenever that input pattern is inputted into the network. Some networks include an additional requirement where the magnitude of the output node must be greater than a specified minimum threshold, such as 0.5 (Yang et al., 2000).

For binary classification issues, feedforward neural networks with a solitary output node are sufficient. If the output of a node is restricted to values between 0 and 1, a value near 1 (more than 0.9) is interpreted as belonging to one of the classes, while a number close to 0 (less than 0.1) signals the other class.

Neural networks have proven to be effective in numerous real-world categorization problems, including the following examples.

i. Identifying printed or written characters
ii. Categorizing loan applicants into groups based on their credit-worthiness.
iii. Examining sonar and radar information to ascertain the characteristics of the signal's origin (Byvatov et al., 2003).

5.6.2. Clustering

Clustering involves the process of categorizing objects that share similarities with one another. In classification issues, the classes and the membership of certain specimens in these classes are predetermined. Clustering problems include only a collection of samples and the distance relationships that may be inferred from the descriptions of these samples. For instance, flowers can be grouped based on characteristics such as their color and the number of petals they possess (Taamneh et al., 2017). The majority of clustering mechanisms rely on a distance measure. An ordered set (vector) of characteristics represents each object. "Similar" things are those that possess almost identical values for various characteristics. Therefore, the objective is to categorize samples in a way that minimizes the distances within each group and maximizes the distances between different groups, while also considering the limitation on the maximum number of clusters (Ayhan & Tokdemir, 2020). A method to quantify intra-cluster distance involves calculating the mean distance between individual samples within a cluster and the cluster's central point. Similarly, the inter-cluster distance can be quantified by calculating the distance between the centroids of distinct clusters. Figure 5.4 illustrates a scenario where previous clustering, resulting in five distinct clusters, proves advantageous in a classification pattern (Liao & Wen, 2007).

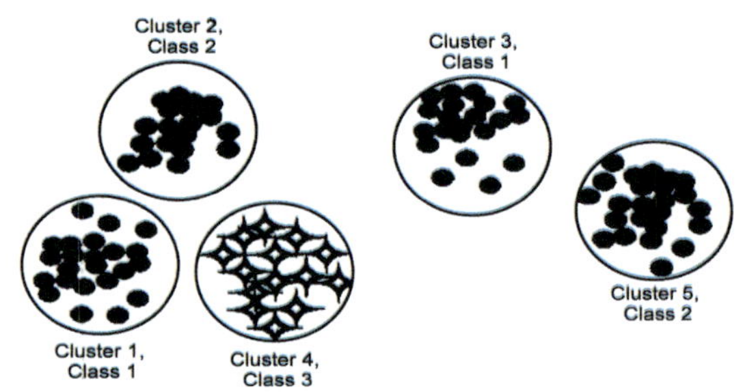

Figure 5.4. *Illustration of five clusters, three classes in two-dimensional input space.*

Source: Kishan Mehrotra, Creative Commons License.

The optimal number of clusters is problem-dependent, although it should be minimized. Figure 5.5 depicts three methods of clustering the identical dataset, with the first method being the most favorable as it strikes a balance between having an excessive or insufficient number of clusters. Some neural networks achieve clustering through the following approach. At first, every node responds in a random manner to the introduction of input samples. Nodes with more outputs to a given input exhibit increased responsiveness to that particular sample and to additional input samples in close proximity. Through this process, various nodes develop specific expertise, exhibiting a strong response to distinct groups of input data (Wang et al., 2010).

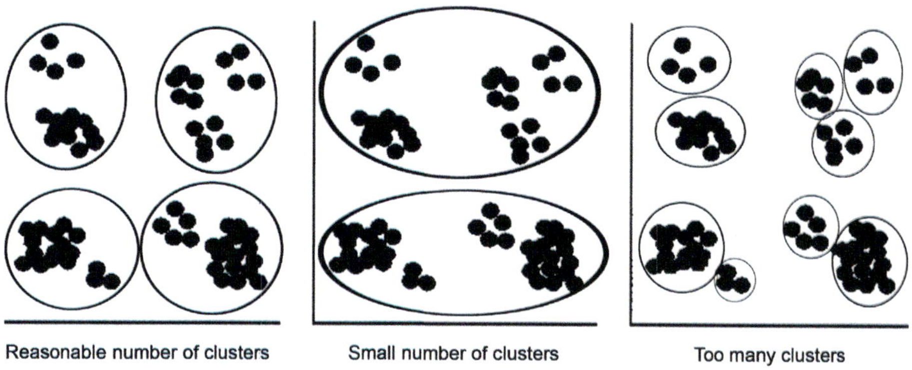

Figure 5.5. *Schematic of three different ways of clustering the same set of sample points.*

Source: Sanjay Ranka, Creative Commons License.

5.6.3. Vector Quantization

Neural networks have been employed to condense extensive input data into a limited set of weight vectors linked to nodes in the networks.

Every input sample is linked to the closest weight vector based on the lowest Euclidean distance. Vector quantization involves partitioning space into many interconnected parts known as "Voronoi regions," which is a task akin to clustering.

A "codebook vector" is used to represent each region individually (Lu & Shin, 1992). Figure 5.6 illustrates a Voronoi diagram, which is a split of space in two dimensions into Voronoi regions, sometimes known as a "tessellation." In two-dimensional input spaces, the borders of Voronoi regions are determined by drawing the perpendicular bisectors of the paths that connect nearby codebook vectors (Martinetz et al., 1993).

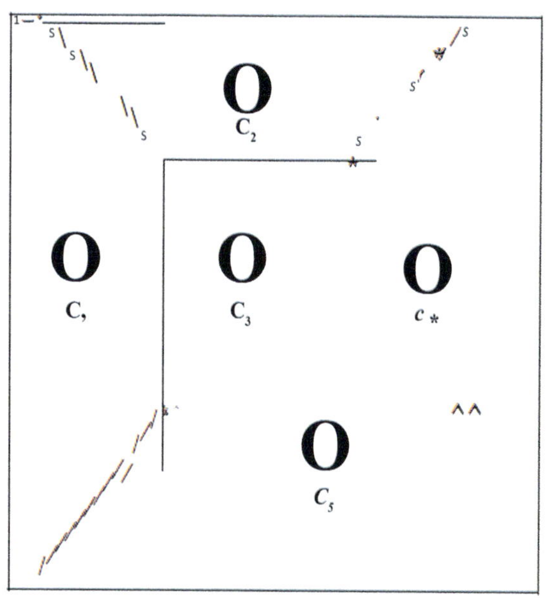

Figure 5.6. *Schematic of voronoi diagram in two-dimensional space, widi five Voronoi regions, and codebook vectors.*

Source: Mohan, Creative Commons License.

5.6.4. Pattern Association

In the context of pattern association, neural networks have the capability to generate a certain output pattern when presented with an input sample.

In tasks involving auto-association or memory for associations (refer to figure 5.7), the sample of input is assumed to be a distorted, noisy, or incomplete replica of the intended result pattern. In hetero-association, the output pattern can be any random pattern that is linked to a set of patterns for input. An instance of an auto-associative job is generating an intact image, like a face, from a distorted version (Carpenter, 1989).

Figure 5.7. *Illustration of Auto-association.*

Source: Mohan, Creative Commons License.

An instance of hetero-association occurs when a name is generated in response to an input of a face image. In the field of neural networks, the term "auto/hetero-association" pertains to the process of establishing weights that represent the relationships between input and output patterns.

Each input pattern dimension is represented by a node, and during the recall process, the node outputs are modified iteratively until the end product pattern stabilizes. In order to achieve hetero-associative recall, it is necessary to incorporate an additional layer of nodes that will construct the output pattern that corresponds to a given input pattern (Chon et al., 1996).

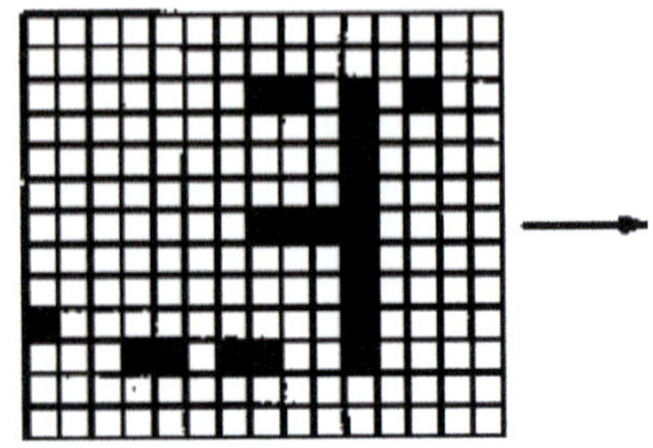

Figure 5.8. *Illustration of Hetero-association.*

Source: Kishan Mehrotra, Creative Commons License.

5.6.5. Function Approximation

Several computational frameworks can be characterized as functions that transfer numerical input vectors onto numerical outputs. While one may have access to training data that provides the outputs for certain input vectors, the underlying mathematical function that governs the relationship between the inputs and outputs remains unknown. Function approximation refers to the process of learning or creating a function that produces outputs similar to the ones generated by the modeled process, using the available training data (Zhang & Barrion, 2006).

Figure 5.9 demonstrates that a single finite number of samples can be utilized to generate multiple distinct functions, all of which exhibit satisfactory performance on the provided set of points. Given that there are infinitely many functions that align with a finite set of points, it is imperative to establish additional criteria to determine which of those functions are preferable. Typically, the function must possess continuity and smoothness. In accordance with accepted scientific methodology, a crucial factor to consider is the simplicity of the model, meaning that the neural network should possess the minimum number of parameters (Mhaskar, 1996).

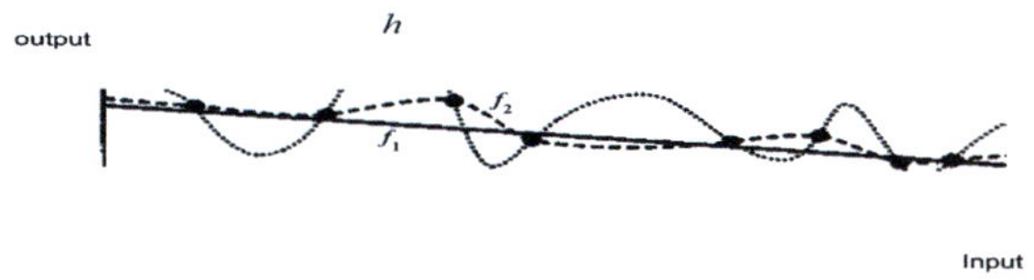

Figure 5.9. *Representation of function approximation: different networks implement functions that have the same behavior on training samples.*

Source: Sanjay Ranka, Creative Commons License.

Occasionally, these criteria conflict with the efficiency criterion of reducing error. This sample set has one outlier that exhibits a substantial deviation from the behavior of the other samples.

The function fo, which includes all the points in the graph, is the most comprehensive and effective. However, the function f, which excludes the outlier, is simpler and hence more desirable. In the case seen in Figure 5.9, the straight line demonstrates satisfactory performance, while f_1 and f_2 exhibit superior performance by achieving zero error (Ge et al., 2002).

Out of the two options mentioned, fa is highly desirable due to its smoother nature and ability to be symbolized by a network with fewer variables. The assumption underlying such comparisons is that the provided samples may contain mistakes resulting from the methodology employed in their acquisition or from environmental influences.

Numerous industrial or manufacturing issues entail the task of stabilizing the actions of an object or monitoring the behavior of a mobile object. These can alternatively be interpreted as problems of approximating functions, where the function to be approximated is the changing behavior of the item in question over time (Wedge et al., 2006).

5.6.6. Forecasting

There exist numerous practical issues in which the anticipation of future occurrences relies on the analysis of past happenings. One example challenge involves forecasting the movements of indexes of the stock market.

Weigend and Huberman assert that prediction relies on two forms of knowledge: understanding of fundamental principles, which is a very effective and precise method of forecasting, and the identification of robust empirical patterns in measurements of a specific system. Nevertheless, the fundamental principles governing the actions of a system are not readily uncovered, and observable patterns or recurring patterns are not always apparent, and can frequently be obscured by random fluctuations (Thirumalaiah & Deo, 1998).

While achieving perfect prediction is rarely feasible, neural networks can be employed to provide reasonably accurate predictions in certain scenarios. Neural networks, for example, have successfully learned the 11-year pattern in sunspot data (figure 5.10) without prior knowledge of the existence of this cycle (Mitrea et al., 2009).

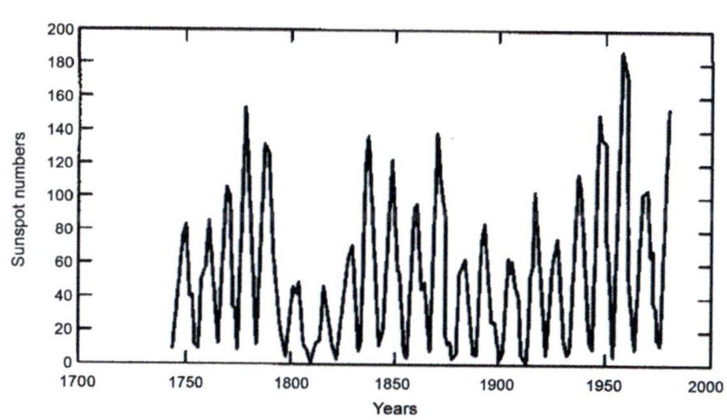

Figure 5.10. *Representation of yearly sunspot numbers, showing cyclic fluctuations.*

Source: Qilin Hua, Creative Commons License.

At a macroscopic level, the issue of prediction can be seen as a specific instance of approximation of function problems, where the function values are expressed as time series.

A time series is a sequential set of measurements taken over a period of time, either in distinct or uninterrupted time intervals. For example, let S = {v(t): 1 < t < N) denote a group of N observations gathered at specific moments t = 1, 2..., N. To create a network that predicts based on the most recent values of a variable, extract a training set of (d + l)-tuples from S. Each tuple in S consists of d + 1 consecutive elements. The first d elements represent network inputs, while the last element indicates the intended output for those inputs. During each iteration of the training phase, the network is supplied with a d-tuple of input data, which represents the recent history. The network endeavors to forecast the subsequent value in the temporal sequence. Thus, the forecasting problem is simplified to a problem of approximating a function (Charytoniuk & Chen, 2000).

Researching multiple linked factors in conjunction is sometimes more effective than researching a single variable when seeking a deeper comprehension of complex problems. A time series that is multivariate is a collection of data that includes multiple variables, each of which changes over time. The variables being tracked may exhibit a strong correlation, for example, when similar properties are being evaluated at various points in the world. By considering differences in the other variables, more accurate predictions can be made for each variable. In order to achieve success, forecasting must rely on all existing connections and empirical connections among various temporal sequences (Zealand et al., 1999).

5.6.7. Control Applications

Several industrial and commercial uses exhibit intricate implicit connections between inputs and outputs. Control is the process that sets the values of the input variables so as to attain the targets for output variables. This topic can also be classified as a function estimation problem, which has been effectively addressed using feedforward, recurrent, and certain specialized neural networks. Adaptive control approaches have been created to address systems that experience significant fluctuations in parameter values, ambient circumstances, and signal inputs. Neural networks may be utilized in adaptive systems of control to deliver rapid reactions, without necessitating human intervention.

Control challenges involve modeling systems that can be classified as either static or dynamic. In dynamic systems, the mapping of inputs to outputs is time-dependent, and this mapping can change over time. An illustrative instance of a static control system involves the conversion of voltage inputs into physical displacements of a robotic arm (Hussain, 1999).

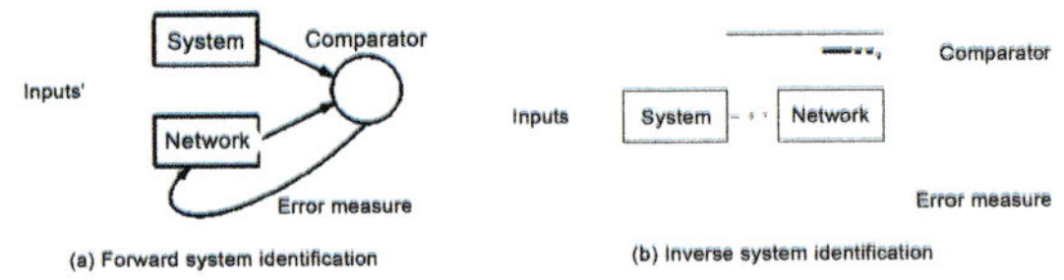

Figure 5.11. *Illustration of forward and inverse control problems.*

Source: Yaxin Li, Creative Commons License.

Neural networks are employed for two control-related tasks, where learning is supervised due to the neural network's objective being determined by the system's behavior. The tasks, depicted in Figure 5.11, are as follows.

System identification refers to the process of estimating the actions of a system by utilizing a neural network or another learning technique. Forward identification is performed by a feedforward neural network when the system maps a set of input variables to output variables. The network's inputs correspond to the input variables and its outputs correspond to the output variables. The network is taught to minimize an error measure that quantifies the difference between the network outputs and the actual control system outputs (Seginer, 1997).

Inverse identification refers to the process of acquiring knowledge about the opposite behavior of a system, which may involve the utilization of neural networks. For example, when a specific force is exerted on an autonomous arm system, the system's response is a displacement of a particular magnitude.

In this situation, the inverse problem involves determining the force necessary to achieve a specific amount of displacement. This can be accomplished by utilizing a feedforward network that takes parts of O as its inputs and elements of the arm as its outputs. The network employs an error measure that quantifies the disparity between the actual system inputs (i) and the outcome (N(S(i))) obtained by applying the actual system to those inputs, and then the neural network.

Once the neural network has been effectively trained for inverse system verification, it is capable of producing the necessary system input values to achieve the intended system outputs. If the behavior of the system changes over time, the network used to generate inputs for the system can also be continuously trained online. If the input-output mapping of the system is not fully understood or changes over time, neural networks may need to be continuously trained to adapt to changes in the system's behavior. A system with feedback is suitable in this case, where the discrepancy between the actual desired system output is utilized to adjust the input signal, so achieving the desired behavior.

Feedforward neural networks are being utilized in several control scenarios, including pole balancing, robotic arm management, vehicle backing-up, and reverse robot kinematics. The success of these systems can be attributed to the following characteristics.

i. Achieving rapid choice-making and control with parallel computation.
ii. Capacity to adjust to a wide range of parameters.
iii. The distributed presentation of information provides inherent fault tolerance.
iv. Networks exhibit robustness to unmodeled parameter alterations due to their generalization capabilities (Sun et al., 2003).

5.6.8. Optimization

Optimization issues are commonly used in both commercial and academic modeling to reflect various challenges. These problems include optimizing (either maximizing or minimizing) specific functions while adhering to certain restrictions. One instance is the duty of organizing elements on the board in a manner that minimizes the overall length of wires. This task also includes extra restrictions that specify some components must be connected to specific others, as depicted in Figure 5.12. Neural networks can also be employed to tackle certain types of difficulties.

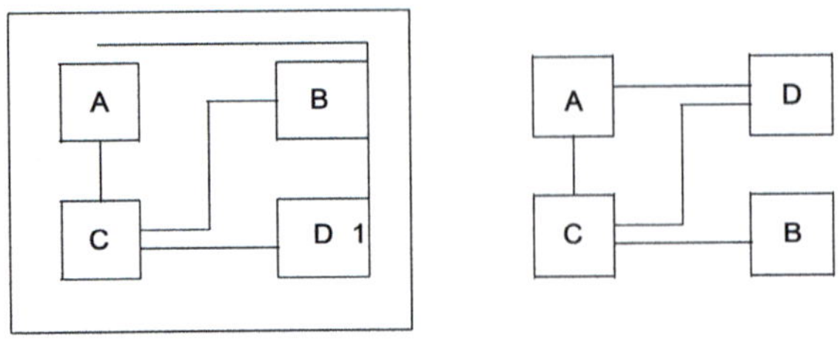

Figure 5.12. *Illustration of two layouts of components on a circuit board with different wire lengths, but with the same inter-component connections.*

Source: Sanjay Ranka, Creative Commons License.

Complex optimization issues are best solved utilizing networks that exhibit stochastic behavior, where the network activity incorporates an important random or probabilistic element (Schweidtmann & Mitsos, 2019).

5.6.9. Search

Search issues and their answers are a focal point in the field of Artificial Intelligence. Search issues are defined by a collection of states, a specification of how transition (or moves) can be performed between distinct states, and techniques for making moves that enable the achievement of a goal, perhaps reducing the total number of steps or computing cost. The problems discussed in the previous subsections, which were resolved using neural networks, can be seen as search problems. In this context, each "state" in a neural network represents a potential weight matrix, each "move" corresponds to a possible alteration in the weight matrix that can be made by the algorithm for learning, and the ultimate objective is to reach a "goal" state where the mean squared error is minimized locally (Schneider et al., 1998).

Neural networks can also be utilized in specific search issues that are often addressed utilizing symbolic reasoning techniques. When tackling a search problem with neural networks, the initial and most challenging step is to get an appropriate representation of the area of search in terms of node and weight within a network. In the context of a neural network designed for playing a game, the inputs provided to the network represent the current state of a board game, while the intended output pattern indicates the optimal move to be made. The network's weights can be trained by evaluating the quality of prior motions performed by the network according to different input patterns (Sexton et al., 1998).

ACTIVITY 5.1.

i. Create a diagram of a feedforward neural network with one hidden layer containing three neurons. Label the input layer, hidden layer, and output layer.

ii. Explain how backpropagation is used to train this network. What is the role of gradient descent in this process

SUMMARY

- This chapter presents Artificial Neural Networks (ANNs), which are essential elements of artificial intelligence. ANNs are motivated by the neural structures of the human brain. The chapter elucidates the pivotal function of Artificial Neural Networks (ANNs) in resolving intricate issues, including tasks such as pattern identification, image and speech analysis, prognostication, and management systems. The chapter provides an overview of the fundamental ideas involved in designing neural networks, including topics such as neurons and synapses, functions for activation, network structure, and training techniques. It highlights the significance of these ideas in constructing efficient and transferable networks. The text also explores different network architectures, such as Convolutional Neural Networks (CNNs), Feedforward Neural Networks, and Recurrent Neural Networks (RNNs). Each structure is defined by its distinct uses and strengths, emphasizing the importance of selecting the suitable architecture for various data kinds and workloads.
- The chapter also discusses the perceptron, an essential part of artificial neural networks (ANNs), providing a detailed explanation of its input-output principles. The Adaline model, also known as the Adaptive Linear Neuron, is a development of the perceptron model. It is designed to handle continuous output and utilizes the Least Mean Squares learning technique. The chapter examines the various uses of ANNs, including sorting, grouping, vector quantization, function approximations, pattern association, forecasting, and control uses. These applications exemplify the tangible influence of artificial neural networks (ANNs) and their capacity to tackle real-life issues.

REVIEW QUESTIONS

1. What are some key applications of artificial neural networks in modern technology?
2. What are the main components of a neuron in an artificial neural network?
3. Describe the architecture of a typical neural network, including input, hidden, and output layers?

4. What is a perceptron, and how does it perform binary classification?
5. How does the Adaline model differ from the perceptron in terms of output and activation function?
6. How are ANNs used in classification and clustering tasks?

MULTIPLE CHOICE QUESTIONS

1. **Which of the following is a primary function of artificial neural networks?**
   a. Word processing
   b. Image and speech recognition
   c. Spreadsheet calculations
   d. Internet browsing
2. **What is the main role of activation functions in a neural network?**
   a. To initialize the weights
   b. To introduce non-linearity
   c. To store data
   d. To reduce overfitting
3. **In which type of neural network does data flow in only one direction, from input to output?**
   a. Recurrent Neural Network (RNN)
   b. Convolutional Neural Network (CNN)
   c. Feedforward Neural Network
   d. Self-organizing Map (SOM)
4. **The perceptron is primarily used for which type of task?**
   a. Multiclass classification
   b. Regression
   c. Binary classification
   d. Clustering
5. **Which learning algorithm is used by the Adaline model to minimize error?**
   a. Gradient descent
   b. Least Mean Squares (LMS)
   c. Backpropagation
   d. Genetic algorithm
6. **Which application of ANNs involves categorizing data into predefined classes?**
   a. Classification
   b. Clustering

c. Vector quantization
d. Function approximation

Answers to Multiple Choice Questions

1. (b); 2. (b); 3. (c); 4. (c); 5. (b); 6. (a)

REFERENCES

1. Anderson, D., & McNeill, G. (1992). *Artificial Neural Networks Technology*. Kaman Sciences Corporation, *258*(6), 1–83.
2. Asadollahfardi, G., & Asadollahfardi, G. (2015). Artificial neural network. In *Water Quality Management: Assessment and Interpretation*, *8*(1), 77–91.
3. Ayhan, B. U., & Tokdemir, O. B. (2020). Accident analysis for construction safety using latent class clustering and artificial neural networks. *Journal of Construction Engineering and Management*, *146*(3), 4019114.
4. Barrow, H. (1996). Connectionism and neural networks. In *Artificial intelligence* (Vol. 2, pp. 135–155). Academic Press.
5. Basheer, I. A., & Hajmeer, M. (2000). Artificial neural networks: Fundamentals, computing, design, and application. *Journal of Microbiological Methods*, *43*(1), 3–31.
6. Baxt, W. G. (1995). Application of artificial neural networks to clinical medicine. *The Lancet*, *346*(8983), 1135–1138.
7. Bielecki, A., & Bielecki, A. (2019). Foundations of artificial neural networks. In *Models of Neurons and Perceptrons: Selected Problems and Challenges*, *5*(1), 15–28.
8. Buscema, P. M., Massini, G., Breda, M., Lodwick, W. A., Newman, F., Asadi-Zeydabadi, M., & Asadi-Zeydabadi, M. (2018). Artificial neural networks. In *Artificial Adaptive Systems Using Auto Contractive Maps: Theory, Applications and Extensions*, *3*(2), 11–35.
9. Byvatov, E., Fechner, U., Sadowski, J., & Schneider, G. (2003). Comparison of support vector machine and artificial neural network systems for drug/nondrug classification. *Journal of Chemical Information and Computer Sciences*, *43*(6), 1882–1889.
10. Carpenter, G. A. (1989). Neural network models for pattern recognition and associative memory. *Neural Networks*, *2*(4), 243–257.
11. Charytoniuk, W., & Chen, M. S. (2000). Very short-term load forecasting using artificial neural networks. *IEEE Transactions on Power Systems*, *15*(1), 263–268.
12. Chen, C. P. (1996). A rapid supervised learning neural network for function interpolation and approximation. *IEEE Transactions on Neural Networks*, *7*(5), 1220–1230.
13. Chon, T. S., Park, Y. S., Moon, K. H., & Cha, E. Y. (1996). Patternizing communities by using an artificial neural network. *Ecological Modelling*, *90*(1), 69–78.
14. Dayhoff, J. E., & DeLeo, J. M. (2001). Artificial neural networks: Opening the black box. *Cancer: Interdisciplinary International Journal of the American Cancer Society*, *91*(S8), 1615–1635.

15. Dedecker, A. P., Goethals, P. L., Gabriels, W., & De Pauw, N. (2004). Optimization of artificial neural network (ANN) model design for prediction of macroinvertebrates in the Zwalm River basin (Flanders, Belgium). *Ecological Modelling, 174*(1), 161–173.

16. Dehuri, S., Roy, R., Cho, S. B., & Ghosh, A. (2012). An improved swarm optimized functional link artificial neural network (ISO-FLANN) for classification. *Journal of Systems and Software, 85*(6), 1333–1345.

17. Ding, L., & Yue, Y. (2004). Novel ANN-based feature recognition incorporating design by features. *Computers in Industry, 55*(2), 197–222.

18. Dongare, A. D., Kharde, R. R., & Kachare, A. D. (2012). Introduction to artificial neural network. *International Journal of Engineering and Innovative Technology (IJEIT), 2*(1), 189–194.

19. Estahbanati, H. K., & Bouduhi, N. (2002). Role of artificial neural networks in prediction of survival of burn patients—A new approach. *Burns, 28*(6), 579–586.

20. Faris, H., Aljarah, I., & Mirjalili, S. (2016). Training feedforward neural networks using multi-verse optimizer for binary classification problems. *Applied Intelligence, 45*, 322–332.

21. Ge, S. S., Hang, C. C., Lee, T. H., Zhang, T., Ge, S. S., Hang, C. C., & Zhang, T. (2002). Neural networks and function approximation. In *Stable Adaptive Neural Network Control* (pp. 27–46).

22. Goel, A., Goel, A. K., & Kumar, A. (2023). The role of artificial neural network and machine learning in utilizing spatial information. *Spatial Information Research, 31*(3), 275–285.

23. Grossi, E., & Buscema, M. (2007). Introduction to artificial neural networks. *European Journal of Gastroenterology & Hepatology, 19*(12), 1046–1054.

24. Guillod, T., Papamanolis, P., & Kolar, J. W. (2020). Artificial neural network (ANN) based fast and accurate inductor modeling and design. *IEEE Open Journal of Power Electronics, 1*, 284–299.

25. Hussain, M. A. (1999). Review of the applications of neural networks in chemical process control—Simulation and online implementation. *Artificial Intelligence in Engineering, 13*(1), 55–68.

26. Kavzoglu, T., & Mather, P. M. (2002). The role of feature selection in artificial neural network applications. *International Journal of Remote Sensing, 23*(15), 2919–2937.

27. Kermani, B. G., Schiffman, S. S., & Nagle, H. T. (2005). Performance of the Levenberg–Marquardt neural network training method in electronic nose applications. *Sensors and Actuators B: Chemical, 110*(1), 13–22.

28. Khan, W. A., Chung, S. H., Awan, M. U., & Wen, X. (2020). Machine learning facilitated business intelligence (Part I): Neural networks learning algorithms and applications. *Industrial Management & Data Systems, 120*(1), 164–195.

29. Krenker, A., Bešter, J., & Kos, A. (2011). Introduction to artificial neural networks. In *Artificial Neural Networks: Methodological Advances and Biomedical Applications* (pp. 1–18). InTech.

30. Kumar, K., & Thakur, G. S. M. (2012). Advanced applications of neural networks

and artificial intelligence: A review. *International Journal of Information Technology and Computer Science, 4*(6), 57–68.

31. Kumar, N., Singh, B., & Panigrahi, B. K. (2019). PNKLMF-based neural network control and learning-based HC MPPT technique for Mult objective grid integrated solar PV based distributed generating system. *IEEE Transactions on Industrial Informatics, 15*(6), 3732–3742.
32. Li, Y., & Ma, W. (2010). Applications of artificial neural networks in financial economics: A survey. In *2010 International Symposium on Computational Intelligence and Design* (Vol. 1, pp. 211–214). IEEE.
33. Liao, S. H., & Wen, C. H. (2007). Artificial neural networks classification and clustering of methodologies and applications–Literature analysis from 1995 to 2005. *Expert Systems with Applications, 32*(1), 1–11.
34. Lu, C. C., & Shin, Y. H. (1992). Neural networks for classified vector quantization of images. *Engineering Applications of Artificial Intelligence, 5*(5), 451–456.
35. Martinetz, T. M., Berkovich, S. G., & Schulten, K. J. (1993). 'Neural-gas' network for vector quantization and its application to time-series prediction. *IEEE Transactions on Neural Networks, 4*(4), 558–569.
36. Mhaskar, H. N. (1996). Neural networks for optimal approximation of smooth and analytic functions. *Neural Computation, 8*(1), 164–177.
37. Mitrea, C. A., Lee, C. K. M., & Wu, Z. (2009). A comparison between neural networks and traditional forecasting methods: A case study. *International Journal of Engineering Business Management, 1*, 11–13.
38. Montesinos López, O. A., Montesinos López, A., & Crossa, J. (2022). Fundamentals of artificial neural networks and deep learning. In *Multivariate Statistical Machine Learning Methods for Genomic Prediction* (Vol. 1, pp. 379–425). Springer International Publishing.
39. Muralikrishnan, G., & Mohanty, N. K. (2019). Modified shunt active line conditioner using enhanced self-restoring technique with step size error elimination algorithm. In *International Conference on Intelligent Computing and Applications: Proceedings of ICICA 2018* (Vol. 1, pp. 237–259). Springer Singapore.
40. Nguyen, H. X., Tran, T. N. C., Park, J. W., & Jeon, J. W. (2018). An adaptive linear-neuron-based third-order PLL to improve the accuracy of absolute magnetic encoders. *IEEE Transactions on Industrial Electronics, 66*(6), 4639–4649.
41. Passos, P., Araújo, D., Davids, K., Gouveia, L., & Serpa, S. (2006). Interpersonal dynamics in sport: The role of artificial neural networks and 3-D analysis. *Behavior Research Methods, 38*, 683–691.
42. Paturi, U. M. R., Cheruku, S., & Reddy, N. S. (2022). The role of artificial neural networks in prediction of mechanical and tribological properties of composites—A comprehensive review. *Archives of Computational Methods in Engineering, 29*(5), 3109–3149.
43. Priddy, K. L., & Keller, P. E. (2005). *Artificial Neural Networks: An Introduction*. SPIE Press.
44. Rumelhart, D. E., Widrow, B., & Lehr, M. A. (1994). The basic ideas in neural networks. *Communications of the ACM, 37*(3), 87–93.

45. Schneider, G., Schrödl, W., Wallukat, G., Müller, J., Nissen, E., Rönspeck, W., & Kunze, R. (1998). Peptide design by artificial neural networks and computer-based evolutionary search. *Proceedings of the National Academy of Sciences, 95*(21), 12179–12184.
46. Schweidtmann, A. M., & Mitsos, A. (2019). Deterministic global optimization with artificial neural networks embedded. *Journal of Optimization Theory and Applications, 180*(3), 925–948.
47. Seginer, I. (1997). Some artificial neural network applications to greenhouse environmental control. *Computers and Electronics in Agriculture, 18*(2–3), 167–186.
48. Sexton, R. S., Alidaee, B., Dorsey, R. E., & Johnson, J. D. (1998). Global optimization for artificial neural networks: A tabu search application. *European Journal of Operational Research, 106*(2–3), 570–584.
49. Sun, Y., Peng, Y., Chen, Y., & Shukla, A. J. (2003). Application of artificial neural networks in the design of controlled release drug delivery systems. *Advanced Drug Delivery Reviews, 55*(9), 1201–1215.
50. Taamneh, M., Taamneh, S., & Alkheder, S. (2017). Clustering-based classification of road traffic accidents using hierarchical clustering and artificial neural networks. *International Journal of Injury Control and Safety Promotion, 24*(3), 388–395.
51. Teodorescu, H. N., & Bonciu, C. (1997). Learning algorithm for RBF networks as features extractors. In *Proceedings of 1st International Conference on Conventional and Knowledge Based Intelligent Electronic Systems (KES'97)* (Vol. 1, pp. 201–208). IEEE.
52. Thirumalaiah, K., & Deo, M. C. (1998). River stage forecasting using artificial neural networks. *Journal of Hydrologic Engineering, 3*(1), 26–32.
53. Uhrig, R. E. (1995). Introduction to artificial neural networks. In *Proceedings of IECON'95-21st Annual Conference on IEEE Industrial Electronics* (Vol. 1, pp. 33–37). IEEE.
54. Wang, G., Hao, J., Ma, J., & Huang, L. (2010). A new approach to intrusion detection using artificial neural networks and fuzzy clustering. *Expert Systems with Applications, 37*(9), 6225–6232.
55. Wedge, D., Ingram, D., McLean, D., Mingham, C., & Bandar, Z. (2006). On global–local artificial neural networks for function approximation. *IEEE Transactions on Neural Networks, 17*(4), 942–952.
56. Yang, C. C., Prasher, S. O., Landry, J. A., & DiTommaso, A. (2000). Application of artificial neural networks in image recognition and classification of crop and weeds. *Canadian Agricultural Engineering, 42*(3), 147–152.
57. Yegnanarayana, B. (1994). Artificial neural networks. *Prentice Hall*

CHAPTER

6 Reinforcement Learning

LEARNING OBJECTIVES

After studying this chapter, you will be able to:

- Understand the fundamentals of reinforcement learning;
- Identify and comprehend the domains of reinforcement learning such as reward function, policy, value function, and model;
- Learn about examples of reinforcement learning applications in various domains such as gaming, robotics, and recommendation systems; and
- Understand reinforcement learning with the help of the example of tic-tac-toe..

KEY TERMS FROM THIS CHAPTER

Model	Policy
Reinforcement learning	Reward function
Tic-tac-toe	Value function

UNIT INTRODUCTION

This chapter offers a thorough introduction to reinforcement learning, which is a sort of machine learning whereby an agent learns to make decisions by doing actions in a setting to maximize the total reward (François-Lavet et al., 2018). Reinforcement learning is a type of learning that differs from supervised and unsupervised learning. It specifically emphasizes learning by interacting with the environment and making adjustments based on trial and error (Naeem et al., 2020).

Reinforcement learning is the process of instructing an agent to make a series of choices based on feedback received from the surrounding environment. The agent engages in a sequence of activities, monitors the resulting outcomes, and adapts its strategy to maximize the potential reward (Kaelbling et al., 1995). The process of learning is motivated by incentives and punishments, which incentivize the agent to discover the most effective strategy for selecting actions. The components of reinforcement learning comprise policy, reward function, value function, and model. Reinforcement learning is effective and adaptable in a range of domains. Illustrative instances encompass instructing agents to engage in games such as Chess and Go, refining robotic systems for control, and constructing recommendation systems (Morales & Zaragoza, 2012). The chapter provides a concrete demonstration by presenting a detailed example of applying reinforcement learning for playing Tic-Tac-Toe. The agent acquires the ability to engage in the game by experimenting with various methods, earning prizes for successful plays, and facing penalties for unsuccessful moves. This example effectively illustrates the ideas and components of reinforcement learning in a straightforward and comprehensible manner (Wiering & Van Otterlo, 2012).

6.1. FUNDAMENTALS OF REINFORCEMENT LEARNING

Reinforcement learning involves acquiring knowledge on how to effectively associate conditions with actions to optimize a numerical reward signal. In contrast to typical kinds of machine learning, the learner is not provided with explicit instructions on which actions to do. Instead, the learner must autonomously determine which behaviors result in the highest level of reward through trial and error (Lei et al., 2020). In complex and stimulating scenarios, actions might have an impact not just on the immediate outcome but also on the subsequent situation and, therefore, on all future rewards. The differentiating characteristics of reinforcement learning include experimentation search and delayed reward (Ding et al., 2020). The definition of reinforcement learning is based on identifying a learning problem rather than characterizing learning algorithms. Any method that is highly suitable for solving that problem is classified as a reinforcement learning algorithm. The fundamental concept is to effectively capture the essential elements of the actual challenge that a learning agent encounters while interacting with its surroundings to accomplish a specific objective (Ris-Ala, 2023). Undoubtedly, an agent must possess the capability to perceive the condition of the environment to a certain degree and have the ability to execute actions that have an impact on that condition. The agent must also possess objectives about the condition of the environment. The definition aims to encompass only these three elements - sensation, action, and objective - in the most basic form conceivable, without diminishing the significance of any of them (Xiong et al., 2019). There is a distinction between reinforcement learning and supervised learning, which is the primary focus of the majority of the research that is being done in machine learning, pattern recognition, and artificial neural networks at the moment. Through the process of supervised learning, one can acquire knowledge by gaining exposure to examples that are provided by an external supervisor who is knowledgeable about the topic matter (Sahu et al., 2023). Even though this kind of learning is significant, it is not adequate on its own for learning through touch. The majority of the time, it is not possible to obtain instances of desired behavior that are not only appropriate but also representative of all the situations in which the agent is required to act while dealing with interactive problems. The ability to acquire knowledge from one's own firsthand experiences is essential for an agent to have when operating in an uncharted area, which is where one would assume the greatest opportunity for learning to be found (Dong et al., 2020).

The agent must utilize its existing knowledge to acquire rewards, while simultaneously engaging in exploration to improve its future decision-making. The predicament lies in the fact that neither the act of exploiting nor the act of exploring can be conducted solely without failing to accomplish the job (Li, 2023). The agent is required to attempt a range of activities and gradually prioritize those that seem to be the most optimal. In a stochastic task, it is necessary to repeatedly attempt each action to accurately predict its anticipated reward. Mathematicians have extensively researched the exploration-exploitation conundrum for several decades. Currently, it can be acknowledged that the concept of balancing exploitation with exploration is not relevant in supervised learning because it is commonly characterized (Zhang et al., 2020).

Did you know?

The algorithm AlphaGo, developed by DeepMind, used reinforcement learning to defeat a world champion Go player in 2016. This was a significant milestone in AI.

Reinforcement learning explicitly takes into account the entire challenge of a goal-directed agent dealing with an uncertain setting. This is contrary to many techniques that focus on solving smaller problems without considering how they can be integrated into a broader context. For instance, it was previously stated that a significant portion of machine learning research focuses on supervised learning, but the practical applications of this capability have not been properly explained (Morales et al., 2021). Previous scholars have formulated theories of planning that encompass broad objectives, although they have neglected to address the significance of planning in immediate decision-making or the origin of the predictive models required for planning. While these methods have produced numerous valuable outcomes, their concentration on individual subproblems poses a notable constraint (Harmon & Harmon, 1996).

Reinforcement learning adopts a contrasting approach by commencing with a fully functional agent that actively seeks goals through interaction. Reinforcement learning agents possess stated objectives, possess the ability to see elements of their surroundings and possess the ability to select behaviors that can impact their surroundings (Shakya et al., 2023). Furthermore, it is commonly believed from the outset that the agent must function despite substantial uncertainty regarding the environment it encounters. To advance learning research, it is crucial to identify and examine significant subproblems. These subproblems should be driven by distinct functions within comprehensive, interactive, and goal-oriented agents, even if the finer aspects of the complete agent are not yet fully understood (Kordabad et al., 2023).

Reinforcement learning is part of a bigger trend that involves increased interaction between AI and other technical fields. Until recently, artificial intelligence was mostly considered distinct from control theory and statistics. The subject matter pertained to logic and symbols, rather than numerical values. Artificial intelligence primarily consisted of extensive LISP programs, rather than being based on linear algebra, differential calculus, or statistics. In recent decades, this perspective has increasingly diminished (Lobbezoo et al., 2021). Contemporary artificial intelligence researchers acknowledge statistics and control-theory algorithms as pertinent rival methodologies or merely as instruments of their profession. The hitherto overlooked domains situated at the intersection of AI and conventional engineering have become highly dynamic, encompassing emerging disciplines like intelligent control, neural networks, and the subject of this discussion, reinforcement learning. Reinforcement learning builds upon concepts from the theory of optimal control and stochastic approximations to tackle the wider and more ambitious objectives of AI (Xiang & Foo, 2021).

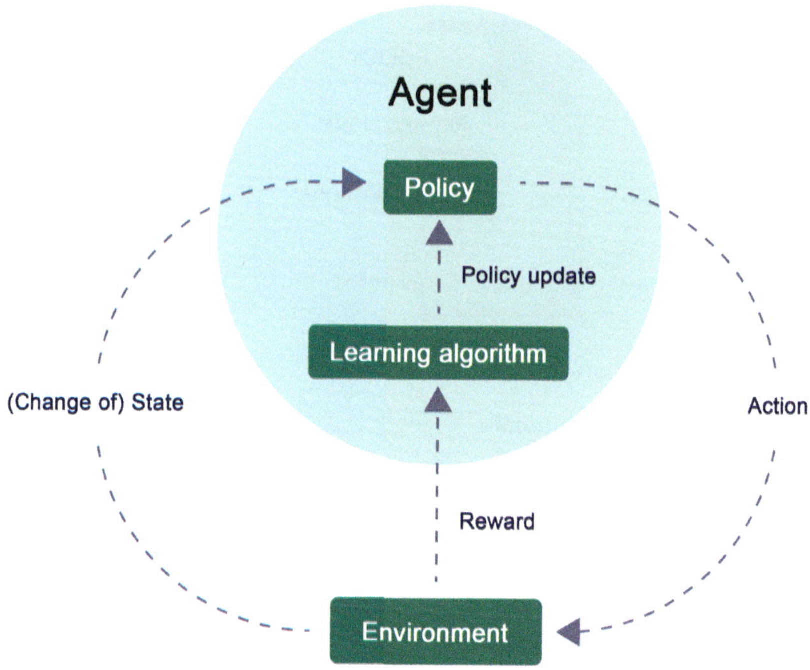

Figure 6.1. *Illustration of the general framework of reinforcement learning.*

Source: Scribbr, Creative Commons License.

6.2. ELEMENTS OF REINFORCEMENT LEARNING

A policy, a reward function, a value function, and, if desired, a model are the four basic sub-elements that make up a reinforcement learning system. These sub-elements are in addition to the agent and the environment (Sequeira & Gervasio, 2020).

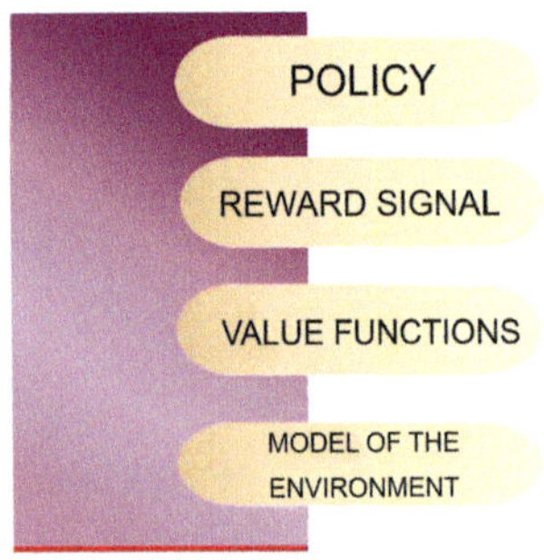

Figure 6.2. *Illustration of the elements of reinforcement learning.*

Source: Akhista, Creative Commons License.

6.2.1. Policy

A policy defines the behavioral strategy of a learning agent at a certain point in time. Essentially, a policy is a function that links observed environmental situations to the corresponding actions to be carried out in such states (Nachum et al., 2017). In the field of psychology, it might be defined as a compilation of stimulus-response rules or correlations. At times, the policy can serve as a simple tool or a reference table, but in other cases, it may require intricate computations, such as a search algorithm. The policy is the essential element of a reinforcement learning agent as it is entirely accountable for determining behavior. Usually, policies can display random behavior (Yu & Sun, 2020).

6.2.2. Reward Function

A reward function defines the goal in a reinforcement learning problem. Essentially, it assigns a numerical value, referred to as a reward, to the perceived states or combinations of states and actions in the environment, reflecting the inherent desirability of the condition (Icarte et al., 2022). The main objective of a reinforcement-learning agent is to maximize its total reward over a long duration. The reward function dictates the favorable and unfavorable consequences for the agent. It is sensible to link rewards with happiness and pain in a biological system (Matignon et al., 2006). The agent encounters these elements, which are the most immediate and defining aspects of the circumstance. Thus, the reward function must remain unchanged. However, it can be used as a basis for making changes to the policy. For example, if a policy's chosen action leads to a very small reward, the policy can be adjusted to choose a different action in similar instances in the future. Reward functions often display stochastic behavior (Camacho et al., 2019).

6.2.3. Value Function

While a reward function denotes what is beneficial in the short term, a value function determines what is advantageous in the long term. Essentially, the value of a state refers to the whole reward that an agent might anticipate gathering in the future, commencing from that particular state. Rewards assess the immediate, inherent appeal of environmental conditions, while values evaluate the long-term appeal of conditions by considering the subsequent states and rewards that may be obtained. For instance, a state may consistently produce a small immediate benefit, yet possess a substantial value due to its frequent association with subsequent states that offer significant rewards (Szepesvári & Littman, 1999). Alternatively, the opposite could be the case. In human terms, rewards can be compared to intense pleasure when they are high, and to discomfort or pain when they are low. On the other hand, values represent a more sophisticated and forward-thinking assessment of human level of satisfaction or dissatisfaction with the state of surroundings. Stated in this manner, it is expected to be evident that value functions codify a fundamental and well-known concept. Rewards might be considered primary, whereas values, which are anticipations of rewards, are auxiliary. Rewards are essential for the existence of values, as the whole goal of assessing values is to attain more rewards (Csáji & Monostori, 2008). However, the primary focus while making and assessing decisions lies in the realm of values. Action choices are determined by assessments of worth. Humans strive for acts that result in the attainment of the most valuable states, rather than actions that alone yield the highest rewards. This is because these actions ultimately lead to the acquisition of the greatest number of rewards in the long term. When making decisions and planning, the quantity that is the most focused on is termed value. Regrettably, ascertaining values is considerably more challenging than determining rewards (Taylor & Stone, 2005).

Rewards are mostly bestowed by the environment, while values necessitate estimation and re-estimation based on the sequences of observations made by an agent throughout its whole lifespan. Efficiently estimating values is a crucial element in nearly all reinforcement learning methods (Boyan & Moore, 1994).

While value function estimation is a crucial aspect of reinforcement learning approaches, it is not an absolute requirement for solving reinforcement learning issues. Search techniques including genetic programming, genetic algorithms, simulated annealing, and additional function optimization methods have been employed to address reinforcement learning challenges. These approaches directly explore the space of policies without relying on value functions (Van Niekerk et al., 2019). These approaches are regarded as evolutionary methods because they function similarly to biological evolution, creating animals with proficient behavior without the need for individual learning during their existence. If the universe of policies is suitably limited or can be organized in a way that facilitates the discovery of optimal policies, evolutionary approaches tend to be highly effective. Furthermore, evolutionary approaches offer benefits when dealing with challenges when the learning agent is unable to precisely perceive the state of its surroundings (Geramifard et al., 2015).

However, reinforcement learning refers to the process of learning through interaction with the environment, which is not a characteristic of evolutionary approaches. It should be firmly believed that techniques capable of leveraging the intricacies of individual behavioral interactions can be significantly more effective than evolutionary methods in numerous instances. Evolutionary methods disregard a significant portion of the valuable structure inherent in the reinforcement learning problem (Dietterich, 2000). They fail to utilize the fact that the policy being sought is a function that maps states to actions. Additionally, they do not take into account the states that an individual traverses during its lifespan or the actions it chooses. While there are instances where this information can be deceptive, such as when states are inaccurately interpreted, it generally facilitates more effective search processes. While evolution and learning have similarities and can complement each other in natural systems, evolutionary methods are not viewed as particularly suitable for reinforcement learning problems on their own (Taylor & Parr, 2009).

6.2.4. Model

A crucial component in certain reinforcement learning systems is the inclusion of an environment model, which serves as the fourth and final element. This is an emulation of environmental behavior. For instance, when provided with a specific state and actions, the model has the capability to forecast the subsequent state and reward (Qiang & Zhongli, 2011). Models are utilized for the purpose of strategic planning, which involves making informed decisions about a course of action based on the anticipation of potential future scenarios before they occur in reality. The integration of models and strategy into the systems is a recently emerged advancement (Doll et al., 2012). Early systems were primarily characterized as trial-and-error learners, with their approach being considered nearly the antithesis of planning. Furthermore, it was discovered that these approaches are tightly linked to state-space planning methods. Contemporary reinforcement learning covers a wide range of learning methods, starting from basic trial-and-error learning to more advanced planning techniques (Doya et al., 2002).

6.3. EXAMPLES OF REINFORCEMENT LEARNING

Following are some of the most relevant examples:

i. A skilled chess player executes a move. The decision is influenced by careful preparation, which involves considering potential responses and counter-responses, as well as relying on immediate, instinctive assessments of the attractiveness of specific stances and actions (Padakandla, 2021).

ii. A dynamic controller modifies the parameters of a hydrocarbon refinery's process in real-time. The controller maximizes the balance between yield, cost, and quality by considering stated marginal costs, while deviating from the initially proposed set points by human engineers (Alharin et al., 2020).

iii. A gazelle calf quickly stands up shortly after being born. After 30 minutes, the speed of the animal increases to 30 miles per hour (Kormushev et al., 2013).

iv. A mobile robot determines whether to enter a new room to hunt for additional debris to gather or initiate the process of returning to its battery recharge station. The selection is determined by the efficiency and speed with which the recharger has been located in previous instances (Littman & Moore, 1996).

v. Phil is preparing his breakfast. Upon close examination, this seemingly ordinary activity unveils itself as an intricate network of conditional actions and interconnected interactions between goals and subgoals: walking towards the cabinet, opening it, choosing a cereal box, and subsequently reaching for, gripping, and retrieving the box (Gosavi, 2009). Additional intricate, calibrated, interacting patterns of behavior are necessary to acquire a spoon, bowl, and milk jug. The process consists of a sequence of ocular movements to gather information and direct reaching and movement (Coronato et al., 2020). Swift assessments are constantly made on how to transport the goods or whether it is more advantageous to transport a few of them to the dinner table before acquiring others. Every action is driven by certain objectives, such as picking up a spoon or reaching the fridge, and is aimed at fulfilling additional objectives, such as getting the spoon ready for eating once the breakfast cereal is prepared, and finally achieving sustenance (Sutton & Barto, 1999).

These instances possess fundamental characteristics that are so elementary that they are prone to being disregarded. All entail the interaction between a proactive decision-making entity and its surroundings, in which the entity strives to accomplish a goal despite uncertainties regarding its environment. The agent is allowed to influence the future condition of the environment, such as the subsequent chess position, the reservoir levels of the refinery, or the future placement of the robot. As a result, this affects the choices and possibilities that the agent will have in the future. Making the correct decision involves considering the indirect and delayed effects of actions, which may include having foresight or preparation (Sutton, 1995).

Did you know?

Self-driving cars use reinforcement learning to navigate and make real-time decisions. They learn from vast amounts of driving data to improve safety and efficiency.

In all of these examples, the consequences of actions cannot be completely foreseen, necessitating the agent to regularly observe its surroundings and respond accordingly. For instance, Phil must carefully monitor the amount of milk he pours into his cereal dish to prevent it from spilling over. All of these examples feature goals that are explicit, meaning that the agent can assess its progress towards the goal based on the information it can directly perceive (Barto, 1997). The chess player have knowledge of their victory or defeat, the refinery controller possesses knowledge of the precise quantity of petroleum being produced, the mobile robot possesses knowledge of the moment its batteries deplete, and Phil possesses knowledge of his level of enjoyment during breakfast (Thrun & Littman, 2000). Across all of these instances, the agent has the ability to enhance its performance over time by utilizing its accumulated knowledge and expertise. The chess player enhances their ability to assess positions, therefore enhancing their gameplay; the gazelle calf enhances its running efficiency; Phil learns to optimize his breakfast preparation (Kaelbling et al., 1996). The initial knowledge possessed by the agent, whether acquired through prior experience or inherent in its design or evolution, has an impact on what is deemed valuable or easily learnable. However, it is crucial for the agent to interact with the environment in order to adapt its behavior and effectively utilize the specific characteristics of the task (Khan et al., 2012).

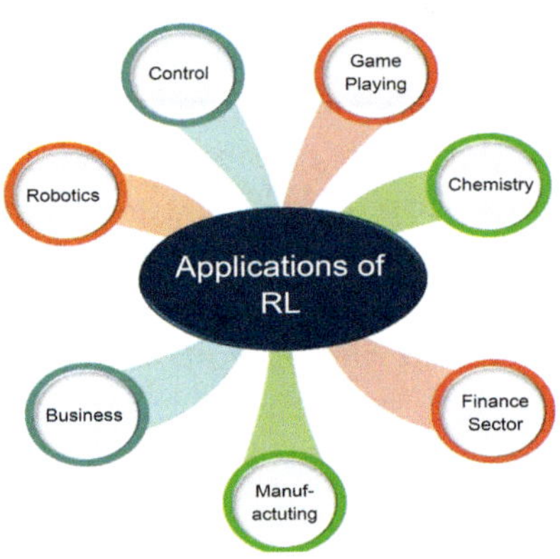

Figure 6.3. *Applications of reinforcement learning.*

Source: Javatpoint, Creative Commons License.

6.4. AN EXTENDED EXAMPLE: TIC-TAC-TOE

In order to elucidate the fundamental concept of reinforcement learning and highlight its distinctions from alternative methodologies, this section will now delve into a specific instance with further scrutiny (Crowley & Siegler, 1993).

Examine the well-known game of Tic-Tac-Toe. Two players alternate turns on a 3x3 grid. In this game, two players take turns placing their respective markings, ‘X’ and ‘Ø’, on a grid. The objective is to be the first player to create a line of three of their marks in a row, either vertically, diagonally, or horizontally. The ‘X’ player has achieved this in the current round (Pilgrim, 1995):

X	O	O
O	X	X
		X

If the game board becomes completely occupied without either player achieving a sequence of three marks in succession, the game is considered a draw. Assuming playing against an imperfect player, who occasionally makes mistakes and gives the opportunity to win, it can be infered that a highly talented player can consistently avoid losing. Currently, consider draws and losses as equally detrimental to this situation. How can a player be designed that can identify flaws in its opponent's gameplay and adapt its strategy to increase its likelihood of winning (Paul, 1978)?

Despite its simplicity, this problem cannot be effectively solved using traditional methods. For instance, the conventional “minimax” approach derived from game theory is not applicable in this case as it presupposes a certain opponent strategy. For instance, a minimax player would always avoid reaching a game state where it could potentially lose, even if it had a guaranteed win due to the opponent's mistakes. Classical optimization techniques, such as dynamic programming, can determine the best possible solution for sequential choice problems. However, they necessitate a comprehensive description of the opponent, which includes the probability associated with each move the opponent makes in every board state. Assume that this data is not known in advance for this problem, as is the case for most practical cases. Alternatively, one can derive such information using empirical means, such as engaging in numerous games versus the adversary. To effectively address this challenge, it is advisable to initially acquire knowledge about the adversary's actions, up to a certain degree of certainty. Subsequently, one can employ dynamic programming techniques to calculate the best possible solution based on the estimated adversary model (Kalra, 2022).

An evolutionary strategy to address this issue would involve systematically exploring the range of potential strategies to identify one that has a high likelihood of achieving victory over the adversary. A policy is a set of instructions that dictates the optimal move for every possible state of the game, encompassing all potential arrangements of X's and Ø's on the three-by-three board. To assess the likelihood of success for each policy under consideration, a determination of its probability of winning would be derived by engaging in a series of games versus the adversary. This assessment would thereafter determine whether policy or policies were subsequently taken into account. A conventional evolutionary approach involves iteratively developing and assessing policies in policy space, to achieve gradual enhancements like hill climbing. Alternatively, a genetic algorithm could be employed to manage and assess a group of policies. Numerous optimization algorithms might potentially be utilized (Glynn-Adey, 2022).

The tic-tac-toe problem can be tackled by employing reinforcement learning techniques and utilizing approximation value functions. Initially, establish a tabular representation consisting of numerical values, with each value corresponding to a potential game state. Each number will represent the most recent estimation of the likelihood of victory from that particular state. The estimate is regarded as the present value of the state, whereas the entire table represents the learned value function. State A is deemed superior to State B if the current estimation of the probability of victory is higher in A than in B. If consistently played as X, then in all states when there are three consecutive X's, the probability of victory is 1, as the victory has already been secured. Likewise, in the case of states containing three consecutive empty spaces or being completely occupied, the probability of winning is 0 since it is impossible to win from those situations. The initial values of all the nonterminal states are set to 0.5, indicating a preliminary estimate that there is a 50% probability of winning (Golomb & Hales, 2000).

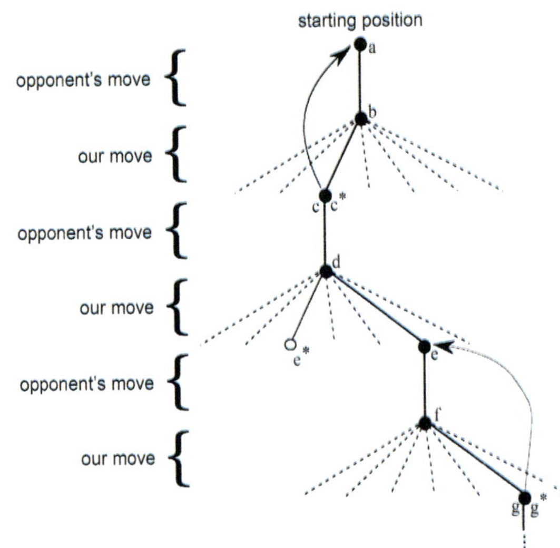

Figure 6.4. *Sequence of tic-tac-toe moves. The solid lines represent the moves taken during a game; the dashed lines represent moves that the reinforcement learning player considered but did not make.*

Source: Richard S. Sutton, Creative Commons License.

In order to determine moves, analyze the potential outcomes of each possible move (corresponding to each empty space on the board) and consult the table to obtain their current values. Typically, humans make decisions in a self-interested manner, choosing the action that results in the state with the highest value, meaning the one with the greatest anticipated likelihood of winning. At times, humans opt for a random selection among alternative moves; these are referred to as exploratory moves as they allow to encounter states that may not have been encountered otherwise. The process of making and analyzing plays in a game can be visually represented in a diagram, as shown in Figure 6.4 (Tisdell, 2020).

By engaging in the game, humans modify the variables of the states that they encounter. They strive to enhance the precision of the estimates regarding the odds of winning from those particular states. To accomplish this, they store the value of the state before each greedy step, as indicated by the arrows in Figure 6.4. To clarify, the current value of the previous state is adjusted to be more similar to the value of the subsequent state. This is done by gradually changing the value of the earlier state to approach the value of the later state. If the state before the greedy move is represented as s, and the state after as s′, then the update to the estimated value of s, denoted as V(s), can be expressed as (Dewdney, 1989):

$$V(s) \leftarrow V(s) + \alpha[V(s') - V(s)],$$

where; α represents the step-size parameter, which affects the speed at which learning occurs. This update rule exemplifies a temporal-difference learning technique, named as such due to its modifications being derived from the disparity between estimates at two distinct time points.

The aforementioned technique exhibits excellent performance on this job. If the step-size variable is appropriately decreased over time, the strategy will converge, regardless of the opponent, to the accurate probability of winning in each condition when the player plays optimally. In addition, the subsequent movements made (excluding exploratory moves) are indeed the most advantageous actions against the opponent. Put simply, the technique reaches the optimum strategy for playing the game. When the step-size parameter is not completely diminished over time, this player also performs effectively against opponents who gradually alter their playing style.

This example demonstrates the disparities between evolutionary techniques and value function learning approaches. To assess a strategy, an evolutionary approach requires keeping it constant and engaging in numerous games versus the opponent, or simulating multiple games using an example of the opponent. The frequency of victories provides an impartial estimation of the likelihood of winning with a certain strategy and can be utilized to guide the subsequent selection of strategies. However, each policy change is implemented solely based on the ultimate outcome of multiple games, disregarding any events or occurrences that transpire throughout the games. For instance, if the player emerges victorious, all of their actions in the game are acknowledged, regardless of the individual movements that may have been crucial for the victory. Even maneuvers that never happened are still credited. Value function approaches, on the other hand, enable the evaluation of specific states (Hirsch et al., 1981).

This example is highly straightforward, yet it effectively demonstrates some fundamental characteristics of reinforcement learning techniques. Firstly, there is a strong focus on acquiring knowledge and skills by active engagement with a specific setting, specifically in this context, through interaction with an adversary. Furthermore, it is essential to have a well-defined objective, and proper conduct necessitates careful consideration and anticipation of the long-term consequences of one's decisions.

For instance, the basic reinforcement learning player might acquire the ability to strategically arrange multi-move traps to exploit the limited foresight of an opponent. An impressive aspect of the reinforcement learning method is its ability to obtain the benefits of planning and lookahead without relying on a model of the opponent or doing a deliberate search of potential future states and actions (Widyantoro & Vembrina, 2009). While this example showcases various crucial elements of reinforcement learning, its simplicity could lead to the mistaken belief that reinforcement learning has more limitations than it truly does. Although Tic-Tac-Toe usually requires two players, reinforcement learning can also be utilized in scenarios when there is no distinct external adversary, such as in a "game against nature." Reinforcement learning is not restricted to problems that can be segmented into separate episodes, such as individual games of Tic-Tac-Toe, where incentives are solely provided at the conclusion of each episode. The principle remains applicable in situations where behavior continues indefinitely and where rewards of varying degrees can be acquired at any one moment. Tic-Tac-Toe has a predefined and predetermined number of potential states, but reinforcement learning can be applied to state sets that are significantly larger or even infinite. Gerry Tesauro (1992, 1995) combined the previously mentioned method with an artificial neural network to develop the capability to play backgammon, a game with a large number of possible situations. It is important to acknowledge that, given the vast number of nations, it is impractical to thoroughly investigate more than a fraction of them. Tesauro's software outperformed all previous programs and today runs at the same level of skill as the world's best human players. The neural network allows the software to draw conclusions based on its previous encounters. By using its network, the system can utilize stored information from previous similar events to make well-informed decisions in novel scenarios. The efficacy of a reinforcement learning agent in scenarios with extensive sets of states relies on its capacity to efficiently extrapolate from previous encounters. The integration of supervised learning methodologies with reinforcement learning is essential in this specific role. Neural networks are not the exclusive or fundamentally superior approach to accomplish this objective (Ambrosetti & Cantamesse, 2018). In this particular instance of Tic-Tac-Toe, the learning process began without any existing information other than the basic principles of the game. However, it is important to note that reinforcement learning does not imply a completely blank slate approach to learning and intelligence. Conversely, previous knowledge can be integrated into reinforcement learning using several methods that are crucial for effective learning. In the Tic-Tac-Toe example, the complete knowledge of the true state was known. However, reinforcement learning can also be used when certain parts of the state are concealed or when the learner perceives several states as identical. Ultimately, the Tic-Tac-Toe player achieved the ability to anticipate and comprehend the outcomes that would arise from every potential move it could make. To accomplish this, the system needed to possess a comprehensive game model that enables it to anticipate the potential alterations in its environment resulting from hypothetical plays it may never execute. Several issues exhibit this characteristic, although in certain cases there is a deficiency in having a concise representation of the consequences of actions in the short term. Reinforcement learning is applicable in both cases. While not mandatory, models can be readily utilized if they are accessible or can be acquired through learning (Van De Steeg et al., 2015).

ACTIVITY 6.1.

- **Objective:** Explore the role of the reward function in reinforcement learning.
- **Instructions:**

i. `Individually or in pairs, choose a simple game or task (e.g., navigating a maze).

ii. Define a reward function that incentivizes the agent to complete the task efficiently.

iii. Implement the reward function using pseudocode or a simple programming language.

iv. Share and discuss the reward functions with the class, highlighting the reasoning behind the chosen rewards and penalties

SUMMARY

- This chapter primarily emphasizes the fundamental elements of reinforcement learning, including the ideas of value and value functions. Value functions are essential for optimizing search within policy domains. Reinforcement learning methods are distinguished from evolutionary methods by their use of value functions. Reinforcement learning methods differ from evolutionary approaches in that they do not explicitly search in policy space using scalar assessments of entire policies. Instead, they rely on value functions.
- Reinforcement learning is an algorithmic method used to understand and automate the method of learning and decision-making with specific goals in mind. It distinguishes itself from other computational systems by emphasizing individual learning via direct interaction with surroundings, without requiring supervision or full models of the world. Reinforcement learning is a pioneering field that effectively addresses the computational difficulties that arise when learning through interactions with an environment to achieve long-term goals.
- Reinforcement learning utilizes a well-defined framework that outlines the interaction between an agent and its surroundings, focusing on states, actions, and rewards. This framework is specifically developed to offer a concise and precise approach to expressing the core features of the AI challenge. These features include the capacity to comprehend the correlation between actions and their outcomes, the existence of unpredictability and absence of determinism, and the existence of well-defined objectives. The salient feature of Markov decision processes is their formalism, which provides a precise and impartial approach to incorporate the fundamental properties.

REVIEW QUESTIONS

1. What is reinforcement learning, and how does it differ from supervised and unsupervised learning?
2. Explain the role of the reward function in reinforcement learning. Why is it crucial for the learning process?
3. What is the value function, and how does it guide the agent's decision-making process?
4. Provide an example of reinforcement learning used in gaming. How does the agent learn to play the game effectively?
5. How does the reward function work in the Tic-Tac-Toe example to reinforce winning moves and discourage losing moves?

MULTIPLE CHOICE QUESTIONS

1. **What is the primary goal of reinforcement learning?**
   a. To classify data into predefined categories

b. To predict future data points
c. To learn optimal actions through trial and error to maximize cumulative reward
d. To reduce the dimensionality of data

2. **Which of the following best describes a policy in reinforcement learning?**
   a. A function that maps states to actions
   b. A function that predicts future rewards
   c. A model of the environment's dynamics
   d. A method for scaling features
3. **In reinforcement learning, what does the reward function do?**
   a. It maps states to actions
   b. It provides feedback to the agent based on the actions taken
   c. It estimates the long-term value of actions
   d. It represents the environment's dynamics
4. **What is the value function in reinforcement learning?**
   a. A function that defines the agent's behavior
   b. A function that assigns a numerical value to each action taken
   c. A function that estimates the expected cumulative reward for each state
   d. A function that predicts the next state and reward
5. **Which of the following is an example of an application of reinforcement learning in robotics?**
   a. Predicting maintenance needs
   b. Classifying objects based on visual input
   c. Optimizing control systems for autonomous movement
   d. Reducing the dimensionality of sensor data

Answers to Multiple Choice Questions

1. (c); 2. (a); 3. (b); 4. (c); 5. (c)

REFERENCES

1. Alharin, A., Doan, T. N., & Sartipi, M. (2020). Reinforcement learning interpretation methods: A survey. *IEEE Access, 8*, 171058–171077.
2. Ambrosetti, N., & Cantamesse, M. (2018). The Basic Dream of the PC, or "Did You Ever Play Tic-Tac-Toe"? In *This Changes Everything–ICT and Climate Change: What Can We Do? 13th IFIP TC 9 International Conference on Human Choice and Computers, HCC13 2018, Held at the 24th IFIP World Computer Congress, WCC 2018, Poznan, Poland, September 19–21, 2018, Proceedings* (Vol. 2, pp. 3–15). Springer International Publishing.

3. Barto, A. G. (1997). Reinforcement learning. In *Neural Systems for Control* (Vol. 1, pp. 7–30). Academic Press.
4. Boyan, J., & Moore, A. (1994). Generalization in reinforcement learning: Safely approximating the value function. *Advances in Neural Information Processing Systems, 7*, 6514.
5. Camacho, A., Icarte, R. T., Klassen, T. Q., Valenzano, R. A., & McIlraith, S. A. (2019). LTL and Beyond: Formal Languages for Reward Function Specification in Reinforcement Learning. In *IJCAI* (Vol. 19, pp. 6065–6073).
6. Coronato, A., Naeem, M., De Pietro, G., & Paragliola, G. (2020). Reinforcement learning for intelligent healthcare applications: A survey. *Artificial Intelligence in Medicine, 109*, 101964.
7. Crowley, K., & Siegler, R. S. (1993). Flexible strategy uses in young children's tic-tac-toe. *Cognitive Science, 17*(4), 531–561.
8. Csáji, B. C., & Monostori, L. (2008). Value function-based reinforcement learning in changing Markovian environments. *Journal of Machine Learning Research, 9*(8), 987–990.
9. Dewdney, A. K. (1989). A tinkertoy computer that plays tic-tac-toe. *Scientific American, 261*(4), 120–123.
10. Dietterich, T. G. (2000). Hierarchical reinforcement learning with the MAXQ value function decomposition. *Journal of Artificial Intelligence Research, 13*, 227–303.
11. Ding, Z., Huang, Y., Yuan, H., & Dong, H. (2020). Introduction to reinforcement learning. *Deep Reinforcement Learning: Fundamentals, Research and Applications, 5*(2), 47–123.
12. Doll, B. B., Simon, D. A., & Daw, N. D. (2012). The ubiquity of model-based reinforcement learning. *Current Opinion in Neurobiology, 22*(6), 1075–1081.
13. Dong, H., Dong, H., Ding, Z., Zhang, S., & Chang, T. (2020). *Deep Reinforcement Learning*. Singapore: Springer Singapore. (Vol. 2, pp. 98–100).
14. Doya, K., Samejima, K., Katagiri, K. I., & Kawato, M. (2002). Multiple model-based reinforcement learning. *Neural Computation, 14*(6), 1347–1369.
15. François-Lavet, V., Henderson, P., Islam, R., Bellemare, M. G., & Pineau, J. (2018). An introduction to deep reinforcement learning. *Foundations and Trends® in Machine Learning, 11*(3–4), 219–354.
16. Geramifard, A., Dann, C., Klein, R. H., Dabney, W., & How, J. P. (2015). RLPy: A value-function-based reinforcement learning framework for education and research. *Journal of Machine Learning Research, 16*(1), 1573–1578.
17. Glynn-Adey, P. (2022). A Potential Strategy for Huge Tic-Tac-Toe. *Math Horizons, 30*(2), 16–19.
18. Golomb, S. W., & Hales, A. W. (2000). Hypercube tic-tac-toe. In *More Games of No Chance, Proceedings of MSRI Workshop on Combinatorial Games* (Vol. 1, pp. 167–182).
19. Gosavi, A. (2009). Reinforcement learning: A tutorial survey and recent advances. *INFORMS Journal on Computing, 21*(2), 178–192.
20. Harmon, M. E., & Harmon, S. S. (1996). Reinforcement learning: A tutorial. WL/AAFC, WPAFB Ohio, *45433*, 237–285.

21. Hirsch, C., Yates, D., & Miller, W. A. (1981). Activities: Calculator Tic-Tac-Toe: A Game of Estimation. *The Mathematics Teacher, 74*(9), 713–724.

22. Icarte, R. T., Klassen, T. Q., Valenzano, R., & McIlraith, S. A. (2022). Reward machines: Exploiting reward function structure in reinforcement learning. *Journal of Artificial Intelligence Research, 73*, 173–208.

23. Kaelbling, L. P., Littman, M. L., & Moore, A. W. (1995). An introduction to reinforcement learning. *The Biology and Technology of Intelligent Autonomous Agents, 4*(30), 90–127.

24. Kaelbling, L. P., Littman, M. L., & Moore, A. W. (1996). Reinforcement learning: A survey. *Journal of Artificial Intelligence Research, 4*, 237–285.

25. Kalra, B. (2022). Generalized agent for solving higher board states of tic tac toe using reinforcement learning. In *2022 Seventh International Conference on Parallel, Distributed and Grid Computing (PDGC)* (Vol. 2, pp. 715–720). IEEE.

26. Khan, S. G., Herrmann, G., Lewis, F. L., Pipe, T., & Melhuish, C. (2012). Reinforcement learning and optimal adaptive control: An overview and implementation examples. *Annual Reviews in Control, 36*(1), 42–59.

27. Kordabad, A. B., Reinhardt, D., Anand, A. S., & Gros, S. (2023). Reinforcement learning for MPC: Fundamentals and current challenges. *IFAC-PapersOnLine, 56*(2), 5773–5780.

28. Kormushev, P., Calinon, S., & Caldwell, D. G. (2013). Reinforcement learning in robotics: Applications and real-world challenges. *Robotics, 2*(3), 122–148.

29. Lei, K., Zhang, B., Li, Y., Yang, M., & Shen, Y. (2020). Time-driven feature-aware jointly deep reinforcement learning for financial signal representation and algorithmic trading. *Expert Systems with Applications, 140*, 112872.

30. Li, S. E. (2023). *Reinforcement Learning for Sequential Decision and Optimal Control*. Berlin/Heidelberg, Germany: Springer. (Vol. 1, pp. 1–449).

31. Littman, M. L., & Moore, A. W. (1996). Reinforcement learning: A survey. *Journal of Artificial Intelligence Research, 4*(1), 237–285.

32. Lobbezoo, A., Qian, Y., & Kwon, H. J. (2021). Reinforcement learning for pick and place operations in robotics: A survey. *Robotics, 10*(3), 105.

33. Matignon, L., Laurent, G. J., & Le Fort-Piat, N. (2006). Reward function and initial values: Better choices for accelerated goal-directed reinforcement learning. In *International Conference on Artificial Neural Networks*. Berlin, Heidelberg: Springer Berlin Heidelberg. (Vol. 3, pp. 840–849).

34. Morales, E. F., & Zaragoza, J. H. (2012). An introduction to reinforcement learning. In *Decision Theory Models for Applications in Artificial Intelligence: Concepts and Solutions*. IGI Global. (Vol. 1, pp. 63–80).

35. Morales, E. F., Murrieta-Cid, R., Becerra, I., & Esquivel-Basaldua, M. A. (2021). A survey on deep learning and deep reinforcement learning in robotics with a tutorial on deep reinforcement learning. *Intelligent Service Robotics, 14*(5), 773–805.

36. Nachum, O., Norouzi, M., Xu, K., & Schuurmans, D. (2017). Bridging the gap between value and policy-based reinforcement learning. *Advances in Neural Information Processing Systems, 30*, 98–100.

37. Naeem, M., Rizvi, S. T. H., & Coronato, A. (2020). A gentle introduction to reinforcement learning and its application in different fields. *IEEE Access, 8*, 209320–209344.

38. Padakandla, S. (2021). A survey of reinforcement learning algorithms for dynamically varying environments. *ACM Computing Surveys (CSUR), 54*(6), 1–25.

39. Paul, J. L. (1978). Tic-tac-toe in n-dimensions. *Mathematics Magazine, 51*(1), 45–49.

40. Pilgrim, R. A. (1995). TIC-TAC-TOE: Introducing expert systems to middle school students. *ACM SIGCSE Bulletin, 27*(1), 340–344.

41. Qiang, W., & Zhongli, Z. (2011). Reinforcement learning model, algorithms and its application. In *2011 International Conference on Mechatronic Science, Electric Engineering and Computer (MEC)* (Vol. 4, pp. 1143–1146). IEEE.

42. Ris-Ala, R. (2023). *Fundamentals of Reinforcement Learning*. Springer. (Vol. 2, pp. 1–88).

43. Sahu, S. K., Mokhade, A., & Bokde, N. D. (2023). An overview of machine learning, deep learning, and reinforcement learning-based techniques in quantitative finance: Recent progress and challenges. *Applied Sciences, 13*(3), 1956.

44. Sequeira, P., & Gervasio, M. (2020). Interestingness elements for explainable reinforcement learning: Understanding agents' capabilities and limitations. *Artificial Intelligence, 288*, 103367.

45. Shakya, A. K., Pillai, G., & Chakrabarty, S. (2023). Reinforcement learning algorithms: A brief survey. *Expert Systems with Applications, 231*, 120495.

46. Sutton, R. S. (1995). Generalization in reinforcement learning: Successful examples using sparse coarse coding. *Advances in Neural Information Processing Systems, 8*, 987.

47. Sutton, R. S., & Barto, A. G. (1999). Reinforcement learning: An introduction. *Robotica, 17*(2), 229–235.

48. Szepesvári, C., & Littman, M. L. (1999). A unified analysis of value-function-based reinforcement-learning algorithms. *Neural Computation, 11*(8), 2017–2060.

49. Taylor, G., & Parr, R. (2009). Kernelized value function approximation for reinforcement learning. In *Proceedings of the 26th Annual International Conference on Machine Learning* (Vol. 2, pp. 1017–1024).

50. Taylor, M. E., & Stone, P. (2005). Behavior transfer for value-function-based reinforcement learning. In *Proceedings of the Fourth International Joint Conference on Autonomous Agents and Multiagent Systems* (Vol. 2, pp. 53–59).

51. Thrun, S., & Littman, M. L. (2000). Reinforcement learning: An introduction. *AI Magazine, 21*(1), 103–103.

52. Tisdell, C. C. (2020). Tic-Tac-Toe and repeated integration by parts: Alternative pedagogical perspectives to Lima's integral challenge. *International Journal of Mathematical Education in Science and Technology, 51*(3), 424–430.

53. Van De Steeg, M., Drugan, M. M., & Wiering, M. (2015). Temporal difference learning for the game tic-tac-toe 3d: Applying structure to neural networks. In *2015 IEEE Symposium Series on Computational Intelligence* (Vol. 2, pp. 564–570). IEEE.

54. Van Niekerk, B., James, S., Earle, A., & Rosman, B. (2019). Composing value

functions in reinforcement learning. In *International Conference on Machine Learning*. PMLR. (Vol. 1, pp. 6401–6409).

55. Widyantoro, D. H., & Vembrina, Y. G. (2009). Learning to play Tic-tac-toe. In *2009 International Conference on Electrical Engineering and Informatics* (Vol. 1, pp. 276–280). IEEE.
56. Wiering, M. A., & Van Otterlo, M. (2012). Reinforcement learning. *Adaptation, Learning, and Optimization, 12*(3), 729.
57. Xiang, X., & Foo, S. (2021). Recent advances in deep reinforcement learning applications for solving partially observable Markov decision processes (POMDP) problems: Part 1—Fundamentals and applications in games, robotics and natural language processing. *Machine Learning and Knowledge Extraction, 3*(3), 554–581.
58. Xiong, Z., Zhang, Y., Niyato, D., Deng, R., Wang, P., & Wang, L. C. (2019). Deep reinforcement learning for mobile 5G and beyond: Fundamentals, applications, and challenges. *IEEE Vehicular Technology Magazine, 14*(2), 44–52.
59. Yu, M., & Sun, S. (2020). Policy-based reinforcement learning for time series anomaly detection. *Engineering Applications of Artificial Intelligence, 95*, 103919.
60. Zhang, W., Zhao, X., Zhao, L., Yin, D., Yang, G. H., & Beutel, A. (2020). Deep reinforcement learning for information retrieval: Fundamentals and advances. In *Proceedings of the 43rd International ACM SIGIR Conference on Research and Development in Information Retrieval* (Vol. 1, pp. 2468–2471).

CHAPTER 7

Applications of Machine Learning in Industrial Sectors

LEARNING OBJECTIVES

After studying this chapter, you will be able to:

- Applications of machine learning in the materials sector;
- Utilization of machine learning in the healthcare sector;
- Applications of machine learning in the information technology sector; and
- Use of machine learning in the consumer services sector.

KEY TERMS FROM THIS CHAPTER

Bioinformatics	Cardiovascular
Chemicals	Cybersecurity
Diabetes	Goods
Information technology	Obesity
Retail	Software

UNIT INTRODUCTION

The fourth Industrial Revolution, also referred to as Industry 4.0 or Industrial Internet of Things, is currently in progress and is significantly influencing various industrial sectors, including automation, automotive, chemical engineering, construction, customer service, energy, banking, health care, computer technology, and telecommunications (Aamer et al., 2020). The volume of industrial data produced by machine controls, sensors, manufacturing systems, and other sources is increasing at an exponential rate. Intelligent systems capable of converting this vast amount of data into intelligence, as expressed in models based on mathematics and statistics, are essential (Sircar et al., 2021). Machine learning is a component of artificial intelligence that enables the construction of these models (Hegde & Rokseth, 2020). Machine learning encompasses several techniques that facilitate this change, allowing software systems to generate valuable insights that can inform optimal decision-making (Narciso & Martins, 2020). These decisions are applicable across various industrial sectors, addressing issues like assessment, preventative maintenance, condition tracking, and asset health management (Carou et al., 2022).

7.1. INDUSTRIAL SECTORS

The industrial sector encompasses the entire process of creating, producing, assembling, distributing, and selling industrial materials, goods, and services. Machine learning techniques are mostly used in this diverse sector to improve industrial goods and procedures (Diez-Olivan et al., 2019).

Industrial goods manufacturing businesses primarily include the production of heavy-duty products, often utilizing advanced automation and integration techniques, such as those seen in the aerospace industry. As a result, almost every business in this sector necessitates substantial quantities of resources and raw materials to enhance their worth (Van Der Heijden, 2022). To achieve profitability, companies must strive for efficient operations characterized by minimal downtimes (i.e., instances when equipment is not functioning due to unexpected failures or lengthy maintenance periods), maximum availability (i.e., ensuring that machine production time closely aligns with total machine uptime), and minimal scrap generation (i.e., reducing the share of parts with quality issues compared to the total number of manufactured parts) (Nabavi et al., 2020). For instance, the utilization of robust manufacturing equipment in the production of cement and other construction aggregates necessitates significant energy consumption, leading to elevated production expenses. In the event of a production halt caused by a malfunction, the expenses for maintenance will cause a significant rise in production costs, leading to a substantial reduction in the profit margin. Conversely, the process of aircraft manufacture necessitates significant quantities of raw materials, including certain ones that are exceedingly costly. If there is a significant proportion of waste material generated during the manufacturing of airplane components, the overall cost of the plane could become too expensive, making it unaffordable (Javanmard & Ghaderi, 2023).

Given the importance of robustness and efficiency, these industries have a shared need to extract practical insights from product and process data to guarantee the profitability of their products and processes. Traditionally, insights are obtained using laborious statistical methods or statistical control of process techniques, which have restricted applicability due to their data-handling capacity (Angelopoulos et al., 2019). With the advancement of computing power, machine-learning approaches are now being effectively utilized in various industrial sectors. However, certain barriers hinder the implementation of machine learning methods that originate from research laboratories or other industrial sectors. These hurdles include challenging surroundings, restricted availability of communication infrastructures, and other crucial issues that need to be addressed (Narciso & Martins, 2020).

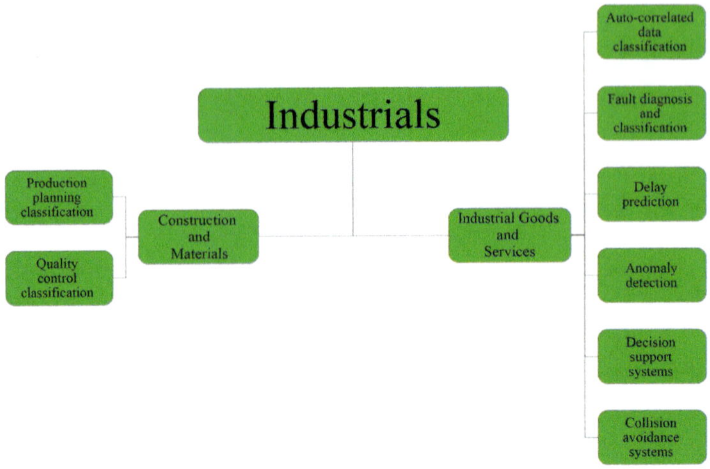

Figure 7.1. *Applications of machine learning in industrial sector.*

Source: Pedro Larranaga, Creative Commons License.

7.1.1. Construction and Materials

In the context of industrial materials production, machine learning is utilized in several manufacturing stages that involve diverse chemical processes associated with the materials themselves and their intended application by the end-user (Sánchez-Garrido et al., 2023). Structural steel is widely utilized in buildings and various other purposes (Kapp et al., 2023). According to the World Steel Association, there exist over 3,500 distinct grades of steel, each possessing unique mechanical and chemical characteristics. Hence, the steel production sector must accurately determine the appropriate processing methods based on factors such as steel grade, breadth, thickness, specific requirements, and relevant tolerances (Bilal & Oyedele, 2020). Stirling and Buntine (1988) explain how a steel company utilizes machine learning approaches to gain an understanding of steel mill operating routes. In this scenario, the company receives an excess of 60 orders daily, accompanied by around 7,500 entries about the product description (Chomacki et al., 2022). These entries outline the various process combinations necessary to achieve the desired product. The total number of distinct route permutations surpasses 10,000 (Farahzadi & Kioumarsi, 2023). To optimize manufacturing quality and delivery speeds, the company has implemented a system that combines rule induction and the use of ID3 and C4.5 algorithms, along with operational knowledge. Halawani (2014) explains that in the field of structural steel manufacturing, classifying tree groupings, such as random forests, are utilized for detecting faults in the manufacturing process (Ramsgaard Thomsen et al., 2020). In addition, feature subset methods of selection are employed to identify the most important features (Akinosho et al., 2020).

7.1.2. Industrial Goods and Services

An exemplary case in the field of industrial electronics manufacturing pertains to the production of electronic semiconductors. In this context, machine learning algorithms are employed to tackle several issues, including the establishment of guidelines for sending the final product during the testing phase. Wang et al. (2005) utilize a combination of classification trees and artificial neural networks to identify the underlying principles that govern the company's testing operations. Hsu and Chien (2007) utilize an artificial neural network to enhance productivity in the field of semiconductor manufacturing (Rao & Jayasree, 2022). The industrial sector has long relied on statistical process control, as previously mentioned. Nevertheless, Chinnam (2002) argues that statistical techniques are not suitable for use in automated manufacturing, including electric and electronic equipment, due to the presence of autocorrelated data, which refers to data that exhibits a delayed copy of its own as a function of delay. Autocorrelated data can lead to the occurrence of false alarms or a decrease in the accuracy of detecting genuine positives in process control. These limits can lead to significant production deviations, particularly in systems with a control system capable of halting output in response to alerts. Chinnam (2002) shows that support vector machines are a successful method for reducing mistakes associated with false alerts and true positive detection rates, resulting in improved accuracy (Romeo et al., 2018). In the field of industrial engineering, applications pertain to manufacturing machinery or components, including pumps, engines, compressors, bearings, and elevators. Kowalski et al. (2017) present a case where they utilize a single-hidden layer feedforward neural network to diagnose faults in a marine engine application. Another instance involves utilizing anomaly detection techniques on data streams to aid in elevator fabrication and maintenance (Ambika, 2020). In the aircraft business, there are two primary areas of application: component production and solutions, including flight control or systems for decision support. Machine learning is mostly utilized for quality assurance in the manufacturing of aerospace components, particularly in cases where a high level of precision is necessary for 100% inspection. In this scenario, the applications bear resemblance to other manufacturing of parts in terms of approach (Gourisaria et al., 2021). Nevertheless, there exist intriguing applications, such as an automated horizon-detecting system designed to aid the pilot throughout a flight. Fefilatyev et al. (2006) discuss the application of support vector machines, C4.5 classification tree, and naive Bayes classifiers. Using a limited number of photos, the accuracy in this example is exceptionally high. In addition to tasks related to classification, feature subset selection strategies that rely on picture processing and ranking based on pixel value are employed (Tarapata et al., 2020).

Did you know?

Some construction companies are using smart helmets equipped with machine learning algorithms to monitor workers' vital signs and ensure their safety on the job site.

7.2. BASIC MATERIALS SECTOR

This division contains chemicals and other basic resources.

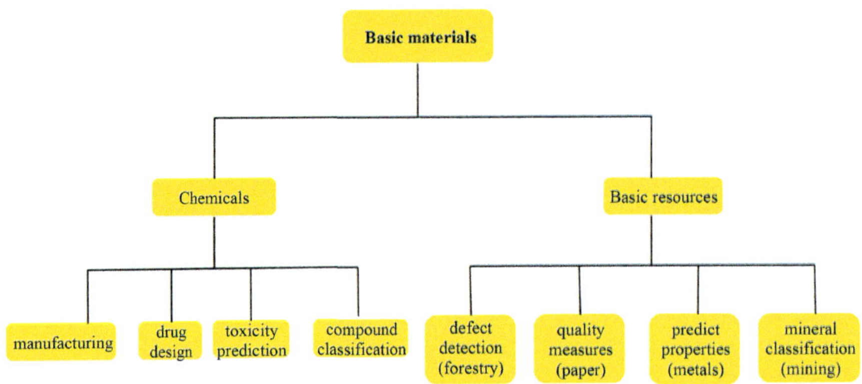

Figure 7.2. *Applications of machine learning in materials sector.*

Source: David Atienza, Creative Commons License.

7.2.1. Chemicals

Similar to other sectors, the chemical business functions within a highly competitive global marketplace, where acquisitions and mergers are frequently utilized to strengthen a company's position. The industrial sector can anticipate significant prospects by using machine learning (Chebila, 2021).

The chemical industry utilizes machine learning in four primary application areas: manufacturing, medicine creation, toxicity prediction, and compound classification. The amount of data that needs to be managed in chemical manufacturing to address optimizing, tracking, and control issues is on the rise. Machine learning has the potential to greatly accelerate processes, discover more environmentally friendly and economically efficient solutions, and create opportunities for new ideas and advancements. Ribeiro (2005) employed artificial neural networks and support vector machines to supervise the accuracy of in-process data in a plastic injection-molding machine (Sun et al., 2022).

The objective of drug design is to discover lead molecules that exhibit substantial activity against a certain biological target. The drug focus is a protein that is regulated by its association with a chemical substance and has the potential to regulate disease. Lead compounds are detected during the drug discovery phase. Subsequently, the compounds undergo optimization throughout the drug formulation phase, leading to a limited selection that is subjected to evaluation in human trials. ML has been employed in the drug discovery process to develop algorithms that assess the likelihood of a chemical compound exhibiting activity against a specific target. It is also used to predict the affinity between a ligand and receptor, as well as to anticipate the structure of the target and the potential side effects of new drugs. Additionally, machine learning is utilized for screening potential targets on cells and in the delivery of drugs. The review conducted by Lima et al. (2016) identifies decision trees, random forests, artificial neural networks, and support vector machines as the primary methodologies employed in the field of new drug development. Additionally, Lavecchia (2015) includes k-nearest neighbors and naive Bayes as other strategies. Machine learning is also valuable for forecasting the pharmacokinetic and toxicological characteristics of chemicals, commonly referred to as ADME-Tox (absorption, distribution, metabolism, excretion, and toxicity) (Feng et al., 2023).

Machine learning is widely employed in various domains to identify and forecast toxicity. Anticipating the toxicity of chemicals is a significant concern in the domains of environmental science and pharmaceutical research. In vitro bioassay data are frequently employed for the prediction of in vivo chemical toxicity. Judson et al. (2008) conducted a comparison between artificial neural networks, k-nearest neighbors, naive Bayes, and support vector machines using filter-based feature selection. Machine learning is employed in the field of drug development to identify toxicities, such as hepatic toxicity, nephrotoxicity, and ototoxicity. There is a lack of studies on cardiotoxicity and neurotoxicity, presenting fresh prospects for researchers in these domains. REACH is a European legislation that governs the registration, examination, licensing, and limitation of chemicals. The implementation of this new legislation has resulted in a rise in the use of computational methods to estimate the toxicity of chemicals manufactured or brought into the European Union. An extensively employed predictive technique is the quantitative structure-activity relationships (QSAR) approach, which relies on artificial neural networks (Nadirgil, 2023).

Machine learning algorithms are more efficient and cost-effective than in vivo experimental studies in accurately predicting genotoxicity. The objective is to identify substances that have a detrimental impact on the process of inheritance in human beings. They can gather a wide range of substances, each of which is identified by distinctive fingerprints and chemical descriptors (Heo et al., 2019).

Supervised classification methods can be used to automatically group thousands of chemical compounds into multiple classes for compound categorization. Smusz et al. (2013) employ the WEKA software to conduct a comparison of 11 classifiers, which includes four metaclassifiers. On the other hand, Lang et al. (2016) utilizes active machine learning to decrease the necessary quantity of training compounds. Active machine learning employs an iterative approach to handle labeled data, avoiding the expensive, error-prone, and time-consuming task of manually collecting class information, which is typically provided by chemists or obtained via experiments. Li et al. (2009) employ support vector machines for categorizing polymers. In their study, Böcker et al.

(2005) employed hierarchical clustering and K-means algorithms to examine extensive compound libraries. Practical objectives in the chemical business involve developing innovative scents that exhibit excellent technical performance (such as non-irritating to the skin and resistant to color change over time), possess pleasant aromas, and stand out as distinctive in the market (Sree Dharinya & Ephzibah, 2020). Master perfumers usually undergo a ten-year training period to achieve proficiency. In their study, Goodwin et al. (2017) employ various classifiers to forecast the gender and average assessment of unfamiliar smells, all of which are distinguished by a specific combination of fragrance notes. The data is transformed into two-dimensional space utilizing t-distributed stochastic neighbor embedding (t-SNE), which is a non-linear technique for reducing dimensionality (Hao et al., 2023). This algorithm identifies clusters of fragrances and areas with missing data, indicating potential combinations of unknown but interesting scent notes. Xu et al. (2007) developed a novel technique for blending colors using an artificial neural network. This method accurately simulates the process of mixing pigments in real life and also facilitates the development of new artificial pigments (Trinh et al., 2021).

7.2.2. Basic Resources

Internal flaw detection in hardwood logs is crucial in forestry due to its impact on the economic value of generated boards and processed wood products. In their study, Sarigul et al. (2005) constructed an artificial neural network using computed tomography pictures of hardwood logs. The purpose was to classify each pixel based on labels such as "knot," "split," and "bark."

The Kappa number is a valuable indicator of the quality of paper pulp in paper manufacture. However, it is challenging to properly detect this parameter using online sensors. In their study, Li and Zhu (2004) discovered that support vector machines are more effective than artificial neural networks in predicting the Kappa number based on data from surrounding sensors. Iglesias et al. (2017) employ a multilayer perceptron (MLP), support vector machines, and classification and regression trees (CART) to forecast specific characteristics of pulp, namely pulp yield, ISO brightness, Kappa number, fiber length, and width. These predictions are based on the proportion of sapwood and heartwood present in the raw material (Mukhamediev et al., 2022).

Pardakhti et al. (2017) employ chemical and morphological descriptors in the field of industrial metals to forecast the adsorption of methane in metal-organic frameworks. To accomplish this, they employ support vector machines, classification trees, and random forests. Rosenbrock et al. (2017) investigate grain boundaries (GB), which are atomic structures that significantly impact several physical characteristics of crystalline materials, such as ductility, strength, resistance to corrosion, crack resistance, and conductivity. Support vector machines and classification trees undergo training separately to predict three distinct features of grain boundaries (GBs): GB energy, temperature-sensitive mobility, and shear-coupled GB migration. This contributes to the production of more robust and less corrosive metals. Defect detection machine learning technologies are utilized in both the steel and wood industries. In these industries, data is initially preprocessed using Principal Component Analysis (PCA). Subsequently, support vector machines with various kernels, random trees, and artificial neural networks are trained. In addition, Bayesian networks are used to forecast the fluctuation of silicon content in molten metals (Nagar et al., 2021). Numerous machine learning applications in the mining industry are used to evaluate ore fragmentation in both underground and open-pit operations. These applications also help in identifying cracked shotcrete, spalling, and plate deformation. Carey et al. (2015) employ machine learning techniques to classify minerals. Harvey and Fotopoulos (2016) employ the techniques of k-nearest neighbors, naive Bayes, random forests, and support vector machines to construct geological maps that accurately classify different rock types in a region where comprehensive ground validation data is available. This enhances the laborious traditional methods used in field expeditions (Nacchia et al., 2021).

Remember

Machine learning accelerates the discovery of new chemical compounds and optimizes mining operations, leading to better resource management and environmental compliance.

7.3. CONSUMER SERVICES SECTOR

This section provides illustrations of machine learning implementation in the retail, media, and tourism industries.

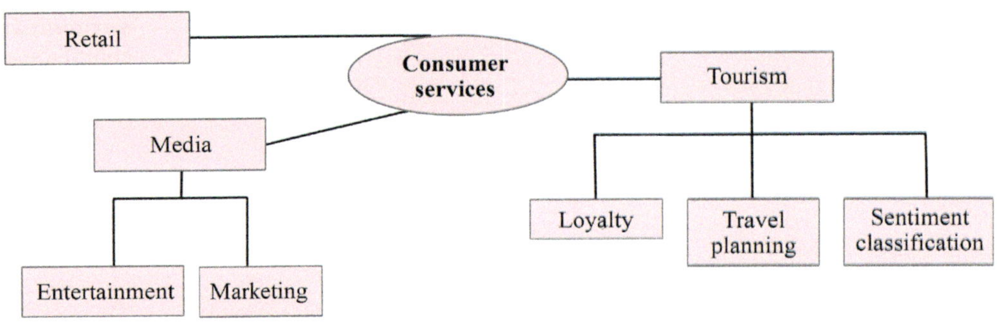

Figure 7.3. *Applications of machine learning in consumer services.*

Source: Concha Bielza, Creative Commons License.

7.3.1. Retail

Machine learning techniques offer retailers a competitive edge by mitigating the expensive issues associated with overstocking or understocking fresh food. They serve as the key to more intelligent fresh food restocking. Furthermore, they can generate demand predictions not only by analyzing past sales data but also by considering other significant elements such as advertising initiatives, store operating hours, local climate conditions, and public holidays (Gopalan et al., 2020).

7.3.2. Media

Machine learning can be beneficial in the domains of entertainment, broadcasting, cinema, and television. Examples include:

i. Utilizing video analysis to track emotions, eeriness, frights, and affection with audio analysis of music and rhythm of voice;
ii. Implementing real-time cataloging and analysis of broadcast coding to offer

advertising partners enhanced visibility, transparency, and accountability;

iii. Creating systems that discover audience interests and provide recommendations for TV shows and movies based on taste (Kongar & Adebayo, 2021);

iv. Enhancing video encoders to deliver exceptional picture quality on 4-inch and 5-inch screens.

An instance of this is the Netflix Prize, a public competition seeking the most optimal algorithm for forecasting user ratings for movies. The competition was initiated in 2006, and in September 2009, a team was awarded a grand prize of $1,000,000 for enhancing Netflix's algorithm by 10% (Mazzei & Ramjattan, 2022).

Marketing can also leverage the real-time analysis of vast amounts of data. Tableau and QlikView offer a diverse range of data visualization tools that are extensively utilized in marketing research. To ensure the success of a marketing campaign, it is crucial to comprehend the specific words, phrases, sentences, and content styles that strongly appeal to individual members of the audience. Machine learning algorithms can be utilized to analyze data from all campaigns to determine the most effective textual introduction for emails sent to a wide audience or even to an individual, thereby enhancing the probability of achieving positive outcomes. Additional instances involve the examination of mobile consumer behavior to assist app publishers in identifying the most devoted customers and forecasting client attrition. With this understanding, marketers may strategically act across various digital platforms to enhance consumer involvement or allocate more resources toward maintaining specific client segments (Chan-Olmsted, 2019).

7.3.3. Tourism

Loyalty is a key objective in strategic marketing as it enables organizations to strengthen their competitive edge by gaining distinct advantages (Imam & Ananda, 2022). This includes customers being more likely to make repeat purchases and recommend items, which can result in revenue growth, higher market share, reduced expenses, and improved employee job satisfaction (Nilashi et al., 2017). Tourism loyalty is determined by various elements, such as the quality of customer service provided by employees, the functionality of the tour website, the perception of consumers regarding the unique features of local tourism, and the level of customer loyalty in terms of repeat visits to a place. Hsu et al. (2009) utilize Bayesian networks to analyze data obtained from tourists who have undergone a tour. The researchers determined that visitors who have a more positive opinion of customer service, web features, and local qualities of the place are more likely to exhibit loyalty towards tourism (Sahebi et al., 2022). This loyalty may manifest in their willingness to revisit the destination or promote it to others. Wong and Chung (2008) utilize classification trees to analyze passenger loyalty among individuals traveling on a domestic airline. They discover distinct categories of both loyal and dishonest passengers (Puri et al., 2023).

Choosing the sightseeing spots to visit in a certain location is a crucial aspect of organizing a journey. While several online travel suggestion systems have emerged in the past 10 years to assist users in organizing their trips, only a limited number of these systems prioritize suggesting personalized tourist attractions. Huang and Bian (2009) present a method for generating tailored recommendations for tourist sites in a new city. Their approach uses a Bayesian network that considers the travel habits of both the user as well as other users (Madzík et al., 2023).

The exponential expansion of Internet tourism apps has resulted in a vast quantity of individual remarks regarding travel-related content on the World Wide Web. These reviews can be presented in many formats such as blogs, wikis, or forum websites. The evaluations contain vital information that can be used for vacation planning purposes. Sentiment classification techniques are employed to extract personal remarks from travel blogs. Ye et al. (2009) conducted a comparative analysis of naive Bayes and support vector machines for sentiment categorization of reviews on travel blogs. The study focused on seven major travel locations in the USA and Europe. Additional significant issues in the tourism industry include the assessment of tourist arrivals, lodging rates, and seasonal pricing, as well as the identification of elements that impact customer happiness in a restaurant (Essien & Chukwukelu, 2022).

7.4. HEALTHCARE SECTOR

The rapid expansion of health-related data offers unparalleled prospects for enhancing patient health. Health-related data originates from several sources, such as personal health records of patients, genomic information from wearable fitness monitors, online evaluations of clinicians, clinical writings, and medical imagery. The implementation of machine learning in healthcare is particularly complex due to a confluence of factors. Initially, there is a significant amount and diverse range of data kinds, ranging from waveforms to unorganized text. Furthermore, investigations in this field encompass the complete learning process, starting from problem definition, followed by feature selection, model training, and final output. At every step of the pipeline, there are difficulties associated with several concerns such as incomplete data, imbalanced classes, temporal coherence, and job diversity. For the technology to have a significant effect, physicians and/or biological researchers must embrace and utilize accurate models.

The benefits of utilizing advanced algorithms to analyze extensive healthcare data and subsequently applying the acquired knowledge to enhance clinical practice are substantial. Machine learning can mitigate the occurrence of diagnosis and therapy errors that are inherent in human medical procedures. Furthermore, a machine learning system can derive valuable insights from a vast pool of patient data to offer immediate guidance for health risk alarms and predictions of health outcomes. Darcy et al. (2016) suggests that there is a significant potential to supervise the implementation of machine learning in the provision of healthcare to patients. The field of medicine, which is still adapting to the use of electronic medical records, must continue to progress with the digital revolution. Bioinformatics serves as a cross-disciplinary tool for prediction (Kaur et al., 2018).

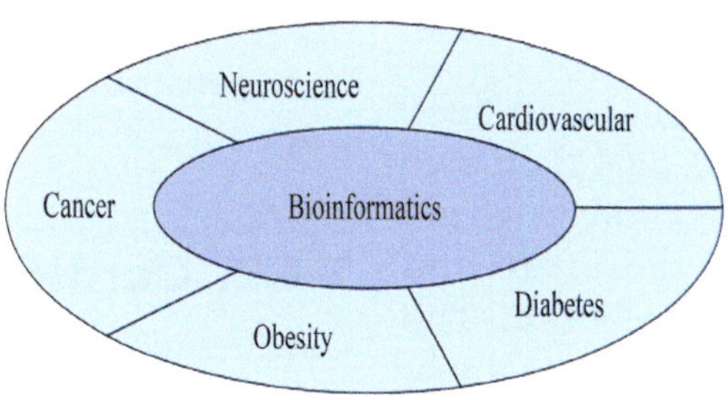

Figure 7.4. *Illustration of healthcare applications of machine learning.*

Source: Alberto Ogbechie, Creative Commons License).

7.4.1. Cancer

Cancer is classified as a heterogeneous illness comprising numerous distinct subgroups. Early detection and assessment of cancer is crucial in studies on cancer, as it might aid in the subsequent clinical treatment of patients. The significance of categorizing those with cancer in high- or low-risk categories is apparent in diagnosing and predicting outcomes, as well as in developing models to understand the advancement and management of malignant illnesses. Machine learning methods have been utilized to tackle three significant issues, including the forecasting of cancer susceptibility, such as estimating the risk of breast cancer. In this case, artificial neural networks were employed to analyze a dataset consisting of over 48,000 mammographic findings, along with demographic risks and tumor characteristics. The ROC curve's area was utilized to evaluate the model's ability to discriminate. Secondly, the prediction of cancer recurrence in oral cancer was done by contrasting Bayesian classifiers with support vector machines, artificial neural networks, classification trees, and random forests. This was done using clinical, imaging tissue, and genomic data, along with multifaceted filter and wrapper approaches for feature subset selection. Third, the prediction of cancer survival involved assessing the survival of women diagnosed with breast cancer. The class variable was survivability, referring to patients who have and have not survived.

Cancer research has extensively utilized Bayesian networks. Sesen et al. (2013) utilized Bayesian networks to conduct individualized predictions of lung cancer survival and recommendations for therapy selection. The study was based on the English Lung Cancer Database, which consisted of about 126,000 patients diagnosed between 2006 and 2010. The model was built using a collection of relevant data that were accessible when a new patient arrived to make a therapy decision. The process of structure learning was conducted through both manual methods, where experts provided input, and automated methods, which utilized a scoring and search technique incorporating the K2 metric and simulated annealing. The automated approach surpassed the manual method in terms of performance. The study conducted by Cruz-Ramírez et al. (2007) examines the efficacy of several Bayesian network classifiers, including naive Bayes and its versions, as well as unrestricted Bayesian network classifiers, in properly diagnosing breast cancer. Gevaert et al. (2006) developed a Bayesian network classifier to predict breast cancer prognosis. They achieved this by combining clinical data (such as age, tumor size, tumor grade, hormonal receptor situation, and the existence of angioinvasion and lymphatic infiltration) with microarray data (which included mRNA expression levels of around 25,000 genes for each individual). The two class values of variables correlate to unfavorable and favorable prognoses. Poor prognosis indicates the occurrence of a relapse within five years following diagnosis, whereas good prognosis indicates at least five years without any signs of the disease. The classifier structure was constructed using the K2 search algorithm in conjunction with the Bayesian Dirichlet scoring metric, based on the Markov blanket. The estimation of parameters was conducted on the assumption of a Dirichlet prior distribution (Priya & Radhika, 2023).

7.4.2. Cardiovascular Diseases

Cardiovascular medicine produces a wide range of biological, clinical, and operational information as part of patient care. These data are frequently kept in several data sources that are not easily accessible for cardiovascular research. Although the use of machine learning methods in cardiovascular disorders is not a recent development, there has been a significant increase in the number of publications published on PubMed that include phrases such as "cardiology" and "machine learning" in recent years. Cardiology datasets may include variables from various cardiac imaging techniques such as echocardiography, magnetic resonance imaging, near-infrared spectroscopy, single-photon emission computed tomography, intravascular ultrasound, and optical coherence tomography. These variables can be combined with molecular entities such as genomics, transcriptomics, and proteomics, as well as data from clinical trials. Clustering techniques can be utilized to categorize chronic complex disorders frequently observed in cardiovascular care, while supervised categorization is valuable for distinguishing between normal and abnormal hearts. Tylman et al. (2016) have created a method for predicting acute cardiovascular events in real-time using input signals such as blood pressure, temperature, pulse-oxymetry, echocardiography, and impedance cardiography. This method utilizes hardware-implemented Bayesian networks (Mohan et al., 2019).

Did you know?

In the healthcare sector, machine learning is revolutionizing drug discovery. AI-driven platforms can screen thousands of compounds in a fraction of the time it would take human researchers.

7.4.3. Diabetes

Diabetes mellitus is a collection of metabolic illnesses that have a substantial impact on global human health. Machine learning has been utilized in the domain of diabetes mellitus to tackle several challenges, including forecasting and diagnosis, complications of diabetes, genetic factors and environmental influences, as well as healthcare and management. Among these, prediction and diagnosis are the most widely studied areas. Kavakiotis et al. (2017) found that the majority of applications, specifically 85%, utilized supervised classification algorithms, while the remaining 15% employed clustering approaches. Support vector machines are the most effective and commonly employed algorithm (Butt et al., 2021).

7.4.4. Obesity

Currently, obesity researchers have abundant access to a vast amount of data. Machine learning algorithms can utilize data from various sources such as sensors, smartphone apps, electronic medical records, massive insurance databases, and public national health statistics to create mathematical models. DeGregory et al. (2006) conducted a study where they compared the effectiveness of logistic regression, artificial neural networks, and classification trees in predicting high levels of body fat percentage. They used anthropometric predictor variables from a sample of over 25,000 medical records obtained from the National Health and Nutrition Examination Survey (NHANES) dataset (Dunstan et al., 2020).

7.4.5. Bioinformatics

In their 2006 study, Larrañaga et al. (2006) examine the utilization of machine learning in several bioinformatics domains. Bioinformatics is defined as a multidisciplinary science that creates techniques and software tools to comprehend biological data. The review encompasses the domains of proteomics, genomics, systems biology, text mining, and various other applications. The text discusses strategies for selecting feature subsets, including filter, wrapper, and hybrid approaches. The clustering approaches that were examined are hierarchical clustering, K-means clustering, and probabilistic clustering. A review is conducted on all supervised classification algorithms, with the exception of rule induction. Bayesian networks and hidden Markov models are included in the analysis (Lan et al., 2018).

7.5. INFORMATION TECHNOLOGY SECTOR

The information technology sector encompasses various industries that are typically linked to the discipline of computer science, including computer hardware, software, the Internet, semiconductors, and office/telecommunications equipment. Machine learning techniques are highly suited for the information technology sector, particularly for jobs that involve a significant amount of data, such as Internet applications (Cioffi et al., 2020).

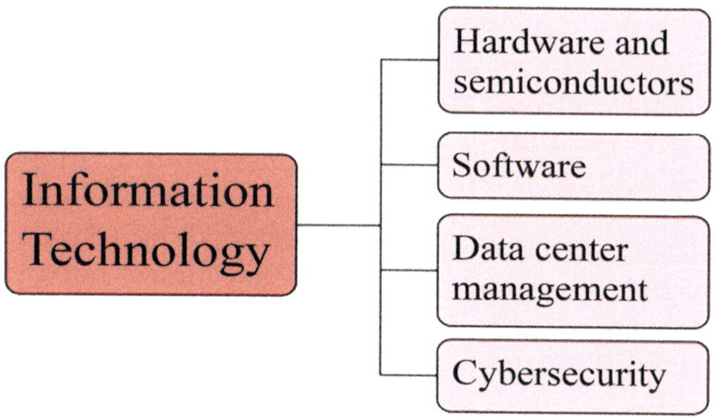

Figure 7.5. *Applications of machine learning in information technology sector.*

Source: Pedro Larranaga, Creative Commons License.

7.5.1. Hardware and Semiconductors

Semiconductor manufacturing is a highly intricate process that encompasses numerous procedures. Failure to identify defective wafers in the early stages of production might lead to higher manufacturing expenses. Several studies have emphasized the efficacy of machine learning methods in identifying defective wafers. Intel, a prominent semiconductor manufacturer, has developed an advanced method that uses deep learning, primarily convolutional neural networks, to identify defects in silicon packaging. The process of silicon packing is intricate and costly, and Intel's method has reached an almost equivalent false negative rate to that of a human.

Furthermore, the literature has examined the identification of hardware failures (Murray et al., 2005). Western Digital, a prominent manufacturer of hard drives, has announced its utilization of machine learning to identify defective hard disks and detect mistakes at the earliest stages of production (Batra et al., 2019).

7.5.2. Software

Machine learning approaches can be utilized by software developers to enhance their outcomes. Zhang and Tsai (2003) present a comprehensive examination of the challenges in the field of software engineering that can be addressed through the application of machine learning techniques. Machine learning can tackle the following challenges:

i. Prediction/Estimation of a Software Project Progress: Key factors to consider in software development include the quality of the software, programming cost, maintenance efforts, software reliability, and reusability. Various machine learning techniques, such as k-nearest neighbors, artificial neural networks, classification trees, and Bayesian networks, have been employed to solve this problem.

ii. Property and Model Discovery: Enumerate characteristics of software entities. This use case has employed artificial neural networks.

iii. Transformation: Automatically alter software to attain an advantage, such as aiding developers by transforming sequential programs into parallel programs. This issue has been addressed with artificial neural networks and a grouping approach based on nearest neighbors.

iv Reuse/Maintenance: Assist with the maintenance endeavors of a software project, such as identifying and utilizing reusable components inside the product. The primary algorithms utilized to address this task are k-nearest neighbors and classification trees.

Systems development is a particular use case in the field of software engineering. This domain typically focuses on software initiatives at a low level, such as the creation of operating systems, compilers, or networking, where performance is a critical factor. In a recent study, Kraska et al. (2017) suggested the potential replacement of conventional data structures with learned index structures that utilize artificial neural networks. These structures provide the advantages of improved speed and reduced memory usage (Zhao et al., 2019).

7.5.3. Data Center Management

Machine learning can also optimize the management of huge computer systems. Google achieved a 40% reduction in its data center cooling expenses by implementing artificial neural networks through training. The artificial neural networks were trained using previous data collected from a multitude of sensors located throughout the data center. These sensors recorded various parameters such as temperatures, power consumption, and pump speeds. Subsequently, they conducted training sessions for three sets of artificial neural networks. An ensemble of artificial neural networks attempts to forecast the average power usage effectiveness in the future. Two further artificial neural network ensembles are tasked with forecasting the future temperature and pressure within the data center. Artificial neural network ensembles can replicate the behavior of data centers to identify the optimal settings for the cooling system while ensuring that the data center operates under the correct conditions (Yang et al., 2022).

7.5.4. Cybersecurity

Cybersecurity exemplifies the utilization of machine learning in an increasingly interconnected environment. Antivirus software is frequently employed as a prevalent remedy in this particular domain. Kaspersky, a provider of cybersecurity and antivirus solutions, is utilizing decision tree ensembles to enhance the detection capabilities of its products. These ensembles are trained in a laboratory using regularly updated sets of files. Additionally, the corporation disclosed its utilization of deep learning models to scrutinize execution logs of dubious files to identify malware. Another cybersecurity activity involves the identification of fraud in Internet apps, particularly those that utilize credit card payments. PayPal is a prominent company that handles online payments and employs machine learning methodologies, including artificial neural networks and deep learning. Visa, a prominent card payment corporation, is said to employ machine learning technologies, including artificial neural networks and other self-improving algorithms, to detect and prevent fraud (Handa et al., 2019).

ACTIVITY 7.1

Compare and contrast the application of machine learning in two different sectors discussed in this chapter. What are the similarities and differences in the data used, techniques applied, and outcomes achieved?

SUMMARY

- This chapter offers a comprehensive examination of the utilization of machine learning in several industrial domains. The text emphasizes the significant influence of machine learning technology on improving operational efficiency, decision-making processes, and fostering creativity. Machine learning enhances the efficiency of construction project management, allocation of resources, and prediction of equipment maintenance. Predictive analytics improve supply chain management by minimizing downtime through the use of predictive maintenance. It facilitates the identification of novel chemical compounds and materials by utilizing predictive modeling and simulations. It enhances operational efficiency and safety by forecasting potential risks and optimizing chemical manufacturing processes. Machine learning improves consumer experience by providing tailored recommendations, implementing dynamic pricing, and optimizing inventory management. Algorithms enhance the customization of content delivery, optimize recommendation systems, and streamline content moderation through automation. Predictive analytics improve customer service by customizing travel recommendations and enhancing demand predictions. Machine learning algorithms aid in the timely identification, diagnosis, and planning of therapy by analyzing images and making predictions. Predictive models facilitate early detection and evaluation of risks, enhancing patient outcomes by tailoring treatment regimens to individual needs. Machine learning improves the management of diabetes by utilizing predictive modeling of blood glucose levels and providing individualized treatment suggestions. It enhances the efficiency of the design and production procedures for semiconductors, resulting in increased output and fewer flaws. In the field of cybersecurity, it improves the ability to detect and respond to threats by finding patterns and anomalies that suggest security breaches.

REVIEW QUESTIONS

1. How is machine learning utilized in the construction and materials sector to improve project management and resource allocation?
2. Explain how machine learning assists in the discovery of new chemical compounds and materials?
3. How do machine learning algorithms assist in the early detection and treatment planning of cancer?
4. Explain the use of predictive models in early diagnosis and risk assessment for cardiovascular diseases?
5. Discuss the applications of machine learning in cybersecurity for threat detection and response?

MULTIPLE CHOICE QUESTIONS

1. Which of the following is a primary application of machine learning in the construction and materials sector?

a. Enhancing customer experience

b. Project management optimization

c. Personalized recommendations

d. Fraud detection

2. How is machine learning utilized in the chemicals sector?

a. For audience engagement analysis

b. For discovery of new chemical compounds

c. For inventory management

d. For dynamic pricing

3. Which of the following sectors uses machine learning for personalized recommendations and inventory management?

a. Healthcare

b. Media

c. Retail

d. Chemicals

4. Machine learning aids in early cancer detection and treatment planning by:

a. Predicting blood glucose levels

b. Image analysis and predictive modeling

c. Dynamic pricing strategies

d. Process optimization

5. **Which sector uses machine learning for the design and manufacturing processes of semiconductors?**
   a. Consumer services
   b. Healthcare
   c. Information technology
   d. Basic resources

Answers to Multiple Choice Questions

1. (b); 2. (b); 3. (c); 4. (b); 5. (c)

REFERENCES

1. Aamer, A., Eka Yani, L., & Alan Priyatna, I. (2020). Data analytics in the supply chain management: Review of machine learning applications in demand forecasting. *Operations and Supply Chain Management: An International Journal, 14*(1), 1–13.
2. Akinosho, T. D., Oyedele, L. O., Bilal, M., Ajayi, A. O., Delgado, M. D., Akinade, O. O., & Ahmed, A. A. (2020). Deep learning in the construction industry: A review of present status and future innovations. *Journal of Building Engineering, 32*, 101827.
3. Ambika, P. (2020). Machine learning and deep learning algorithms on the Industrial Internet of Things (IIoT). *Advances in Computers, 117*(1), 321–338.
4. Angelopoulos, A., Michailidis, E. T., Nomikos, N., Trakadas, P., Hatziefremidis, A., Voliotis, S., & Zahariadis, T. (2019). Tackling faults in the industry 4.0 era—A survey of machine-learning solutions and key aspects. *Sensors, 20*(1), 109.
5. Batra, G., Jacobson, Z., Madhav, S., Queirolo, A., & Santhanam, N. (2019). Artificial-intelligence hardware: New opportunities for semiconductor companies. *McKinsey and Company, 2*, 857–860.
6. Bilal, M., & Oyedele, L. O. (2020). Guidelines for applied machine learning in construction industry—A case of profit margins estimation. *Advanced Engineering Informatics, 43*, 101013.
7. Böcker, A., Derksen, S., Schmidt, E., Teckentrup, A., & Schneider, G. (2005). A hierarchical clustering approach for large compound libraries. *Journal of Chemical Information and Modeling, 45*(4), 807–815.
8. Butt, U. M., Letchmunan, S., Ali, M., Hassan, F. H., Baqir, A., & Sherazi, H. H. R. (2021). Machine learning based diabetes classification and prediction for healthcare applications. *Journal of Healthcare Engineering, 2021*(1), 9930985.
9. Carey, C., Boucher, T., Mahadevan, S., Bartholomew, P., & Dyar, M. D. (2015). Machine learning tools for mineral recognition and classification from Raman spectroscopy. *Journal of Raman Spectroscopy, 46*(10), 894–903.
10. Carou, D., Sartal, A., & Davim, J. P. (2022). Machine learning and artificial intelligence with industrial applications. *Springer. 10*, 978–980.

11. Chan-Olmsted, S. M. (2019). A review of artificial intelligence adoptions in the media industry. *International Journal on Media Management, 21*(3–4), 193–215.

12. Chebila, M. (2021). Predicting the consequences of accidents involving dangerous substances using machine learning. *Ecotoxicology and Environmental Safety, 208*, 111470.

13. Chinnam, R. B. (2002). Support vector machines for recognizing shifts in correlated and other manufacturing processes. *International Journal of Production Research, 40*(17), 4449–4466.

14. Chomacki, L., Rusek, J., & Słowik, L. (2022). Machine learning methods in damage prediction of masonry development exposed to the industrial environment of mines. *Energies, 15*(11), 3958.

15. Cioffi, R., Travaglioni, M., Piscitelli, G., Petrillo, A., & De Felice, F. (2020). Artificial intelligence and machine learning applications in smart production: Progress, trends, and directions. *Sustainability, 12*(2), 492.

16. Cruz-Ramirez, N., Acosta-Mesa, H. G., Carrillo-Calvet, H., Nava-Fernández, L. A., & Barrientos-Martinez, R. E. (2007). Diagnosis of breast cancer using Bayesian networks: A case study. *Computers in Biology and Medicine, 37*(11), 1553–1564.

17. Darcy, A. M., Louie, A. K., & Roberts, L. W. (2016). Machine learning and the profession of medicine. *JAMA, 315*(6), 551–552.

18. DeGregory, K. W., Kuiper, P., DeSilvio, T., Pleuss, J. D., Miller, R., Roginski, J. W., & Thomas, D. M. (2018). A review of machine learning in obesity. *Obesity Reviews, 19*(5), 668–685.

19. Diez-Olivan, A., Del Ser, J., Galar, D., & Sierra, B. (2019). Data fusion and machine learning for industrial prognosis: Trends and perspectives towards Industry 4.0. *Information Fusion, 50*, 92–111.

20. Dunstan, J., Aguirre, M., Bastías, M., Nau, C., Glass, T. A., & Tobar, F. (2020). Predicting nationwide obesity from food sales using machine learning. *Health Informatics Journal, 26*(1), 652–663.

21. Essien, A., & Chukwukelu, G. (2022). Deep learning in hospitality and tourism: A research framework agenda for future research. *International Journal of Contemporary Hospitality Management, 34*(12), 4480–4515.

22. Farahzadi, L., & Kioumarsi, M. (2023). Application of machine learning initiatives and intelligent perspectives for CO2 emissions reduction in construction. *Journal of Cleaner Production, 384*, 135504.

23. Fefilatyev, S., Smarodzinava, V., Hall, L. O., & Goldgof, D. B. (2006). Horizon detection using machine learning techniques. In *2006 5th International Conference on Machine Learning and Applications (ICMLA'06)* (Vol. 1, pp. 17–21). IEEE.

24. Feng, R., Xu, X., Yu, Z. T., & Lin, Q. (2023). A machine-learning assisted multi-cluster assessment for decarbonization in the chemical fiber industry toward net-zero: A case study in a Chinese province. *Journal of Cleaner Production, 425*, 138965.

25. Gevaert, O., Smet, F. D., Timmerman, D., Moreau, Y., & Moor, B. D. (2006). Predicting the prognosis of breast cancer by integrating clinical and microarray data with Bayesian networks. *Bioinformatics, 22*(14), 184–190.

26. Goodwin, R., Maria, J., Das, P., Horesh, R., Segal, R., Fu, J., & Harris, C. (2017). AI for fragrance design. In *Proceedings of the Machine Learning for Creativity and Design Workshop at NIPS* (Vol. 8, pp. 741–745).

27. Gopalan, R., Desai, M., & Acharjya, D. (2020). Customer classification in Indian retail sector—A comparative analysis of various machine learning approaches. *International Journal of Operations and Quantitative Management, 26*(1), 1–28.

28. Gourisaria, M. K., Agrawal, R., Harshvardhan, G. M., Pandey, M., & Rautaray, S. S. (2021). Application of machine learning in industry 4.0. *Machine Learning: Theoretical Foundations and Practical Applications, 6*, 57–87.

29. Halawani, S. M. (2014). A study of decision tree ensembles and feature selection for steel plates faults detection. *International Journal of Technical Research and Applications, 2*(4), 127–131.

30. Handa, A., Sharma, A., & Shukla, S. K. (2019). Machine learning in cybersecurity: A review. *Wiley Interdisciplinary Reviews: Data Mining and Knowledge Discovery, 9*(4), 1306.

31. Hao, N., Sun, P., Zhao, W., & Li, X. (2023). Application of a developed triple-classification machine learning model for carcinogenic prediction of hazardous organic chemicals to the US, EU, and WHO based on Chinese database. *Ecotoxicology and Environmental Safety, 255*, 114806.

32. Harvey, A. S., & Fotopoulos, G. (2016). Geological mapping using machine learning algorithms. *The International Archives of the Photogrammetry, Remote Sensing and Spatial Information Sciences, 41*, 423–430.

33. Hegde, J., & Rokseth, B. (2020). Applications of machine learning methods for engineering risk assessment–A review. *Safety Science, 122*, 104492.

34. Heo, S., Safder, U., & Yoo, C. (2019). Deep learning driven QSAR model for environmental toxicology: Effects of endocrine disrupting chemicals on human health. *Environmental Pollution, 253*, 29–38.

35. Hsu, C. I., Shih, M. L., Huang, B. W., Lin, B. Y., & Lin, C. N. (2009). Predicting tourism loyalty using an integrated Bayesian network mechanism. *Expert Systems with Applications, 36*(9), 11760–11763.

36. Hsu, S. C., & Chien, C. F. (2007). Hybrid data mining approach for pattern extraction from wafer bin map to improve yield in semiconductor manufacturing. *International Journal of Production Economics, 107*(1), 88–103.

37. Huang, Y., & Bian, L. (2009). A Bayesian network and analytic hierarchy process based personalized recommendations for tourist attractions over the Internet. *Expert Systems with Applications, 36*(1), 933–943.

38. Iglesias, C., Santos, A. J. A., Martínez, J., Pereira, H., & Anjos, O. (2017). Influence of heartwood on wood density and pulp properties explained by machine learning techniques. *Forests, 8*(1), 20.

39. Imam, T., & Ananda, J. (2022). Machine learning for characterizing growth in tourism employment in developing economies: An assessment of tourism employment in Sri Lanka. *Current Issues in Tourism, 25*(16), 2695–2716.

40. Javanmard, M. E., & Ghaderi, S. F. (2023). Energy demand forecasting in seven

sectors by an optimization model based on machine learning algorithms. *Sustainable Cities and Society, 95*, 104623.

41. Judson, R., Elloumi, F., Setzer, R. W., Li, Z., & Shah, I. (2008). A comparison of machine learning algorithms for chemical toxicity classification using a simulated multi-scale data model. *BMC Bioinformatics, 9*, 1–16.

42. Kapp, S., Choi, J. K., & Hong, T. (2023). Predicting industrial building energy consumption with statistical and machine-learning models informed by physical system parameters. *Renewable and Sustainable Energy Reviews, 172*, 113045.

43. Kaur, P., Sharma, M., & Mittal, M. (2018). Big data and machine learning based secure healthcare framework. *Procedia Computer Science, 132*, 1049–1059.

44. Kavakiotis, I., Tsave, O., Salifoglou, A., Maglaveras, N., Vlahavas, I., & Chouvarda, I. (2017). Machine learning and data mining methods in diabetes research. *Computational and Structural Biotechnology Journal, 15*, 104–116.

45. Kongar, E., & Adebayo, O. (2021). Impact of social media marketing on business performance: A hybrid performance measurement approach using data analytics and machine learning. *IEEE Engineering Management Review, 49*(1), 133–147.

46. Kowalski, J., Krawczyk, B., & Wo⊠niak, M. (2017). Fault diagnosis of marine 4-stroke diesel engines using a one-vs-one extreme learning ensemble. *Engineering Applications of Artificial Intelligence, 57*, 134–141.

47. Kraska, T., Beutel, A., Chi, E. H., Dean, J., & Polyzotis, N. (2018). The case for learned index structures. In *Proceedings of the 2018 International Conference on Management of Data* (Vol. 1, pp. 489–504).

48. Lan, K., Wang, D. T., Fong, S., Liu, L. S., Wong, K. K., & Dey, N. (2018). A survey of data mining and deep learning in bioinformatics. *Journal of Medical Systems, 42*, 1–20.

49. Lang, T., Flachsenberg, F., von Luxburg, U., & Rarey, M. (2016). Feasibility of active machine learning for multiclass compound classification. *Journal of Chemical Information and Modeling, 56*(1), 12–20.

50. Larranaga, P., Calvo, B., Santana, R., Bielza, C., Galdiano, J., Inza, I., & Robles, V. (2006). Machine learning in bioinformatics. *Briefings in Bioinformatics, 7*(1), 86–112.

51. Lavecchia, A. (2015). Machine-learning approaches in drug discovery: Methods and applications. *Drug Discovery Today, 20*(3), 318–331.

52. Li, H., & Zhu, X. (2004). Application of support vector machine method in prediction of Kappa number of kraft pulping process. In *Fifth World Congress on Intelligent Control and Automation* (IEEE Cat. No. 04EX788) (Vol. 4, pp. 3325–3330). IEEE.

53. Li, H., Liang, Y., & Xu, Q. (2009). Support vector machines and its applications in chemistry. *Chemometrics and Intelligent Laboratory Systems, 95*(2), 188–198.

54. Lima, A. N., Philot, E. A., Trossini, G. H. G., Scott, L. P. B., Maltarollo, V. G., & Honorio, K. M. (2016). Use of machine learning approaches for novel drug discovery. *Expert Opinion on Drug Discovery, 11*(3), 225–239.

55. Madzík, P., Falát, L., Copuš, L., & Valeri, M. (2023). Digital transformation in tourism: Bibliometric literature review based on machine learning approach. *European Journal of Innovation Management, 26*(7), 177–205.

56. Mazzei, D., & Ramjattan, R. (2022). Machine learning for Industry 4.0: A systematic review using deep learning-based topic modelling. *Sensors, 22*(22), 8641.

57. Mohan, S., Thirumalai, C., & Srivastava, G. (2019). Effective heart disease prediction using hybrid machine learning techniques. *IEEE Access, 7*, 81542–81554.

58. Mukhamediev, R. I., Popova, Y., Kuchin, Y., Zaitseva, E., Kalimoldayev, A., Symagulov, A., & Yelis, M. (2022). Review of artificial intelligence and machine learning technologies: Classification, restrictions, opportunities, and challenges. *Mathematics, 10*(15), 2552.

59. Murray, J. F., Hughes, G. F., Kreutz-Delgado, K., & Schuurmans, D. (2005). Machine learning methods for predicting failures in hard drives: A multiple-instance application. *Journal of Machine Learning Research, 6*(5), 85–90.

60. Nabavi, S. A., Aslani, A., Zaidan, M. A., Zandi, M., Mohammadi, S., & Hossein Motlagh, N. (2020). Machine learning modeling for energy consumption of residential and commercial sectors. *Energies, 13*(19), 5171.

61. Nacchia, M., Fruggiero, F., Lambiase, A., & Bruton, K. (2021). A systematic mapping of the advancing use of machine learning techniques for predictive maintenance in the manufacturing sector. *Applied Sciences, 11*(6), 2546.

62. Nadirgil, O. (2023). The relationship between the contaminating industries and the European carbon price, machine learning approach. *Journal of Cleaner Production, 426*, 139131.

63. Nagar, D., Raghav, S., Bhardwaj, A., Kumar, R., Singh, P. L., & Sindhwani, R. (2021). Machine learning: Best way to sustain the supply chain in the era of Industry 4.0. *Materials Today: Proceedings, 47*, 3676–3682.

64. Narciso, D. A., & Martins, F. G. (2020). Application of machine learning tools for energy efficiency in industry: A review. *Energy Reports, 6*, 1181–1199.

65. Nilashi, M., Bagherifard, K., Rahmani, M., & Rafe, V. (2017). A recommender system for tourism industry using cluster ensemble and prediction machine learning techniques. *Computers & Industrial Engineering, 109*, 357–368.

66. Pardakhti, M., Moharreri, E., Wanik, D., Suib, S. L., & Srivastava, R. (2017). Machine learning using combined structural and chemical descriptors for prediction of methane adsorption performance of metal organic frameworks (MOFs). *ACS Combinatorial Science, 19*(10), 640–645.

67. Priya, G., & Radhika, A. (2023). Deep learning-based breast cancer disease prediction framework for medical industries. *International Journal of Modeling, Simulation, and Scientific Computing, 14*(03), 2350012.

68. Puri, V., Mondal, S., Das, S., & Vrana, V. G. (2023). Blockchain propels tourism industry—An attempt to explore topics and information in smart tourism management through text mining and machine learning. In *Informatics*. MDPI (Vol. 10, pp. 9).

69. Ramsgaard Thomsen, M., Nicholas, P., Tamke, M., Gatz, S., Sinke, Y., & Rossi, G. (2020). Towards machine learning for architectural fabrication in the age of Industry 4.0. *International Journal of Architectural Computing, 18*(4), 335–352.

70. Rao, P. N. V. S., & Jayasree, P. (2022). Predictive maintenance-as-a-Service (PdMaaS)

using industrial Internet of Things (IIoT) and machine learning for mechanical equipment used in the Indian shipbuilding industry. *International Journal of Mechanical Engineering, 7*, 674–687.

71. Ribeiro, B. (2005). Support vector machines for quality monitoring in a plastic injection molding process. *IEEE Transactions on Systems, Man, and Cybernetics, Part C (Applications and Reviews), 35*(3), 401–410.
72. Romeo, L., Paolanti, M., Bocchini, G., Loncarski, J., & Frontoni, E. (2018). An innovative design support system for Industry 4.0 based on machine learning approaches. In *2018 5th International Symposium on Environment-Friendly Energies and Applications (EFEA)* (Vol. 1, pp. 1–6). IEEE.
73. Rosenbrock, C. W., Homer, E. R., Csányi, G., & Hart, G. L. (2017). Discovering the building blocks of atomic systems using machine learning: Application to grain boundaries. *NPJ Computational Materials, 3*(1), 29.
74. Sahebi, A. G., Kordheydari, R., & Aghaei, M. (2022). A new approach in marketing research: Identifying the customer expected value through machine learning and big data analysis in the tourism industry. *Advancement in Management and Technology (AMT), 2*(3), 26–42.
75. Sánchez-Garrido, A. J., Navarro, I. J., García, J., & Yepes, V. (2023). A systematic literature review on modern methods of construction in building: An integrated approach using machine learning. *Journal of Building Engineering, 73*, 106725.
76. Sarigul, E., Abbott, A. L., Schmoldt, D. L., & Araman, P. A. (2005). An interactive machine-learning approach for defect detection in computed tomography (CT) images of hardwood logs. In *Proceedings of Scan Tech 2005 International Conference* (Vol. 5, pp. 15–26). Las Vegas, Nevada.
77. Sesen, M. B., Nicholson, A. E., Banares-Alcantara, R., Kadir, T., & Brady, M. (2013). Bayesian networks for clinical decision support in lung cancer care. *PloS One, 8*(12), 82349.
78. Sircar, A., Yadav, K., Rayavarapu, K., Bist, N., & Oza, H. (2021). Application of machine learning and artificial intelligence in oil and gas industry. *Petroleum Research, 6*(4), 379–391.
79. Smusz, S., Kurczab, R., & Bojarski, A. J. (2013). A multidimensional analysis of machine learning methods performance in the classification of bioactive compounds. *Chemometrics and Intelligent Laboratory Systems, 128*, 89–100.
80. Sree Dharinya, S., & Ephzibah, E. P. (2020). Machine intelligence and automation: Deep learning concepts aiding industrial applications. In *Internet of Things for Industry 4.0: Design, Challenges and Solutions* (pp. 237–248).
81. Stirling, D., & Buntine, W. (1988). Process routings in a steel mill: A challenging induction problem. *Artificial Intelligence Developments and Applications, 5*(2), 301–313.
82. Sun, Y., Wang, X., Ren, N., Liu, Y., & You, S. (2022). Improved machine learning models by data processing for predicting life-cycle environmental impacts of chemicals. *Environmental Science & Technology, 57*(8), 3434–3444.
83. Tarapata, Z., Nowicki, T., Antkiewicz, R., Dudzinski, J., & Janik, K. (2020). Data-

driven machine learning system for optimization of processes supporting the distribution of goods and services–A case study. *Procedia Manufacturing, 44*, 60–67.

84. Trinh, C., Meimaroglou, D., & Hoppe, S. (2021). Machine learning in chemical product engineering: The state of the art and a guide for newcomers. *Processes, 9*(8), 1456.

85. Tylman, W., Waszyrowski, T., Napieralski, A., Kami⊠ski, M., Trafidło, T., Kulesza, Z., & Wenerski, M. (2016). Real-time prediction of acute cardiovascular events using hardware-implemented Bayesian networks. *Computers in Biology and Medicine, 69*, 245–253.

86. Van Der Heijden, H. (2022). Predicting industry sectors from financial statements: An illustration of machine learning in accounting research. *The British Accounting Review, 54*(5), 101096.

87. Wang, K. J., Chen, J. C., & Lin, Y. S. (2005). A hybrid knowledge discovery model using decision tree and neural network for selecting dispatching rules of a semiconductor final testing factory. *Production Planning & Control, 16*(7), 665–680.

88. Wong, J. Y., & Chung, P. H. (2008). Retaining passenger loyalty through data mining: A case study of Taiwanese airlines. *Transportation Journal, 47*(1), 17–29.

89. Xu, S., Tan, H., Jiao, X., Lau, F. C., & Pan, Y. (2007). A generic pigment model for digital painting. In *Computer Graphics Forum* (Vol. 26, pp. 609–618). Oxford, UK: Blackwell Publishing Ltd.

90. Yang, Z., Du, J., Lin, Y., Du, Z., Xia, L., Zhao, Q., & Guan, X. (2022). Increasing the energy efficiency of a data center based on machine learning. *Journal of Industrial Ecology, 26*(1), 323–335.

91. Ye, Q., Zhang, Z., & Law, R. (2009). Sentiment classification of online reviews to travel destinations by supervised machine learning approaches. *Expert Systems with Applications, 36*(3), 6527–6535.

92. Zhang, D., & Tsai, J. J. (2003). Machine learning and software engineering. *Software Quality Journal, 11*, 87–119.

93. Zhao, Y., Li, Y., Zhang, X., Geng, G., Zhang, W., & Sun, Y. (2019). A survey of networking applications applying the software defined networking concept based on machine learning. *IEEE Access, 7*, 95397–95417.

CHAPTER 8

Issues of Machine Learning for Society

LEARNING OBJECTIVES

After studying this chapter, you will be able to:

- Comprehend data privacy concerns in machine learning;
- Recognize sources of bias in machine learning algorithms;
- Comprehend ethical implications related to job displacement, surveillance, and other societal impacts of machine learning;
- Understand the concept of transparency in machine learning systems; and
- Comprehend and contrast human decision-making with machine decision-making capabilities.

KEY TERMS FROM THIS CHAPTER

Adversarial machine learning
Biases
Spoofing
Automation
Ethics
Transparency

UNIT INTRODUCTION

For quite some time now, computers have played a significant role in automating various tasks, including record keeping and invoice management (Jordan & Mitchell, 2015). Undoubtedly, society has greatly benefited from these advancements. However, it is crucial to highlight that the advancements discussed in this book go beyond only task automation (Sharifani & Amini, 2023). They enable machines to acquire knowledge. Their goal is to enable machines to make decisions and interact with the environment in a manner similar to that of human beings. Certainly, in numerous cases, the objective is to educate machines to surpass human capabilities in specific tasks (Sianaki et al., 2018).

The fact that Google's AlphaGo was able to defeat world go champion Ke Jie has already been mentioned. Go is a really complex game. There are too many moves for the computer to compute every scenario (Kim et al., 2016). Using a deep learning approach, AlphaGo was able to imitate and then refine the way the top human players consider their next move. Here, it is important to remember that AlphaGo was not taught how to play Go by its programmers. It was trained to play the game of Go by them (Stahl et al., 2021). There are several challenging difficulties for society when it comes to teaching machines to use data to learn and behave intelligently. The data that machine learning algorithms use is owned by whom? Which biases exist in algorithms used in machine learning (de Miguel et al., 2020)? Can humans teach a machine to discriminate between right and wrong? Should there be greater transparency in the algorithms that underlie machine learning? What effects would it have if humans were no longer the most intelligent species on the planet? These queries will be addressed in this chapter (Pramod et al., 2021).

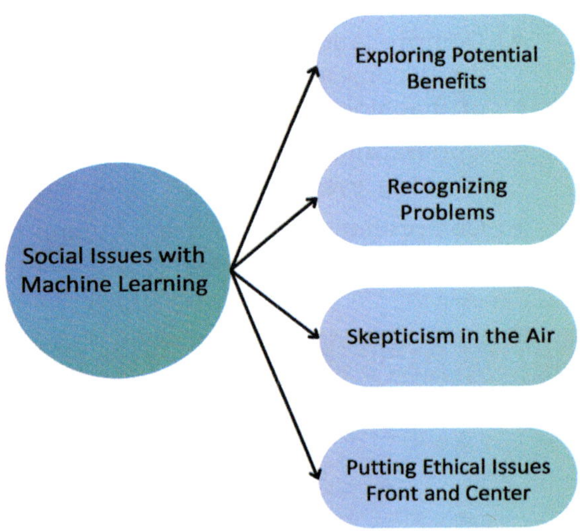

Figure. 8.1. *Representation of social issues with machine learning.*

Source: IABAC, Creative Commons License.

8.1. DATA PRIVACY

Data privacy concerns have garnered significant attention, in part due to the actions of Cambridge Analytica. This corporation provided services to both Donald Trump's 2016 presidential campaign and an organization advocating for the United Kingdom's withdrawal from the European Union (Mühlhoff, 2023). It successfully obtained and utilized personal data from millions of Facebook users without their consent. The data provided sufficient detail for Cambridge Analytica to construct profiles and ascertain the optimal adverts or other measures to advance the objectives of the organizations that had engaged its services (Miyajima et al., 2022).

Data privacy is a pressing concern for many governments. The European Union has taken a proactive approach by implementing the General Data Protection Regulation (GDPR) in May 2018. The importance of data is acknowledged and the following requirements are included (Zhao et al., 2018):

i. Before a business uses a person's data for purposes other than those for which it was originally gathered, the person must give consent to the business.
ii. Notifying all impacted parties of a data breach must happen within 72 hours (Papernot et al., 2018).
iii. When it comes to how algorithms are applied to their data, citizens have a "right to explanation."
iv. Data handling across borders needs to be done safely.
v. Businesses need to designate a data protection officer (Biswas et al., 2021).

A company's worldwide sales, or 4% of it, might be fined up to 20 million euros for violating the GDPR. It is probable that in the future, additional governments might pass laws similar to the GDPR. It is interesting to note that worries regarding the necessity of regulating how businesses use data are not limited to governments. The CEO of Facebook, Mark Zuckerberg, has stated support for GDPR and believes that laws are necessary to regulate the internet (Peyvandi et al., 2022).

Did you know?

While machine learning can personalize user experiences, such as recommending movies or products, it also raises concerns about how personal data is collected, stored, and used.

8.2. BIASES

Biases are inherent in human nature. There are individuals who prefer to play it safe, while others are more inclined to take risks. People's levels of empathy can vary greatly. While some individuals naturally possess a caring nature, others may come across as more insensitive. One potential advantage of machines is their ability to make logical decisions without being influenced by biases. Regrettably, that is not the situation. There are numerous biases that can be observed in machine learning algorithms (Pot et al., 2021).

One bias relates to the obtained data. It may lack representativeness. An example, before the emergence of machine learning, is the effort made by Literary Digest to forecast the outcome of the 1936 United States presidential election (Van Giffen et al., 2022). A survey was conducted by the magazine, with a substantial sample size of 10 million individuals, resulting in 2.4 million responses. The forecast indicated that Landon, a Republican candidate, would defeat Roosevelt, a Democrat candidate, with a margin of 57.1% to 42.9% (Mehrabi et al., 2021).

Indeed, Roosevelt emerged as the victor. What could have possibly gone wrong? It appears that Literary Digest utilized a sample that may have been influenced by certain biases, including the inclusion of their own readers, telephone users, and individuals with car registrations. Most of these individuals were supporters of the Republican party (Sharma & Rathodiya, 2019). In recent times, there have been instances where facial recognition software was primarily trained on images of white individuals, leading to a lack of accurate recognition for other races. This has resulted in misidentifications by police forces utilizing the software (Fuchs, 2018). Machine learning often relies on easily accessible data and has a tendency to favor established practices. It is highly probable that the data used to make future lending decisions will consist of historical loan data. It would be interesting to have insights into the outcomes of loans that were not approved in the past. Unfortunately, such data is not accessible due to its inherent unavailability. Amazon encountered a comparable bias during the development of its recruitment software. The software's bias against women was a result of its predominantly male recruits. Consequently, its usage was terminated (Leavy et al., 2020). Selecting the features to be considered in a machine learning exercise is a crucial task. Typically, it is considered inappropriate to incorporate factors like race, gender, or religious affiliation. However, it is important for data scientists to exercise caution and avoid incorporating additional features that exhibit strong correlations with these sensitive features.

Consider this scenario: if a specific community has a significant number of black residents, incorporating the "residential neighborhood" as a factor in creating a loan decision algorithm could potentially result in racial biases. There are numerous ways in which an analyst can unintentionally display biases while developing a machine learning algorithm. Take into consideration that biases can arise in various aspects of the machine learning process, such as data cleaning, model selection, and result interpretation and utilization (Hutchinson et al., 2020).

8.3. ETHICS

Many ethical questions are raised by machine learning. The Social Credit System, which aims to standardize the manner in which citizens are evaluated, has caused some people to believe that China has gone too far. Is it appropriate to utilize machine learning in fight? Perhaps that will always be the case.

Google and the US Department of Defense collaborated on initiative Maven, an effort to improve drone attack targeting, but the initiative was abandoned when hundreds of Google employees wrote an open letter opposing it. Still, the US and other countries are investigating the possibility of using AI for military applications (Mika et al., 2019).

Is it possible to program machine learning algorithms to exhibit moral and ethical behavior? One approach is to develop a new algorithm for machine learning and expose it to a substantial dataset containing labels such as "ethical" or "non-ethical." This way, the algorithm can be trained to recognize non-ethical data (Malhotra et al., 2018). When new data is received for a specific project, the algorithm is used to determine the ethical suitability of utilizing the data.

The idea behind this concept is that if humans are capable of learning ethical behavior, then machines can also acquire this ability. (Certainly, there are arguments suggesting that machines have the potential to surpass humans in terms of ethical behavior) (Thylstrup, 2022).

With regard to driverless cars, an intriguing moral dilemma occurs. What action should be done if an accident cannot be prevented? How should an algorithm decide which individual to kill, a younger person or an elderly person? How is it supposed to decide between taking the life of a jaywalker and someone who is following the traffic laws? How is it supposed to decide which rider to hit, one using a helmet or not? Problems like this, in which one must decide who survives and who dies, are frequently called the "trolley problem" (Dorsey, 2020).

Did you know?

AI ethics frameworks often draw parallels with established ethical theories, such as utilitarianism or Kantian ethics, to guide decision-making.

When people interact with machine learning systems, it can occasionally produce unexpected results where inappropriate and unethical behavior is learned. Microsoft unveiled Tay (short for "thinking about you") in March 2016. Tay was meant to mimic the linguistic patterns of a 19-year-old American girl by learning from human-to-human interactions on Twitter (Zhang et al., 2021).

Several Twitter users started posting phrases that were considered politically incorrect. Tay learned from these experiences and consequently sent inappropriate and offensive messages to other Twitter users. Microsoft unexpectedly terminated the service only 16 hours after its initial release (Shadowen, 2019).

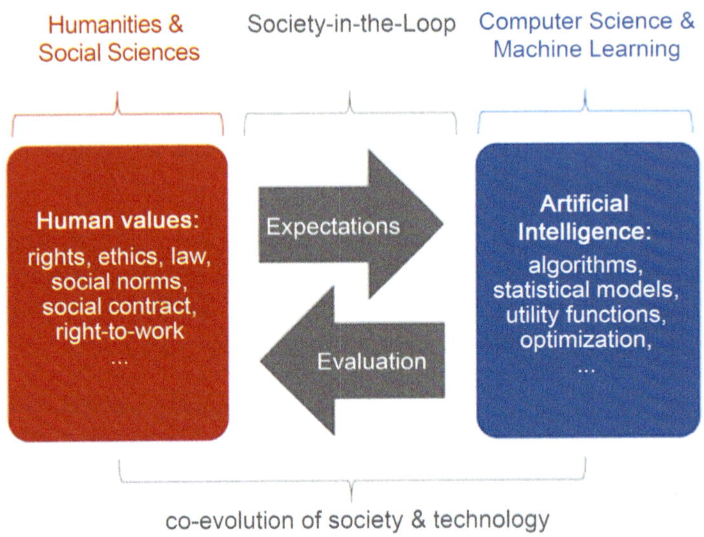

Figure. 8.2. *Relationship of ethics, society, and technology.*

Source: I. Rahwan, Creative Commons License.

8.4. TRANSPARENCY

Machine learning algorithms have come a long way in terms of transparency in recent years (De Laat, 2018). Developing strategies to enable individuals impacted by the outcomes of machine learning algorithms to access the results is crucial when generating predictions. It is essential for firms to understand the algorithms they use in order to have confidence in the rationality of the decisions being made (Goldenfein, 2019). Algorithms could always appear to be making wise choices, but in reality, they could be exploiting hidden correlations. The background (ice, grass, or trees) rather than the pictures of the animals themselves may be used by software to differentiate between polar bears and dogs (Cao & Yousefzadeh, 2023).

8.5. ADVERSARIAL MACHINE LEARNING

Adversarial machine learning relates to the potential for a machine learning algorithm to be targeted with intentionally crafted data in order to deceive it (Rosenberg et al., 2021). Undoubtedly, deceiving a machine is generally simpler than deceiving a human being! An example of this is a person who understands the functioning of a spam filter and devises an email with the intention of avoiding it. Spoofing in algorithmic trading is a type of adversarial machine learning (Biggio & Roli, 2018).

A spoofer feeds the market with buy or sell orders and cancels them before they are executed in an attempt to (illegally) manipulate the market (Finlayson et al., 2019). A malicious person putting a sign next to a road that would confuse the algorithm of the driverless car and cause accidents is another example of adversarial machine learning. Creating examples of adversarial machine learning and teaching the machine to be skeptical of them is one method of preventing it (Finlayson et al., 2019).

To make sure that machine learning algorithms are not being manipulated, it appears likely that humans will need to keep an eye on the algorithms for some time to come (Alotaibi & Rassam, 2023). The risks associated with adversarial machine learning support the arguments previously expressed regarding the need for machine learning algorithms to be more than just transparent black boxes. The output's transparency and interpretability are crucial (Laskov & Lippmann, 2010).

8.6. LEGAL ISSUES

It is believed that machine learning algorithms will give rise to numerous challenges not previously addressed by the legal system. The ownership and usage of data are major concerns that have already been discussed (DoCarmo et al., 2021). Class action lawsuits related to data misuse are expected to increase in frequency as it becomes increasingly apparent that data is a valuable commodity. It has been explained how biases might appear in machine learning algorithms. There will probably be more class action lawsuits filed by groups who believe rightly or wrongly that an algorithm is biased against them (Surden, 2021).

Autonomous vehicles are expected to emerge as a significant means of transportation in the near future. In the event of a driverless car colliding with a pedestrian, the question arises as to which party bears the legal responsibility. It could be any of

i. The individual responsible for programming the algorithm of the car.

ii. The company that produced the car (Helbing, 2019).

iii. The individual who possesses ownership of the car (Zeleznikow, 2023).

In the future, it is possible that contract law will need to undergo modifications due to the increasing prevalence of contracts between machines. These contracts would involve the use of learning algorithms by both machines involved. What happens in the event of a disagreement? Is it possible for a legal dispute to arise regarding the contractual power of a machine in a court of law? In the future, there is a possibility that machines may be granted rights, similar to how companies have rights today (Bacciu et al., 2019). Imagine a scenario where an immense amount of knowledge and expertise, surpassing that of any human, is stored within a particular machine. Is it ethical to give a human the power to deactivate a machine, resulting in the loss of its accumulated experience and intelligence (Drabiak et al., 2023)?

8.7. MAN VERSUS MACHINE

Numerous industrial revolutions have characterized human progress:

i. Steam and water power (1760–1840)
ii. Electricity and mass production (1840–1920)
iii. Computers and digital technology (1950–2000)
iv. Artificial intelligence (2000–present)

Undoubtedly, the initial three industrial revolutions have undeniably produced substantial advantages for humanity. Although the benefits were not immediately apparent, they eventually led to significant enhancements in our quality of life. There have been occasional fears about the possibility of jobs traditionally performed by humans being automated, leading to unemployment. Society experienced disruptions, although they did not result in enduring joblessness (Cummings, 2014).During the initial three industrial revolutions, there was a loss of certain employment opportunities, while simultaneously giving rise to new ones. As an example, the initial industrial revolution led individuals to transition from rural lifestyles to employment in factories. The introduction of assembly lines during the second industrial revolution revolutionized the work done in factories, altering its nature significantly. The advent of the third industrial revolution brought about an increase in employment opportunities that required proficiency in computer usage. The implications of the fourth industrial revolution remain uncertain. It is important to mention that during the third industrial revolution, not all employees were expected to become computer programmers. Many individuals in various professions had to adapt to using computers and navigating software. It is expected that the upcoming fourth industrial revolution will require individuals to acquire new skills in order to effectively utilize artificial intelligence (McRuer, 1980). Machine learning algorithms are now capable of making routine decisions at a level that is equal to or surpasses that of human beings. However, the key term in this context is "routine." The decision and the surroundings must exhibit a resemblance to those in previous situations. Machine learning algorithms cannot generate accurate conclusions if the decision is non-standard or if the environment has changed in a way that makes past data irrelevant. Driverless cars serve as an example in this case. If the regulations governing traffic were altered, such as the guidelines for making right or left turns, it would pose a significant risk to depend on an autonomous vehicle that had been programmed based on the previous regulations (Acemoglu & Restrepo, 2018). An essential responsibility for individuals is likely to involve the management of extensive data sets and the supervision of machine learning algorithms to guarantee that choices are not made using unsuitable data. Similar to how the third industrial revolution did not necessitate that every individual become a computer programmer, the fourth industrial revolution will not necessitate that every individual become a data scientist (Poggio, 1984). However, in numerous professional roles, it is important to grasp the concepts and practices of data science. In today's professional landscape, a significant number of roles require individuals to utilize pre-existing software to accomplish a wide range of tasks. In the future, there may be a need to closely monitor the functioning of machine learning algorithms created by different individuals. The combination of human expertise and advanced machine learning capabilities is expected to outperform either humans or machines working independently for the foreseeable future.However, it is important to not underestimate the potential for future advancements in the field of machine learning. In the future, machines are expected to surpass human intelligence in various aspects. One ongoing challenge faced by humans is how to effectively collaborate with machines in a manner that enhances society instead of causing harm (Margulies & Zemanek, 1983).

ACTIVITY 8.1.

A company faces a lawsuit alleging bias in its AI-driven hiring system. Discuss the legal implications and potential outcomes of the lawsuit. What legal defenses could the company use to justify its algorithmic decisions?

SUMMARY

- This chapter explores the several problems that arise when machine learning is used in society. It specifically focuses on important obstacles and considerations that need to be addressed to guarantee the ethical and efficient utilization of these technologies. Machine learning systems sometimes necessitate huge quantities of data, which gives rise to significant concerns over data privacy. It is essential to handle the gathering, storage, and utilization of personal information with caution in order to safeguard individuals' privacy rights.
- Machine learning algorithms can produce unjust and discriminatory results due to inherent biases. These biases may arise from partial training data, faulty algorithms, or systematic problems in data collection procedures. Ethical considerations encompass the possibility of employment displacement resulting from automation, the utilization of AI in surveillance and security, and the moral obligation of developers and organizations when implementing these technologies.
- Adversarial machine learning refers to planned efforts to fool or manipulate machine learning models using malicious inputs. Adversarial attacks can greatly compromise the dependability and integrity of AI systems, leading to major security risks. The swift progress of machine learning technologies poses several legal challenges.
- These questions revolve around issues of liability for decisions made by AI, ownership of content generated by AI, and adherence to current regulations. The growing abilities of machine learning systems have sparked concerns about the evolving dynamic between humans and machines. These factors encompass the possibility of job displacement, the necessity for human supervision and authority, and the societal consequences of systems becoming more autonomous. Considering the implications for human roles and responsibilities is an important aspect when it comes to the benefits of machine learning.

REVIEW QUESTIONS

1. What are the primary concerns related to data privacy in machine learning applications.
2. What strategies can be implemented to identify and mitigate biases in machine learning systems.
3. What are the key ethical considerations when developing and deploying machine learning technologies.
4. Describe some common techniques used in adversarial attacks on machine learning models.
5. What are the potential impacts of machine learning on the job market and employment.

MULTIPLE CHOICE QUESTIONS

1. **What is a primary concern related to data privacy in machine learning?**
   a. Algorithm efficiency
   b. Data anonymization
   c. Model accuracy
   d. User interface design
2. **What can lead to biases in machine learning algorithms?**
   a. Diverse dataset
   b. Unbiased data collection
   c. Flawed algorithms
   d. Transparent decision-making
3. **What ethical consideration is associated with job displacement due to automation?**
   a. Economic growth
   b. Workforce diversity
   c. Social responsibility
   d. Technological unemployment
4. **What is adversarial machine learning primarily concerned with?**
   a. Improving model accuracy
   b. Protecting user privacy
   c. Defending against cyber threats
   d. Manipulating AI systems
5. **What is a potential societal impact of increasingly autonomous machine learning systems**
   a. Reduced technological innovation
   b. Increased human oversight
   c. Shift in workforce dynamics
   d. Lower consumer demand

Answers to Multiple Choice Questions

1. (b); 2. (c); 3. (d); 4. (d); 5. (c)

REFERENCES

1. Acemoglu, D., & Restrepo, P. (2018). The race between man and machine: Implications of technology for growth, factor shares, and employment. American Economic Review, 108(6), 1488–1542.

2. Alotaibi, A., & Rassam, M. A. (2023). Adversarial machine learning attacks against intrusion detection systems: A survey on strategies and defense. Future Internet, 15(2), 62.
3. Bacciu, D., Biggio, B., Lisboa, P. J., Martin Guerrero, J. D., Oneto, L., & Vellido Alcacena, A. (2019). Societal issues in machine learning: When learning from data is not enough. In ESANN 2019, 27th European Symposium on Artificial Neural Networks, Computational Intelligence and Machine Learning: Bruges, April 24–25–26, 2019: Proceedings (Vol. 2, pp. 455–464). European Symposium on Artificial Neural Networks (ESANN).
4. Biggio, B., & Roli, F. (2018). Wild patterns: Ten years after the rise of adversarial machine learning. In Proceedings of the 2018 ACM SIGSAC Conference on Computer and Communications Security (Vol. 1, pp. 2154–2156).
5. Biswas, S., Khare, N., Agrawal, P., & Jain, P. (2021). Machine learning concepts for correlated Big Data privacy. Journal of Big Data, 8(1), 157.
6. Cao, X., & Yousefzadeh, R. (2023). Extrapolation and AI transparency: Why machine learning models should reveal when they make decisions beyond their training. Big Data & Society, 10(1), 1169731.
7. Cummings, M. M. (2014). Man versus machine or man+ machine? IEEE Intelligent Systems, 29(5), 62–69.
8. De Laat, P. B. (2018). Algorithmic decision-making based on machine learning from big data: Can transparency restore accountability? Philosophy & Technology, 31(4), 525–541.
9. de Miguel, I., Sanz, B., & Lazcoz, G. (2020). Machine learning in the EU health care context: Exploring the ethical, legal, and social issues. Information, Communication & Society, 23(8), 1139–1153.
10. DoCarmo, T., Rea, S., Conaway, E., Emery, J., & Raval, N. (2021). The law in computation: What machine learning, artificial intelligence, and big data mean for law and society scholarship. Law & Policy, 43(2), 170–199.
11. Dorsey, C. (2020). Ethics in artificial intelligence and machine learning: The importance of opening the dialogue for new processes at your organization. Journal of Financial Compliance, 3(3), 233–246.
12. Drabiak, K., Kyzer, S., Nemov, V., & El Naqa, I. (2023). AI and machine learning ethics, law, diversity, and global impact. The British Journal of Radiology, 96(1150), 20220934.
13. Finlayson, S. G., Bowers, J. D., Ito, J., Zittrain, J. L., Beam, A. L., & Kohane, I. S. (2019). Adversarial attacks on medical machine learning. Science, 363(6433), 1287–1289.
14. Fuchs, D. J. (2018). The dangers of human-like bias in machine-learning algorithms. Missouri S&T's Peer to Peer, 2(1), 1–5.
15. Goldenfein, J. (2019). Algorithmic transparency and decision-making accountability: Thoughts for buying machine learning algorithms. In Jake Goldenfein (Ed.), Closer to the Machine: Technical, Social, and Legal Aspects of AI (Vol. 8, pp. 98–100).

16. Helbing, D. (2019). Societal, economic, ethical, and legal challenges of the digital revolution: From big data to deep learning, artificial intelligence, and manipulative technologies (Vol. 2, pp. 47–72).

17. Hutchinson, B., Prabhakaran, V., Denton, E., Webster, K., Zhong, Y., & Denuyl, S. (2020). Unintended machine learning biases as social barriers for persons with disabilities. ACM SIGACCESS Accessibility and Computing, (125), 1–1.

18. Jordan, M. I., & Mitchell, T. M. (2015). Machine learning: Trends, perspectives, and prospects. Science, 349(6245), 255–260.

19. Kim, Y. M., Ahn, K. U., & Park, C. S. (2016). Issues of application of machine learning models for virtual and real-life buildings. Sustainability, 8(6), 543.

20. Laskov, P., & Lippmann, R. (2010). Machine learning in adversarial environments. Machine Learning, 81, 115–119.

21. Leavy, S., Meaney, G., Wade, K., & Greene, D. (2020). Mitigating gender bias in machine learning data sets. In Bias and Social Aspects in Search and Recommendation: First International Workshop, BIAS 2020, Lisbon, Portugal, April 14, Proceedings 1 (Vol. 2, pp. 12–26). Springer International Publishing.

22. Malhotra, C., Kotwal, V., & Dalal, S. (2018). Ethical framework for machine learning. In 2018 ITU Kaleidoscope: Machine Learning for a 5G Future (ITU K) (Vol. 2, pp. 1–8). IEEE.

23. Margulies, F., & Zemanek, H. (1983). Man's role in man-machine systems. Automatica, 19(6), 677–683.

24. McRuer, D. (1980). Human dynamics in man-machine systems. Automatica, 16(3), 237–253.

25. Mehrabi, N., Morstatter, F., Saxena, N., Lerman, K., & Galstyan, A. (2021). A survey on bias and fairness in machine learning. ACM Computing Surveys (CSUR), 54(6), 1–35.

26. Mika, N., Nadezhda, G., Jaana, L., & Raija, K. (2019). Ethical AI for the Governance of the Society: Challenges and Opportunities. In CEUR Workshop Proceedings (Vol. 2505, pp. 20–26).

27. Miyajima, H., Shigei, N., Miyajima, H., & Shiratori, N. (2022). Machine learning with distributed processing using secure divided data: Towards privacy-preserving advanced AI processing in a super-smart society. Journal of Networking and Network Applications, 2(1), 48–60.

28. Mühlhoff, R. (2023). Predictive privacy: Collective data protection in the context of artificial intelligence and big data. Big Data & Society, 10(1), 20539517231166886.

29. Papernot, N., McDaniel, P., Sinha, A., & Wellman, M. P. (2018). SOK: Security and privacy in machine learning. In 2018 IEEE European Symposium on Security and Privacy (EuroS&P) (Vol. 1, pp. 399–414). IEEE.

30. Peyvandi, A., Majidi, B., Peyvandi, S., & Patra, J. C. (2022). Privacy-preserving federated learning for scalable and high data quality computational-intelligence-as-a-service in Society 5.0. Multimedia Tools and Applications, 81(18), 25029–25050.

31. Poggio, T. (1984). Vision by man and machine. Scientific American, 250(4), 106–117.

32. Pot, M., Kieusseyan, N., & Prainsack, B. (2021). Not all biases are bad: Equitable and inequitable biases in machine learning and radiology. Insights into Imaging, 12(1), 13.

33. Pramod, A., Naicker, H. S., & Tyagi, A. K. (2021). Machine learning and deep learning: Open issues and future research directions for the next 10 years. Computational Analysis and Deep Learning for Medical Care: Principles, Methods, and Applications, 4(3), 463–490.

34. Rosenberg, I., Shabtai, A., Elovici, Y., & Rokach, L. (2021). Adversarial machine learning attacks and defense methods in the cyber security domain. ACM Computing Surveys (CSUR), 54(5), 1–36.

35. Shadowen, N. (2019). Ethics and bias in machine learning: A technical study of what makes us "good". The Transhumanism Handbook, 247–261.

36. Sharifani, K., & Amini, M. (2023). Machine learning and deep learning: A review of methods and applications. World Information Technology and Engineering Journal, 10(07), 3897–3904.

37. Sharma, I., & Rathodiya, B. (2019). Bias in machine learning algorithms. Turkish Journal of Computer and Mathematics Education (TURCOMAT), 10(2), 1158–1161.

38. Sianaki, O. A., Yousefi, A., Tabesh, A. R., & Mahdavi, M. (2018). Internet of everything and machine learning applications: Issues and challenges. In 2018 32nd International Conference on Advanced Information Networking and Applications Workshops (WAINA) (Vol. 3, pp. 704–708). IEEE.

39. Stahl, B. C., Andreou, A., Brey, P., Hatzakis, T., Kirichenko, A., Macnish, K., & Wright, D. (2021). Artificial intelligence for human flourishing–Beyond principles for machine learning. Journal of Business Research, 124, 374–388.

40. Surden, H. (2021). Machine learning and law: An overview. In Research Handbook on Big Data Law (Vol. 5, pp. 171–184).

41. Thylstrup, N. B. (2022). The ethics and politics of data sets in the age of machine learning: Deleting traces and encountering remains. Media, Culture & Society, 44(4), 655–671.

42. Van Giffen, B., Herhausen, D., & Fahse, T. (2022). Overcoming the pitfalls and perils of algorithms: A classification of machine learning biases and mitigation methods. Journal of Business Research, 144, 93–106.

43. Zeleznikow, J. (2023). The benefits and dangers of using machine learning to support making legal predictions. Wiley Interdisciplinary Reviews: Data Mining and Knowledge Discovery, 13(4), 1505.

44. Zhang, B., Anderljung, M., Kahn, L., Dreksler, N., Horowitz, M. C., & Dafoe, A. (2021). Ethics and governance of artificial intelligence: Evidence from a survey of machine learning researchers. Journal of Artificial Intelligence Research, 71, 591–666.

45. Zhao, J., Mortier, R., Crowcroft, J., & Wang, L. (2018). Privacy-preserving machine learning based data analytics on edge devices. In Proceedings of the 2018 AAAI/ ACM Conference on AI, Ethics, and Society (Vol. 1, pp. 341–346).

Index

F

G

H

I

L

M

N

U

V

W

Z

Printed and bound by CPI Group (UK) Ltd, Croydon, CR0 4YY

18/09/2026

14965063-0007